ThreeDimensional

Published by
Viction:ary

3d Graphics in Branding and Design

Preface

What happens when branding breaks out of the box – literally? With rendering tools now more accessible than ever and a collective appetite for the surreal, designers today are stepping beyond the flat page and leaping into the wonderfully weird, wildly tactile world of 3D. Once the realm of animation studios and tech demos, 3D is now front and centre in brand storytelling and it's having a moment.

ThreeDimensional is a celebration of that shift. Here, forms bubble, bend, stretch, and spiral. Logos twist into sculptures. Puffy typefaces feel soft to the touch. Clay-like characters pop off the screen, and entire brand worlds unfold in surreal, shimmering technicolour. From slick centrepieces to whimsical campaigns, the projects gathered in these pages show how 3D design isn't just a passing trend – it's a new visual language: one that's playful, expressive, and endlessly adaptable.

Throughout the book, you'll meet a brilliant line-up of creatives reshaping the look and feel of modern branding. Studio Dumbar's explosive motion identity for the Utah Jazz's 50th season (pp. 342-351) takes the energy of the game and dials it up with shimmering, percussive graphics that feel like jazz in motion. Untitled Macau's sprites for the Shenzhen Fringe Festival (pp. 148-157) bounce with quirky charm, turning a performing arts celebration into a full-blown visual party.

There are softer, more reflective moments too. Indego Design's Forest Bath (pp. 128-139) constructs a lush, stylised ecosystem inspired by nature's changing light, while Szu Yu Hou's Fairy Tales A–Z (pp. 498-501) is a typographic playground that taps into nostalgia while reimagining childhood classics for modern eyes. Bito's dreamy visuals for the 58th Golden Horse Awards (pp. 80-87) combine sculptural form with cinematic elegance to honour the richness of Chinese-language cinema.

Elsewhere, you'll find dimensionality used to amplify message and emotion. Aaron Nieh's work for the KISISF festival (pp. 102-109) layers meaning through dramatic, densely detailed visuals. Similarly, Dada Project's Nike_HerRise campaign (pp. 352-361) turns empowerment into something tangible, blending bold textures and forms to mirror strength in motion.

What ties all these projects together isn't just their shared use of 3D – it's how they use it to tell stories, evoke feelings, and challenge the boundaries of traditional design. There's a palpable sense of fun, but also a serious understanding of how dimensionality can communicate at a glance what flat visuals sometimes can't.

So whether you're a designer looking for inspiration, a brand strategist exploring new directions, or simply a curious visual wanderer, we invite you to dive in. ThreeDimensional is more than a catalogue of shiny renders; it's a glimpse into the evolving mindset of design today – a world where imagination and software combine to create identities that don't just sit on a page but move, breathe, and come alive.

Projects (01–33)

[3d]→ Visual Identities / Posters

(pp.008-217)

(01)

[3d]→ Inflatable

Special Credits Luciano Bürger, Mateus Yuzo, Michel Refatti

Studio/Designer Monga Design

Title Sopro Festival Year 2023 Client Sopro Festival

Typeface(s) Custom, Aktiv Grotesk, Franklin Gothic

: Monga Design's identity for Sopro Festival playfully reimagines the public space with an inflatable logo concept. Echoing the spirit of Jeff Koons, the pop design blends bold, bubbly visuals with urban surroundings, turning the city into an accessible open-air gallery. It positioned the festival as both contemporary and inviting – where art interacts directly with the public in unexpected, joyful ways.

UM MÊS
DE EXPOSIÇÃO
SOPRO
FESTIVAL
CHEGA AÍ
QUE É FREE.
01 → 30
07.2024
ACABA NUM
SUSPIRO.
PARQUE
VILLA LOBOS

FREE
01 A 30
JULHO
FREE
Arte.
Inflável.
Pública.
FREE
PARQUE
VILLA LOBOS
FREE

01 A 30
JULHO
FREE
Arte.
Inflável.
Pública.
PARQUE
VILLA LOBOS
FREE

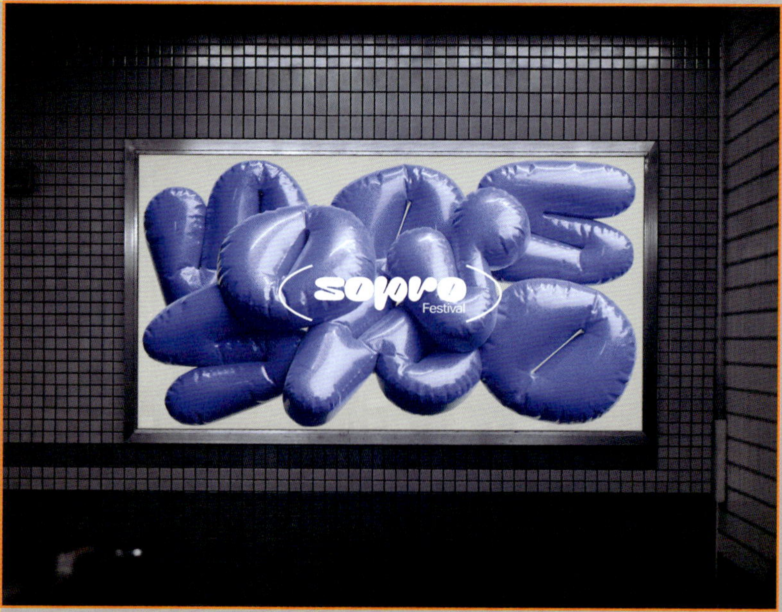
sopro
Festival

Exposições
Line-up
sopro
Festival
PARQUE
VILLA LOBOS
01 → 30
JULHO
Arte
Inflável
Pública

ar
01→30
07.2024
no
CHEGA AÍ
QUE É FREE.
sopro
está
PARQUE
VILLA LOBOS
Cultura

Festival
2024

Festiva
2024

(02)

[3d]→ Pinecone

: For the theatre production of Shakespeare's "A Midsummer Night's Dream", Erich Brechbühl designed a striking new poster that reimagines the play's many iconic themes in a contemporary context. Inspired by the central theme of a love potion, he used Viagra pills arranged as pinecones to symbolise the magical influence of the forest, offering a playful and modern twist on the timeless classic.

Studio/Designer Erich Brechbühl

Title Sommernachtstraum (Midsummer Night's Dream)

Year 2014 Client Junges Theater Sempach

Typeface(s) GT Pressura

SOMMER
NACHTS
TRAUM
JUNGES THEATER SEMPACH SPIELT
EINE GEKÜRZTE FASSUNG VON
ADI BLUM & UELI BLUM
FR 9. MAI BIS
SA 24. MAI 2014
JEWEILS 20 UHR
ZEHNTENSCHEUNE
SEMPACH
VORVERKAUF: GABRIEL
BLUMEN & GARTEN
041 462 55 88
WWW.JUTHE.CH

:   For Hyundai Department Store's Daegu reopening, ACRE designed a vibrant campaign celebrating its Jaime Hayon-designed floor, rooftop garden, and café – where playful geometric visuals represented themes of sustainability, connection, and digital-age friendships. Conceived with motion in mind, the campaign spanned LED screens, billboards, in-store merchandise, and digital plaforms – redefining the visual language of modern retail storytelling.

Studio/Designer ACRE Title Create the Future
Year 2022 Client The Hyundai Typeface(s) Euclid Circular

(03)

[3d]→ Shapes

THE HYUNDAI DAEGU

THE
HYUNDAI
DAEGU
THE
HYUNDAI
DAEGU
LOUIS VUITTON

Create *Worlds*

Create *Friends*

Create *Adventure*

Create *Forests*

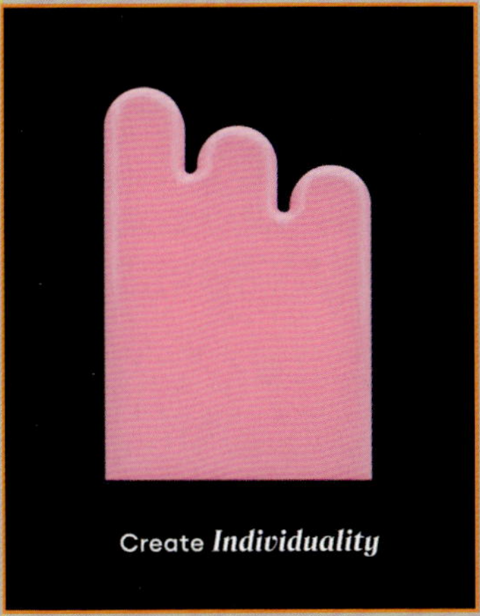
Create *Individuality*

Create *Love*

Create *Opportunities*

Create *Freedom*

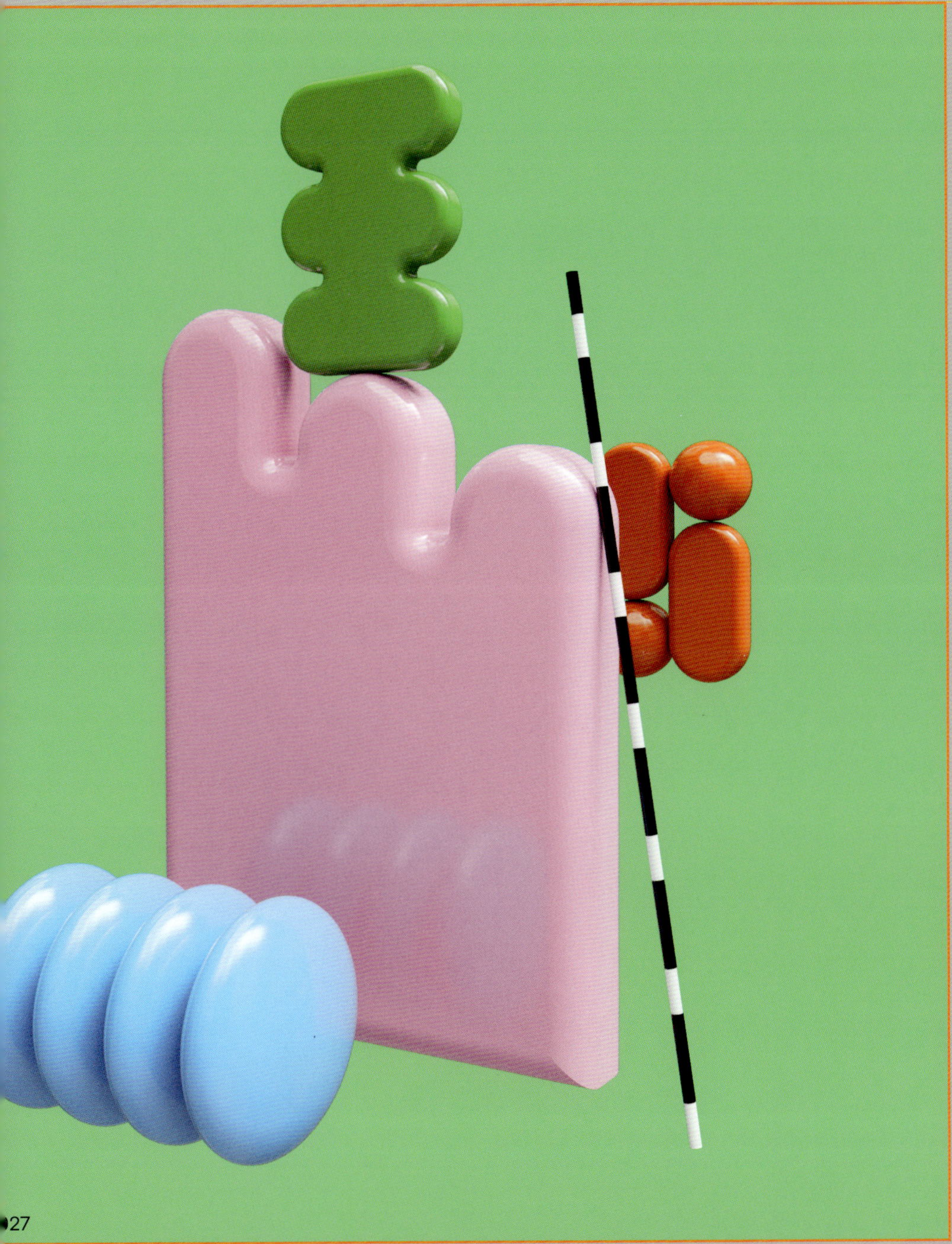

(04) [3d]→ Fluidity

: "Be Water" by Erich Brechbühl channels Bruce Lee's philosophical fluidity into striking typographic architecture. His 2016 poster for Beijing's independent art spaces transforms the martial artist's famous metaphor into visual poetry, where letterforms flow and adapt like liquid mercury. Brechbühl's design philosophy itself mirrors water's adaptability – rigid structure dissolving into organic movement.

Studio/Designer Erich Brechbühl Title Be Water
Year 2016 Client Independent Art Spaces, Beijing
Typeface(s) Suisse Intl.

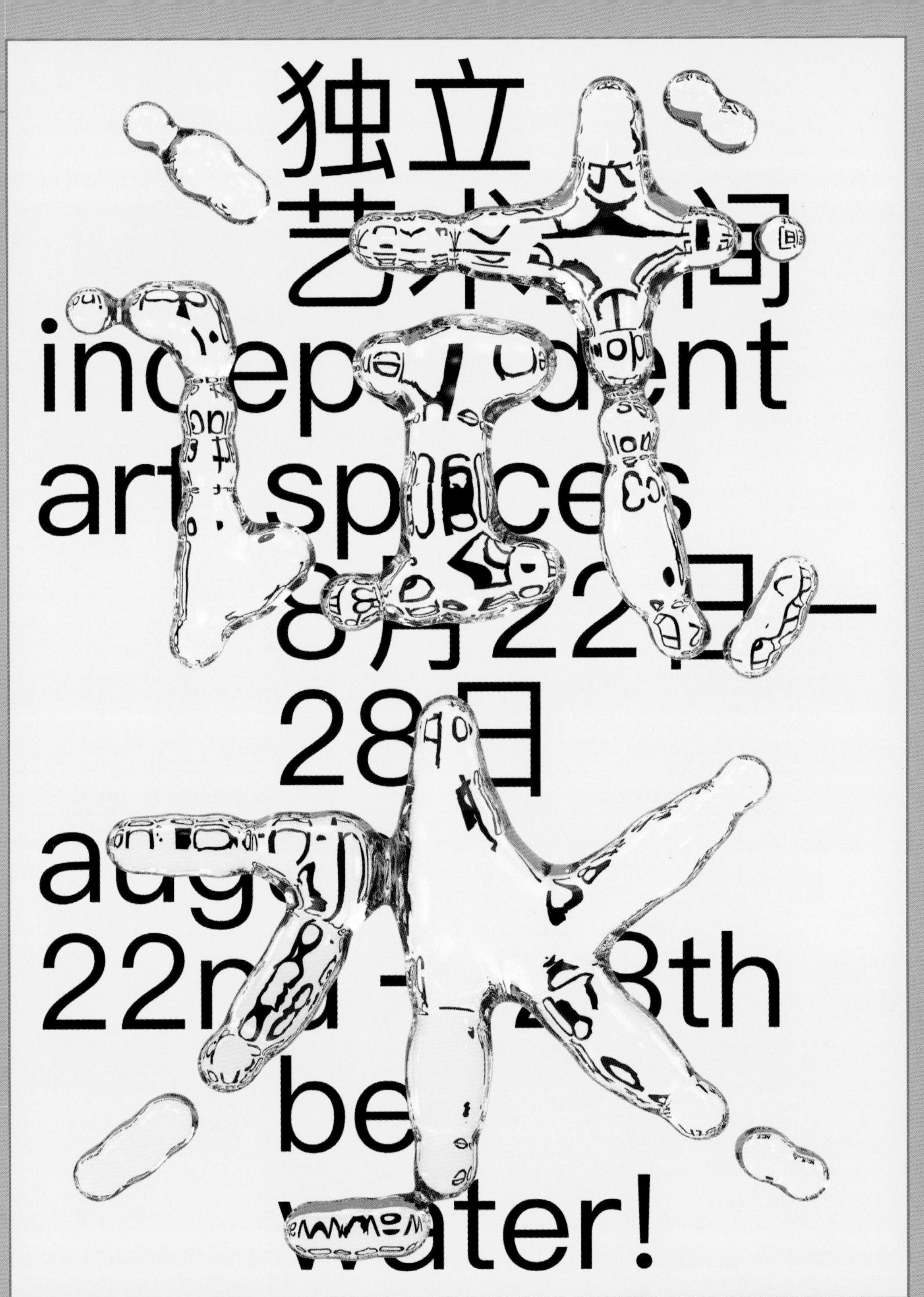
独立
28日
be
water!

Studio/Designer Sebastian Koseda

Title RCA2023 Year 2023 Client Royal College of Art

Typeface(s) Helvetica Neue (Modified)

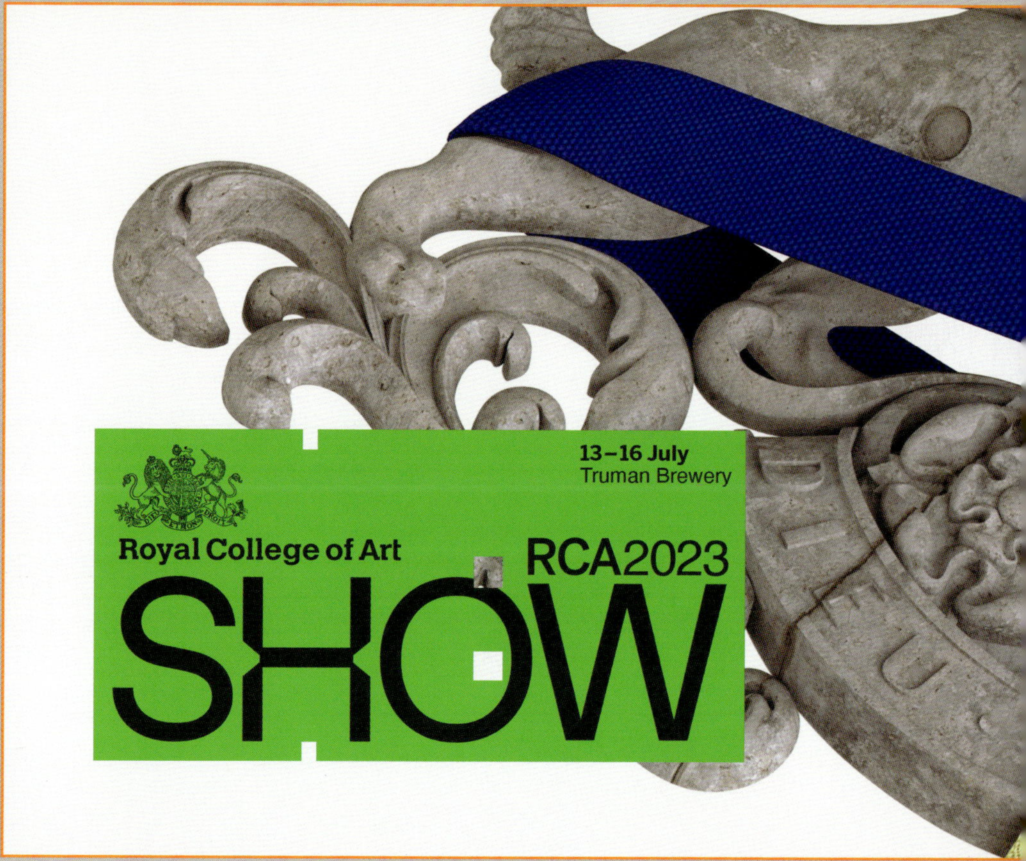

(05)

[3d]→ Deconstructe

Special Credits

(3D Support) William Fairbrother
(Sound Design) James Rogers

: The identity for RCA2023 was built around a deconstructed royal crest, crafted using materials that represent the diverse range of courses at the Royal College of Art. Featured across motion graphics, printed materials, and the exterior vinyl on the Battersea and South Kensington campuses, it also appeared prominently at the Truman Brewery, which housed the RCA MA2 courses.

30 June – 3 July
RCA Battersea
& Kensington
Royal College of Art
/RCA2023
→
Exhibitions/
Events/
Ideas/
Experiences/
Innovation/

Royal College of Art
/RCA2023
Exhibitions/
Events/
Ideas/
Experiences/
Innovation/
2023.rca.ac.uk

Royal College of Art
30 June – 3 July
RCA Battersea
& Kensington
/RCA2023
Exhibitions/
Events/
Ideas/
Experiences/
Innovation/
2023.rca.ac.uk
Animation,
Service Design

Royal College of Art
30 June – 3 July
RCA Battersea
& Kensington
/RCA2023
←
Exhibitions/
Events/
Ideas/
Experiences/
Innovation/
2023.rca.ac.uk
1
2

HOW CAN
DESIGN PRE-
PARE US FOR
DESIGNING
FOR AN AGEING
POPULATION

Studio/Designer Sebastian Koseda

Title RCA2024 Year 2024 Client Royal College of Art

Typeface(s) Helvetica Neue (Modified)

(06) [3d]→ Crests

Special Credits

(3D Support) William Fairbrother
(Sound Design) James Rogers

: Similar to the previous year, the RCA2024 identity featured eight uniquely designed royal crests that each represented a different school within the Royal College of Art. The designs were showcased across the Battersea and South Kensington campuses, as well as the Truman Brewery in Shoreditch as motion graphics, printed materials, and on large-scale vinyl.

Royal College of Art
RCA2024
School of Communication
Festival of Communication

Royal College of Art
RCA2024
School of Design
postgraduate exhibition
and events

Royal College of Art
RCA2024
School of Architecture
postgraduate exhibition
and events

Royal College of Art
School of Arts
& Humanities
postgraduate exhibition
and events
RCA2024

(07)

[3d]→ Details

: Daniel Bornmann's personal poster experiments combine intricate 3D visuals with custom typography. Each piece explores unusual and unexpected compositions, showcasing a hands-on approach to visual storytelling and form-driven design.

Studio/Designer Daniel Bornmann Title Hypnotised
Year 2024-2025 Client Self-initiated

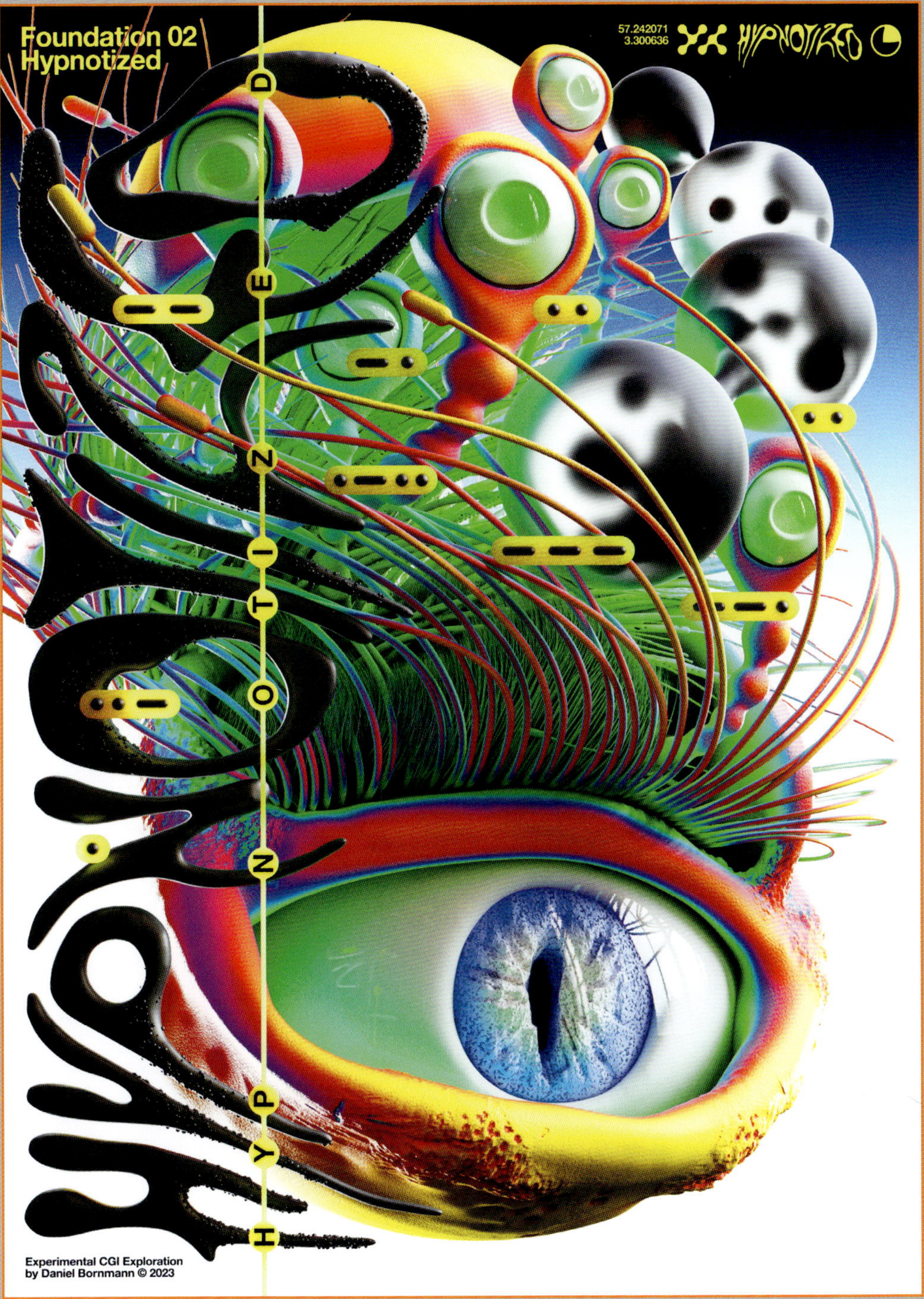
Foundation 02
Hypnotized
57.242071
3.300636
HYPNOTIZED
HYPNOTIZED
Experimental CGI Exploration
by Daniel Bornmann © 2023

Studio/Designer Ordinary People Title Kaleidoscope Eyes Year 2022
Client Leeum Museum of Art Typeface(s) Aktiv Grotesk KR

(08)

[3d]→ Kaleidoscope

: Kaleidoscope Eyes' identity design embodies the exhibition's immersive tech-driven experience. A static poster transforms into a dynamic 3D portal via the Kaleidoscope Eyes symbol, inviting interaction with dematerialised artworks. Extending beyond print, the work also includes animated posters, interactive web visuals, AR wall graphics, and face filters, blurring the lines between physical and virtual worlds.

Special Credits

(Motion Graphics) Particle Field
(Poster Sound) Moonki Jeong
(Interactive Web Poster) Chopsticks Studio
(Trigger Design) Kim Dohyun Studio

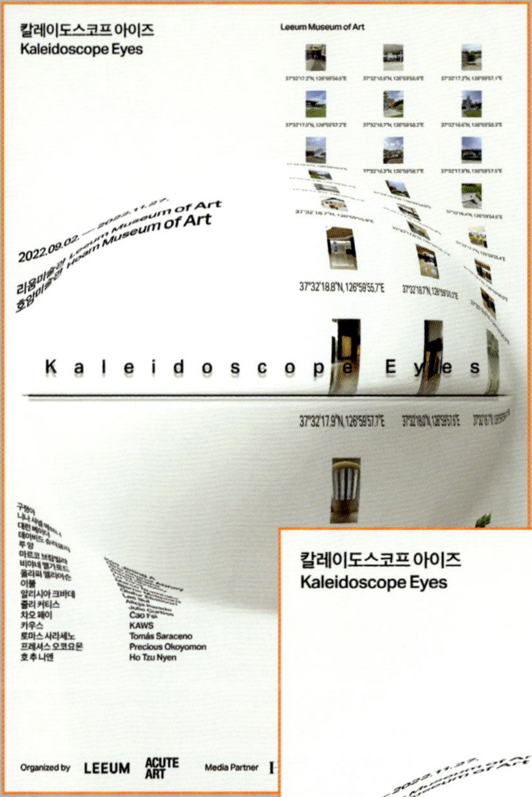
칼레이도스코프 아이즈
Kaleidoscope Eyes
Leeum Museum of Art
2022.09.02. — 2022.11.27.
리움미술관 Leeum Museum of Art
호암미술관 Hoam Museum of Art
Kaleidoscope Eyes
37°32'18.8"N, 126°59'55.7"E
37°32'17.9"N, 126°59'57.7"E
Cao Fei
KAWS
Tomás Saraceno
Precious Okoyomon
Ho Tzu Nyen
Organized by LEEUM ACUTE ART Media Partner

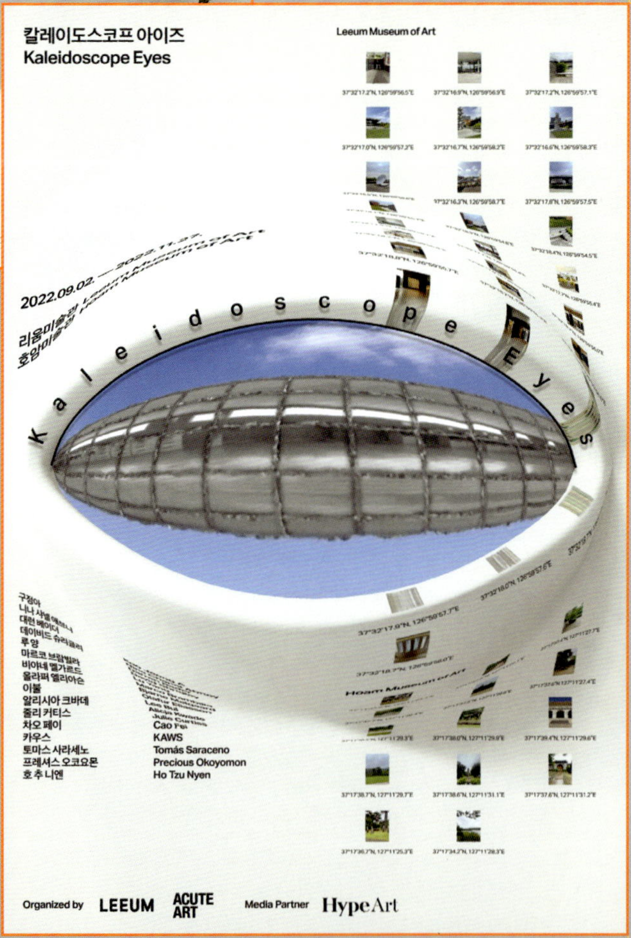
칼레이도스코프 아이즈
Kaleidoscope Eyes
Leeum Museum of Art
2022.09.02. — 2022.11.27.
리움미술관 Leeum Museum of Art
호암미술관 Hoam Museum of Art
Kaleidoscope Eyes
37°32'17.9"N, 126°59'57.7"E
37°32'18.0"N, 126°59'57.6"E
Hoam Museum of Art
구정아
나나 사볼레비스니
대런 베이더
데이비드 슈리글리
루 양
마르코 브람빌라
비야네 멜가드
올라퍼 엘리아슨
이불
알리시아 크바데
줄리 커티스
차오 페이
카우스
토마스 사라세노
프레셔스 오코요몬
호 추 니엔
Cao Fei
KAWS
Tomás Saraceno
Precious Okoyomon
Ho Tzu Nyen
Organized by LEEUM ACUTE ART Media Partner HypeArt

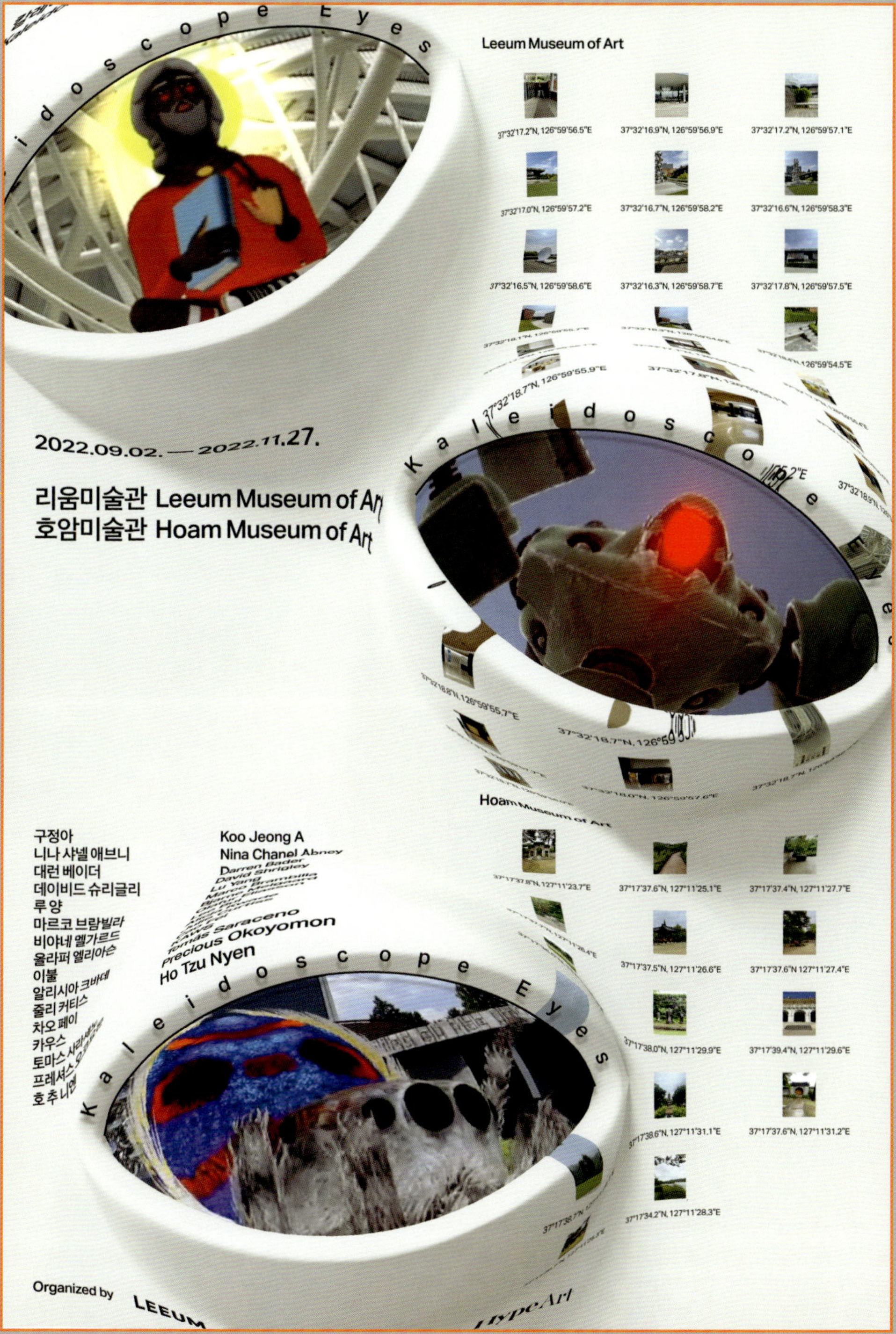
Leeum Museum of Art
37°32'17.2"N, 126°59'56.5"E
37°32'16.9"N, 126°59'56.9"E
37°32'17.2"N, 126°59'57.1"E
37°32'17.0"N, 126°59'57.2"E
37°32'16.7"N, 126°59'58.2"E
37°32'16.6"N, 126°59'58.3"E
37°32'16.5"N, 126°59'58.6"E
37°32'16.3"N, 126°59'58.7"E
37°32'17.8"N, 126°59'57.5"E
2022.09.02. — 2022.11.27.
리움미술관 Leeum Museum of Art
호암미술관 Hoam Museum of Art
Hoam Museum of Art
37°17'37.6"N, 127°11'25.1"E
37°17'37.4"N, 127°11'27.7"E
37°17'37.5"N, 127°11'26.6"E
37°17'37.6"N 127°11'27.4"E
37°17'38.0"N, 127°11'29.9"E
37°17'39.4"N, 127°11'29.6"E
37°17'38.6"N, 127°11'31.1"E
37°17'37.6"N, 127°11'31.2"E
37°17'34.2"N, 127°11'28.3"E
구정아
니나 샤넬 애브니
대런 베이더
데이비드 슈리글리
루 양
마르코 브람빌라
비야네 멜가르드
올라퍼 엘리아슨
이불
알리시아 크바데
줄리 커티스
차오 페이
카우스
토마스
프레셔스
호 추 니엔
Koo Jeong A
Nina Chanel Abney
Darren Bader
David Shrigley
Tomás Saraceno
Precious Okoyomon
Ho Tzu Nyen
Organized by
LEEUM
HypeArt

칼레이도스코프 아이즈
Kaleidoscope Eyes
2022.09.02. — 2022.11.27.
리움미술관 Leeum Museum of Art
호암미술관 Hoam Museum of Art
카우스
토마스 사라세노
프레셔스 오코요몬
호추니엔
Tomás Saraceno
Precious Okoyomon
Ho Tzu Nyen
Media Partner HypeArt
ACUTE ART

칼레이도스코프 아이즈
Kaleidoscope Eyes
2022.09.02. — 2022.11.27.
Leeum Museum of Art
Hoam Museum of Art
Kaleidoscope Eyes
Hoam Museum of Art
37°32'17.2"N, 126°59'57.1"E
37°32'16.6"N, 126°59'58.3"E
37°32'18.7"N, 126°59'56.0"E
37°17'37.4"N, 127°11'27
Lu Yang
Bjarne Melgaard
Olafur Eliasson
Lee Bul
Alicja Kwade
Tomás Saraceno
Precious Okoyomon
Ho Tzu Nyen
카우스
프레셔스 오코요몬
호 추 니엔
Organized by
ACUTE ART
Media Partner
HypeArt

적어도 내게 있어 정밀한 디지털 엔지니어링 기술의
결과물로 탄생한 이 작은 작품은 완전히 새로운 전시와
미술의 영역을 열어주었다. 그해 말, 이 작품은 리젠트 파크로
돌아왔고, 프리즈 조각(Frieze Sculpture)展에 정식으로
출품되었다.
사람들은 대부분 디지털 예술작품이라고 하면 모든
곳이면서 그 어디도 아닌 또 다른 영역에 떠다니는 무언가를
떠올린다. 그러나 구정아의 큐브는 그렇지 않다. 작업이
놓인 특정 위치에서만 이를 감상할 수 있다. 그것은 희귀한
오브제이다. 특정 GPS 좌표와 지상으로부터의 정확한 높이를
갖추고 있으며, 핸드폰으로 보면 실재하는 듯 보인다. 사진을
찍어 다른 이에게 보내주더라도 받아 본 사람 주변의 물체나
사람만큼이나 사실적으로 보인다.
최근 몇 년간 또 다른 예술가들도 이러한 가능성을 깊이
탐구하고 있다. 가장 눈에 띄는 예로는 의심의 여지 없이
카우스(KAWS)의 사례를 들 수 있겠다. 그는 기술적 가능성을
활용하여 전 세계 모든 대륙의 수많은 관객이 즐길 수 있는
참여 예술의 새로운 형태를 확립하였다. 코로나로 인한 봉쇄
중에도 가상 블록버스터를 세상에 내보였다.
신 매체의 출현은 항상 예술의 또 다른 가능성을
열어주며, 각 시대마다 기술과 예술의 창의적인 만남을
보여주는 대표적인 작가들이 있었다. 오늘날의 몰입형
미디어는 예술의 생산 및 유통에 있어 전례 없는 가능성을
제시하였고, 증강현실의 도래는 새로운 비물질적 예술 형태를
탄생시켰다고 해도 과언이 아닐 것이다. 2020년 봄, 카우스는
아시아, 유럽, 아프리카, 호주, 미국의 주요 도시와 장소에서
10점의 커다란 공공조형물 <EXPANDED HOLIDAY>를
전시했다. 이 프로젝트는 이전과는 전혀 다른 국제 전시
형식을 도입한 것이다.
예술가들은 늘 새로운 기술을 수용해 왔다. 그러나
지난 한 세기 동안 이탈리아 미래주의와 러시아 구축주의,
백남준과 1960년대 E.A.T.(예술과 기술의 실험) 단체의
활동을 포함한 기술 낙관주의의 순간들이 있었다고 해도,
현대 기술을 대하는 예술계의 전반적인 태도가 열광적이었다고
말할 수는 없을 것이다. 하지만 몇 해 전부터 올라퍼 엘리아슨
(Olafur Eliasson)과 차오 페이(Cao Fei)와 같은 선구자들이
최신 디지털 도구의 시적 가능성을 탐구하고 있다. 니나 샤넬
애브니(Nina Chanel Abney), 이불, 대런 베이더(Darren
Bader), 마르코 브람빌라(Marco Brambilla), 줄리 커티스
(Julie Curtiss), 알리시아 크바데(Alicja Kwade), 구정아,
비야네 멜가르드(Bjarne Melgaard), 호 추 니엔(Ho Tzu
Nyen), 프레셔스 오코요몬(Precious Okoyomon), 데이비드
슈리글리(David Shrigley), 토마스 사라세노(Tomás
Saraceno), 루 양(Lu Yang) 또한 이와 같은 가능성을
파고들고 있다.
서울의 한 미술관에 있는 당신을 상상해 보라. 지금은
2022년 가을이다. 뻥 뚫린 하늘에 작품이 등장한다. 당신의
핸드폰이라는 프리즘을 통해 모습을 드러낸다. 춤추는 거인,
시를 읽는 꽃, 인공 태양, 땅 가까이 맴도는 작은 구름. 빗방울
또한 떨어진다.
우리는 또 어떤 것들을 기대해 볼 수 있을까? 노랗고 파란
셀로판 꽃이 당신의 머리 위로 높이 솟아오른다면 어떨까.
눈 안에 태양을 담고 있는 소녀를 찾아보라. 그녀는 곧
사라진다…
다니엘 번바움
어큐트 아트 예술감독, 《칼레이도스코프 아이즈》 큐레이터
칼레이도스코프 아이즈
Kaleidoscope Eyes
Kaleidoscope
2022.09.02. — 2022.11.27.
리움미술관 Leeum Museum of Art
호암미술관 Hoam Museum of Art
Organized by
LEEUM
ACUTE ART
Media Partner
HypeArt
Picture yourself in an empty museum.
walls go transparent and works of art
mysteriously in space. Picture yourself
museum. In the garden other immaterial
– ghostlike, spectral.
Picture yourself in a boat on a river,
tangerine trees and marmalade skies.
you, you answer quite slowly. A girl with
eyes.
No matter how adamantly John
insisted that it was a mere coincidence,
were convinced that the title of his 1967
in the Sky with Diamonds" – in which the
about kaleidoscope eyes appear –
mind expanding drug LSD.
These were the days in which
drugs played a key role in psychedelic
In 1966, legendary American Psychologist
Leary established the League for Spiritual
with LSD as its "sacrament." Some years
discovered that psychedelic drugs and
Reality both have the potential to show us
worlds and break the constraints of our
experience. Since its conception, Virtual
been inextricably linked to the idea of
experience. The early discussion around
directly related to psychedelic culture and
capacity of drugs to drastically alter our
Leary believed in what he called
the synthesis of psychedelic drugs and
He was convinced that with this combined
we would be able to reprogram the mind.
as far as changing his popular catchphrase
tune in, drop out" to "turn on, boot up, and

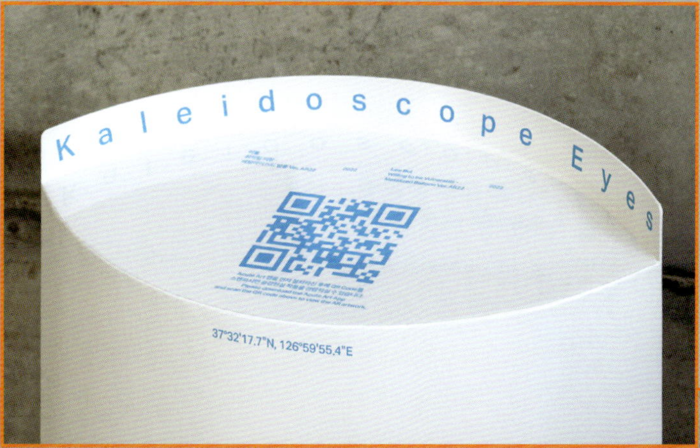
Kaleidoscope Eyes
37°32'17.7"N, 126°59'55.4"E

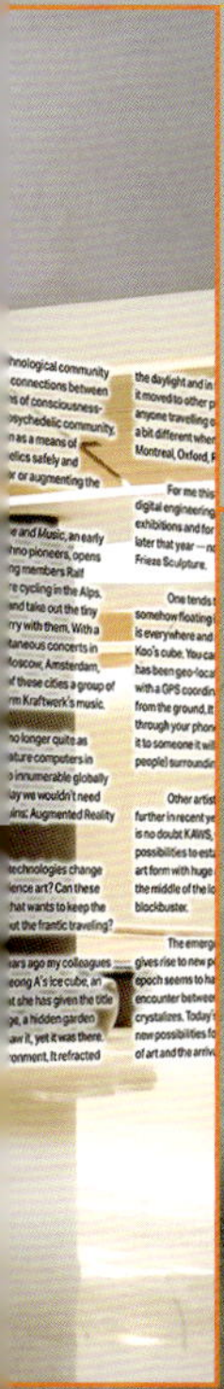

Kaleidoscope Eyes
LEEUM
ACUTE ART
HypeArt

1. 구를 확대하여 눈 안으로 들어가 보세요.
2. 작은 안구를 클릭하여 가상의 전시를 즐겨 보세요.
1. Zoom in on the sphere to go into the eyeball.
2. Enjoy the virtual exhibition by clicking the small eyeballs.
Koo
Nina
Darren
David
Lu Yang
Marco
Bjarne
Olafur Eliasson
Lee Bul
Alicja Kwade
Julie Curtiss
Cao Fei
KAWS
Tomás Saraceno
Precious
Ho Tzu
데이비드 슈리글리
이불
알리시아 크바데
카우스
토마스 사라세노
프레셔스 오코요몬

Lu Yang
Marco Brambilla
Bjarne Melgaard
Olafur Eliasson
Alicja Kwade
Julie Curtiss
KAWS
Tomás Saraceno
Ho Tzu Nyen
루 양
데이비드 슈리글리

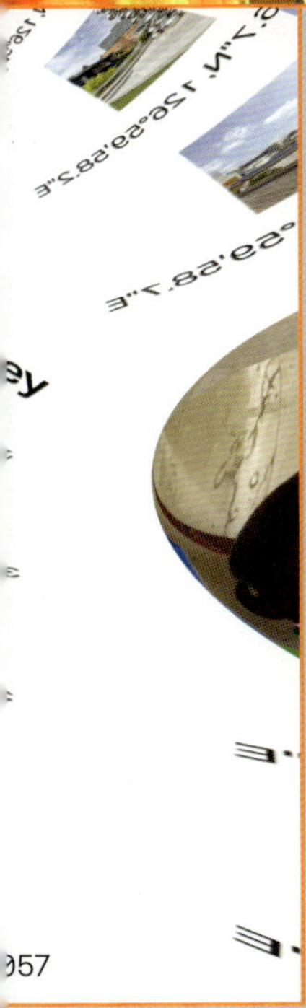

Bundestagswahl 2025
23.02.2025
WAHL
VOTE
WAHL
VOTE
WAHL
VOTE

(09)

[3d]→ Vote

Studio/Designer Dennis Hoelscher Title WAHL | VOTE - 23.02.2025

Year 2025 Client Self-initiated

: Dennis Hoelscher's dynamic poster encouraged civic engagement ahead of Germany's 2025 election by emphasising the importance of personal choice. It features rotating letterforms designed to be legible from multiple angles, reflecting the multifaceted nature of voting and inspiring viewers to take action.

(10)

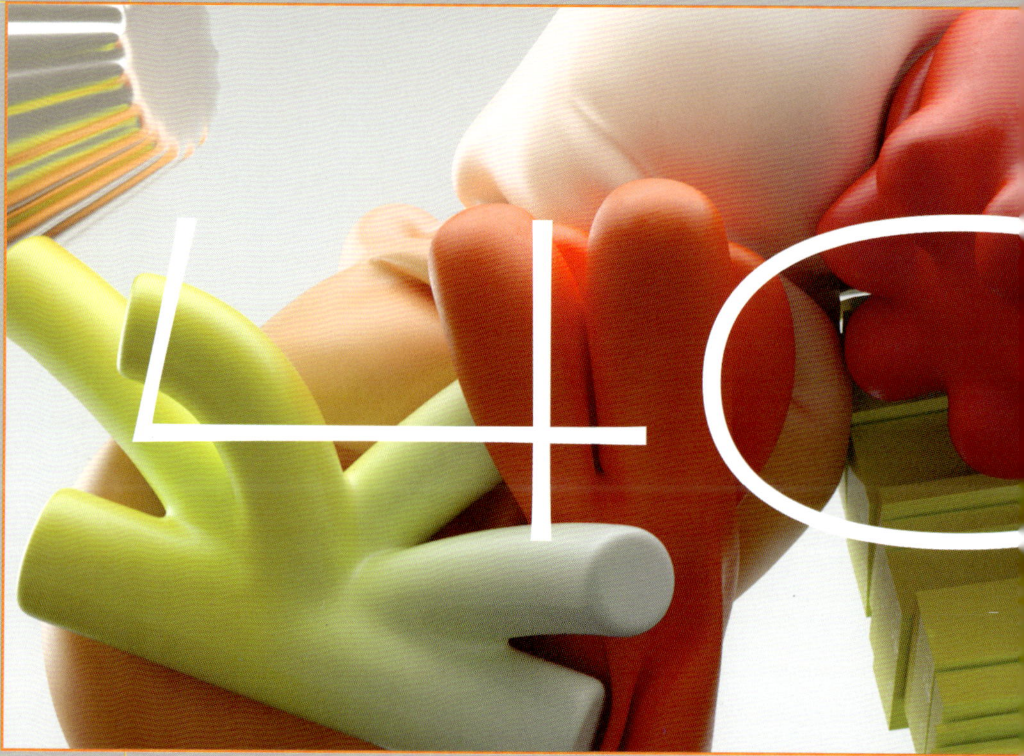

: Kind of Studio's REUNION! campaign for Turkey's 40th GMK Award Ceremony celebrates the joy of coming together after separation. The visuals progress through three phases – Separated, Noticing, and Party Hard – starting with solitary forms that gradually unite, culminating in vibrant, energetic compositions that embody the emotional release and celebration of reunion.

[3d]→ Reunion

Studio/Designer Kaan Iscan Hazal Özkaya Ethem Cem Title Reunion Year 2021 Client GMK (Graphic Design Association of Turkey) Typeface(s) Obviously Wide

40.
GRAFİK
TASARIM
SERGİSİ
BAŞVURULARI
ÇOK YAKINDA!
GMK
GMK
GMK
GMK
GMK
GMK

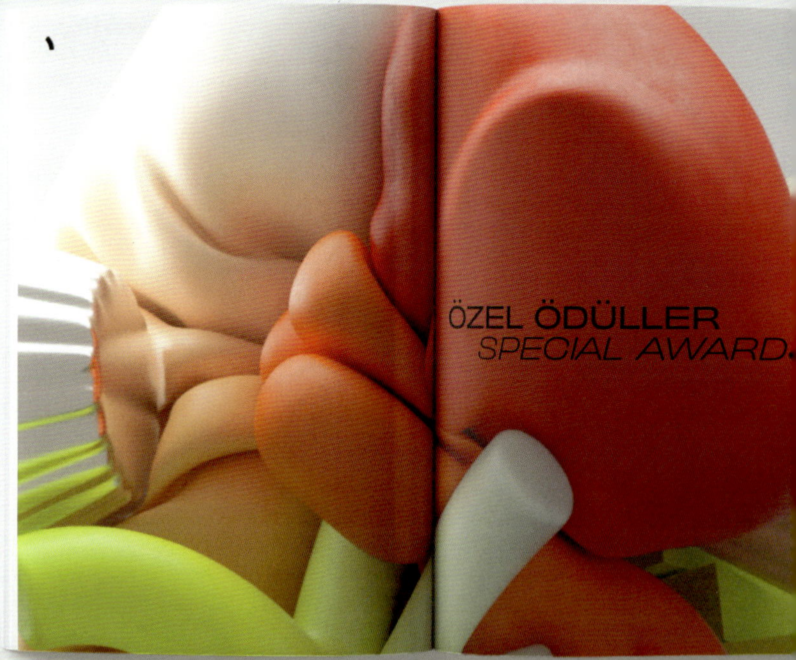
ÖZEL ÖDÜLLER
SPECIAL AWARDS

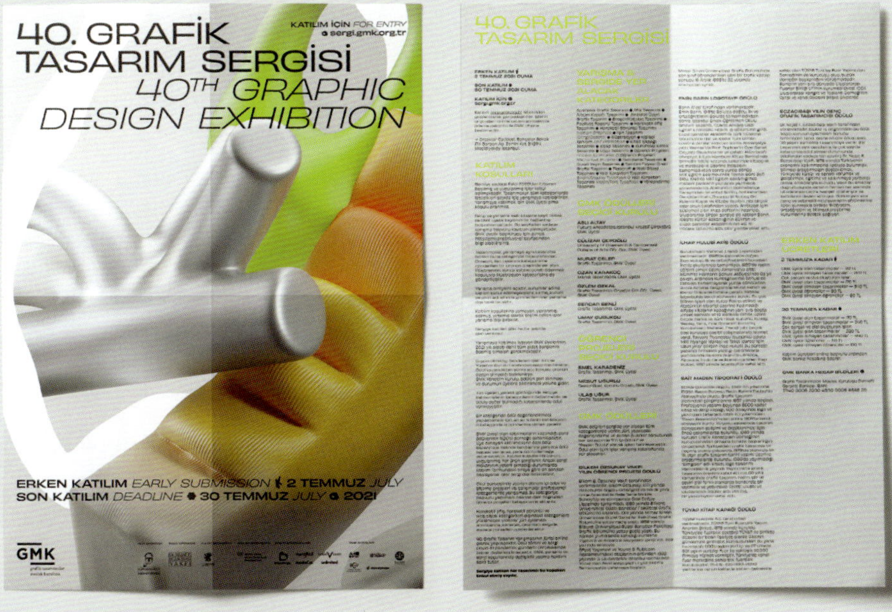
40. GRAFİK TASARIM SERGİSİ
40TH GRAPHIC DESIGN EXHIBITION
KATILIM İÇİN FOR ENTRY
sergi.gmk.org.tr
ERKEN KATILIM EARLY SUBMISSION 2 TEMMUZ JULY
SON KATILIM DEADLINE 30 TEMMUZ JULY 2021
GMK
40. GRAFİK TASARIM SERGİSİ

40. GRAFİK TASARIM
GMK
40. GRAFİK
GMK
AFİŞ
TASARIMI
BAŞARI
ÖDÜLÜ
40. GRAFİK TASARIM SERGİSİ
GMK
BROŞÜR/KATALOG
TASARIMI
BAŞARI ÖDÜLÜ
40. GRAFİK TASARIM SERGİSİ
GMK
FAALİYET RAPORU
TASARIM SERGİSİ
GMK

TASAR
GM
AMBAL
GRAFİ

40. GRAFİK TASARIM SERGİSİ
40TH GRAPHIC DESIGN EXHIBITION
12 EKİM OCTOBER
8 KASIM NOVEMBER 2021
MSGÜ TOPHANE'İ ÂMİRE KSM
GMK

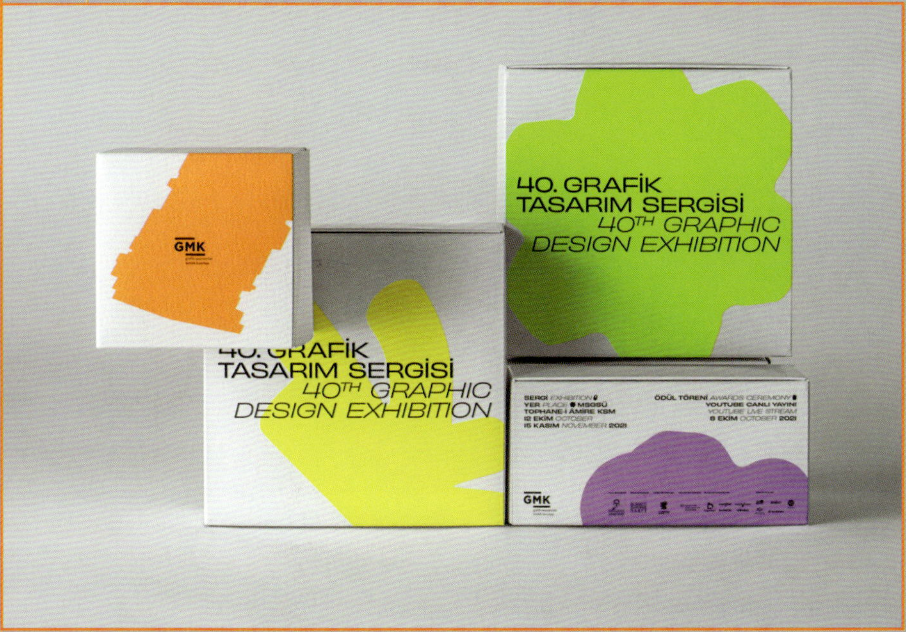
40. GRAFİK
TASARIM SERGİSİ
40TH GRAPHIC
DESIGN EXHIBITION
GMK
SERGİ EXHIBITION
YER PLACE MSGSÜ
TOPHANE-İ ÂMİRE KSM
12 EKİM OCTOBER
15 KASIM NOVEMBER 2021
ÖDÜL TÖRENİ AWARDS CEREMONY
YOUTUBE CANLI YAYINI
YOUTUBE LIVE STREAM
8 EKİM OCTOBER 2021

(11) [3d]→ Cyber-organic

: Daniel Bornmann's poster design for Duat x Concrete at Mensch Meier captures the raw intensity of techno and the industrial spirit of its Berlin venue through a bold and immersive visual language. With abstract forms, rhythmic structures, and layered textures, it reflects the pulsating energy of the music and the atmospheric depth of the space.

Studio/Designer Daniel Bornmann

Title Duat x Concrete at Mensch Meier

Year 2022 Client Duat Records

Typeface(s) Custom, Adina, Helvetica Medium

30.07.22
MENSCH MEIER
23 — 12
CONCRETE
AMIN FALLAHA · DMCG B2B LØUS · DRIVE BY · ELUZID
GUZY · JUST LAUREN · MOIA · RUEDE HAGELSTEIN
SAGAN · TOM PETERS · UNCNSRD · VINYA · YARA

Special Credits

(Creative Direction) Jeff Zemetis
(Motion Design & Music Production) Amigo Total

(12)

[3d]→

Happiness

: Crafted by The Royal Studio, the 2019 Lovie Awards identity celebrates moments of joy and excitement with the expression: yay! The visuals capture physical manifestations of happiness, featured across large-scale installations like BFI walls and mupis to reflect the creative spirit of the awards and Europe's vibrant internet community.

Studio/Designer The Royal Studio Title Lovie Awards
Year 2019 Client The Lovie Awards Typeface(s) Bizarrerie, Brush Script, DomaineDisp-Regular, EckmannDEE, EuropaGroNr2SHOP, Haltrix, Luminari ,Maelstrom , Messapia, PVC Menu

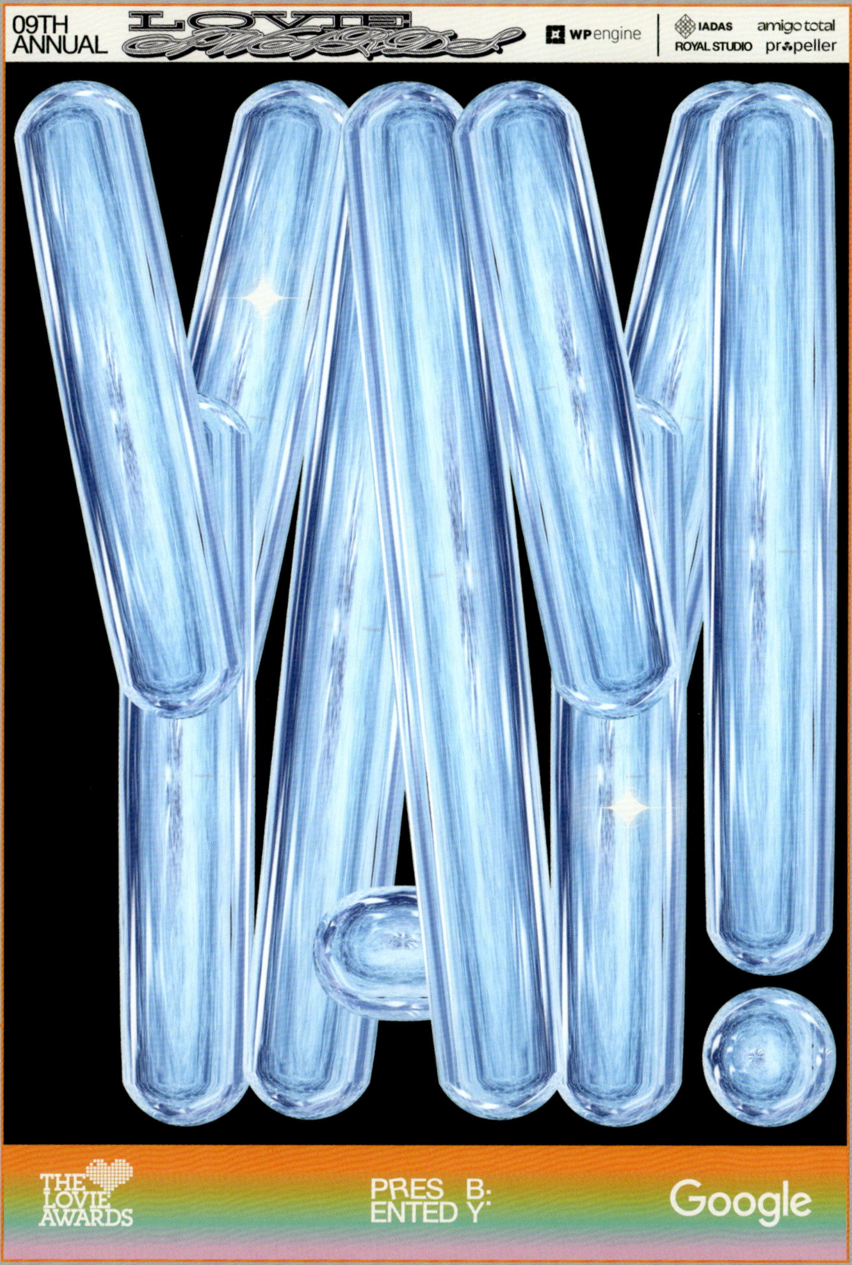

THE LOVIE AWARDS
PRES B:
ENTED Y:
Google
09TH
ANNUAL
WP engine
IADAS
amigo total
ROYAL STUDIO
propeller

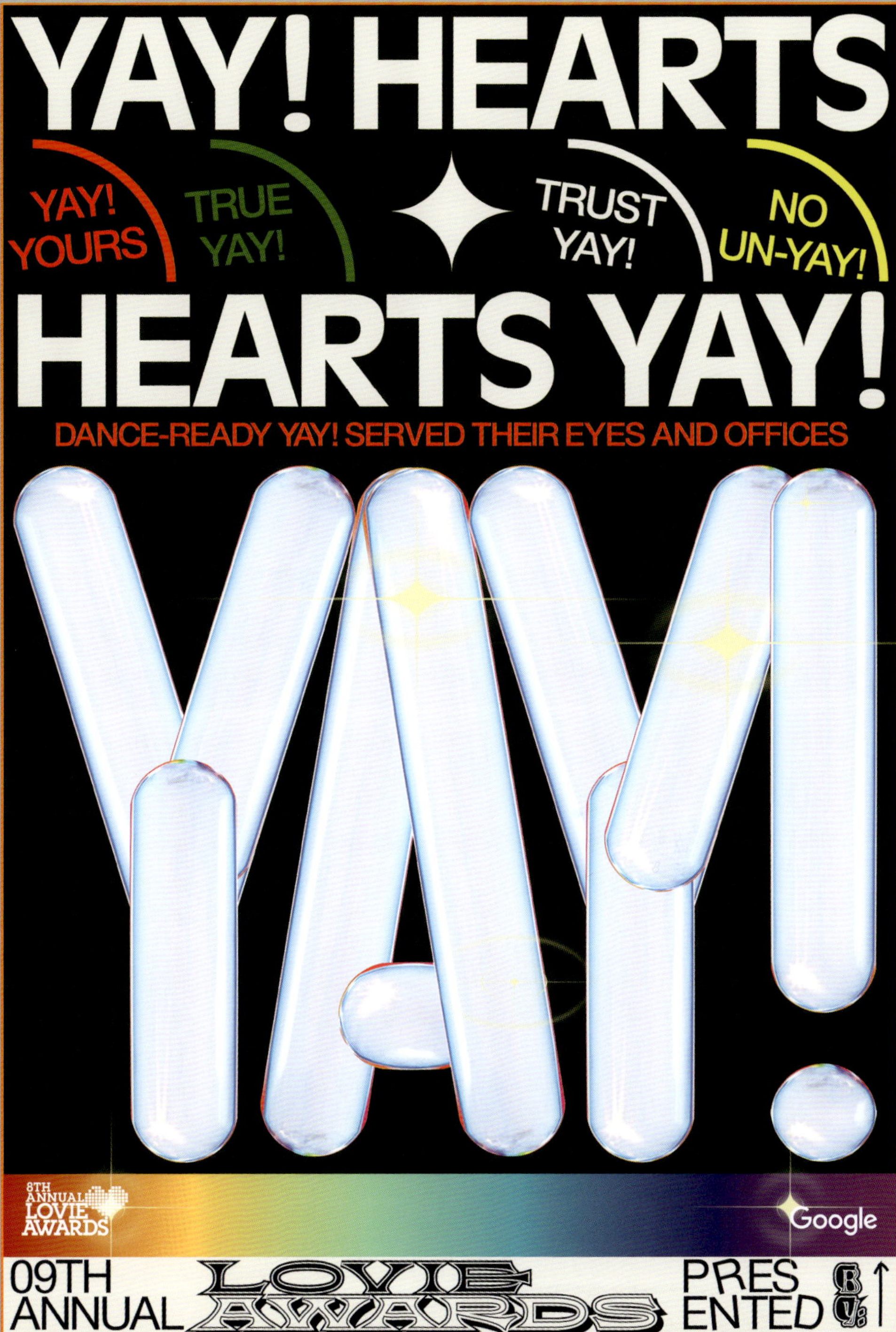
YAY! HEARTS
YAY! YOURS
TRUE YAY!
TRUST YAY!
NO UN-YAY!
HEARTS YAY!
DANCE-READY YAY! SERVED THEIR EYES AND OFFICES
YAY!
8TH ANNUAL LOVIE AWARDS
Google
09TH ANNUAL
LOVIE AWARDS
PRES ENTED BY:

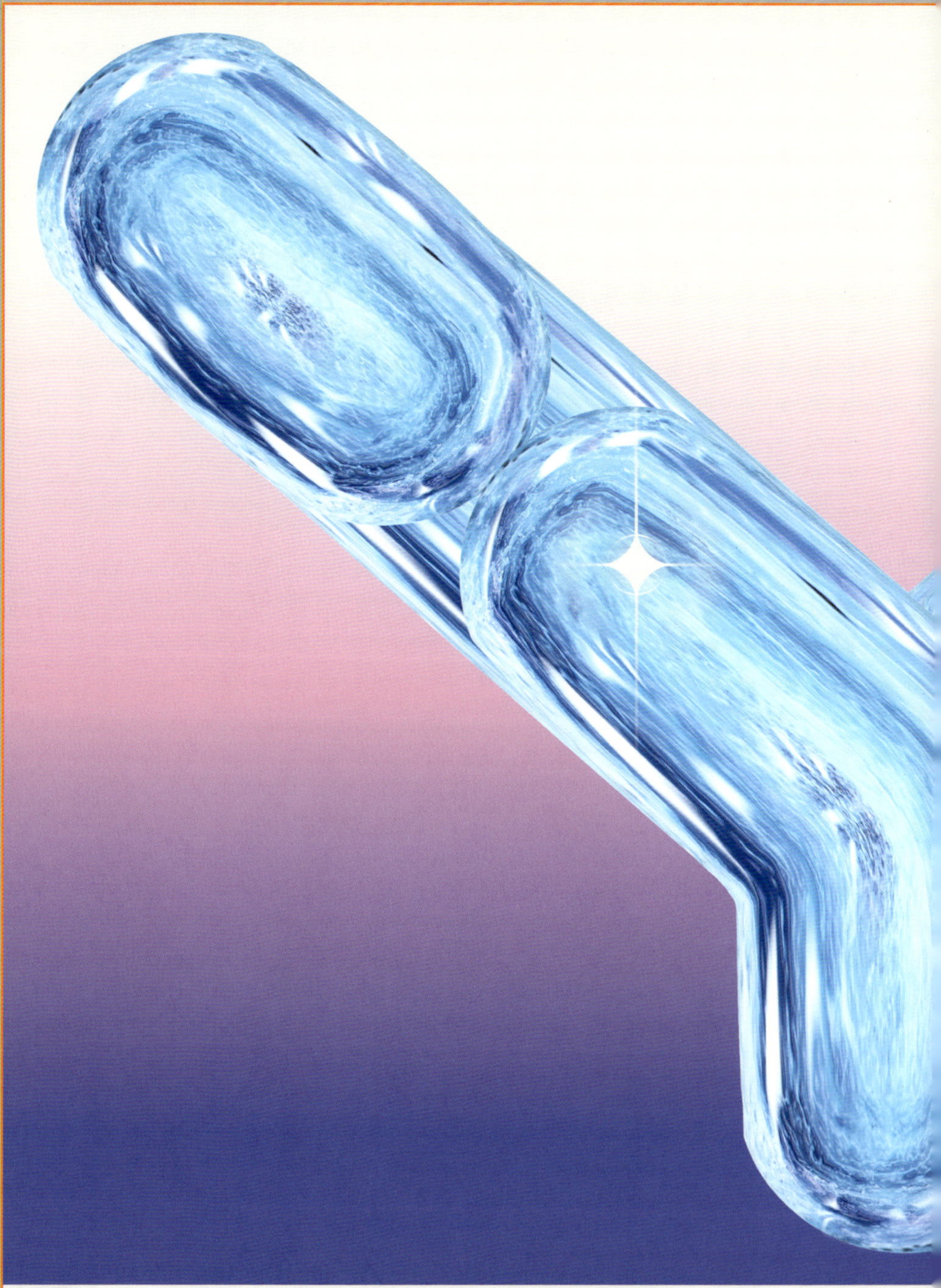

09TH ANNUAL LOVIE THE LOVIE AWARDS

PRESENTED BY:
Google
WP engine
IADAS
amigo total
ROYAL STUDIO
propeller

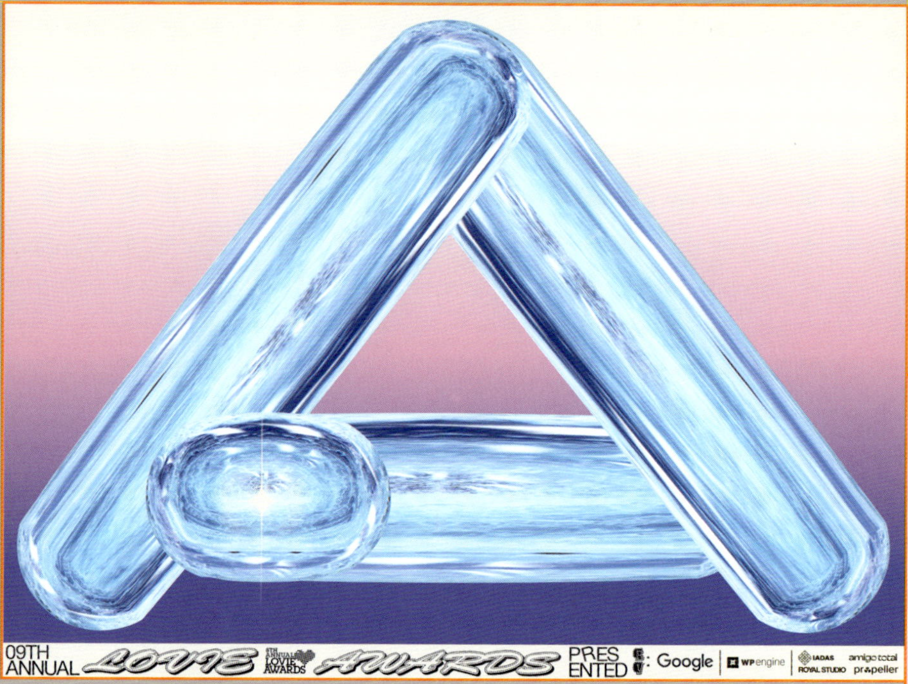
09TH
ANNUAL
LOVIE
AWARDS
PRES
ENTED
Google
WP engine
IADAS
ROYAL STUDIO
amigo total
propeller

09TH
ANNUAL

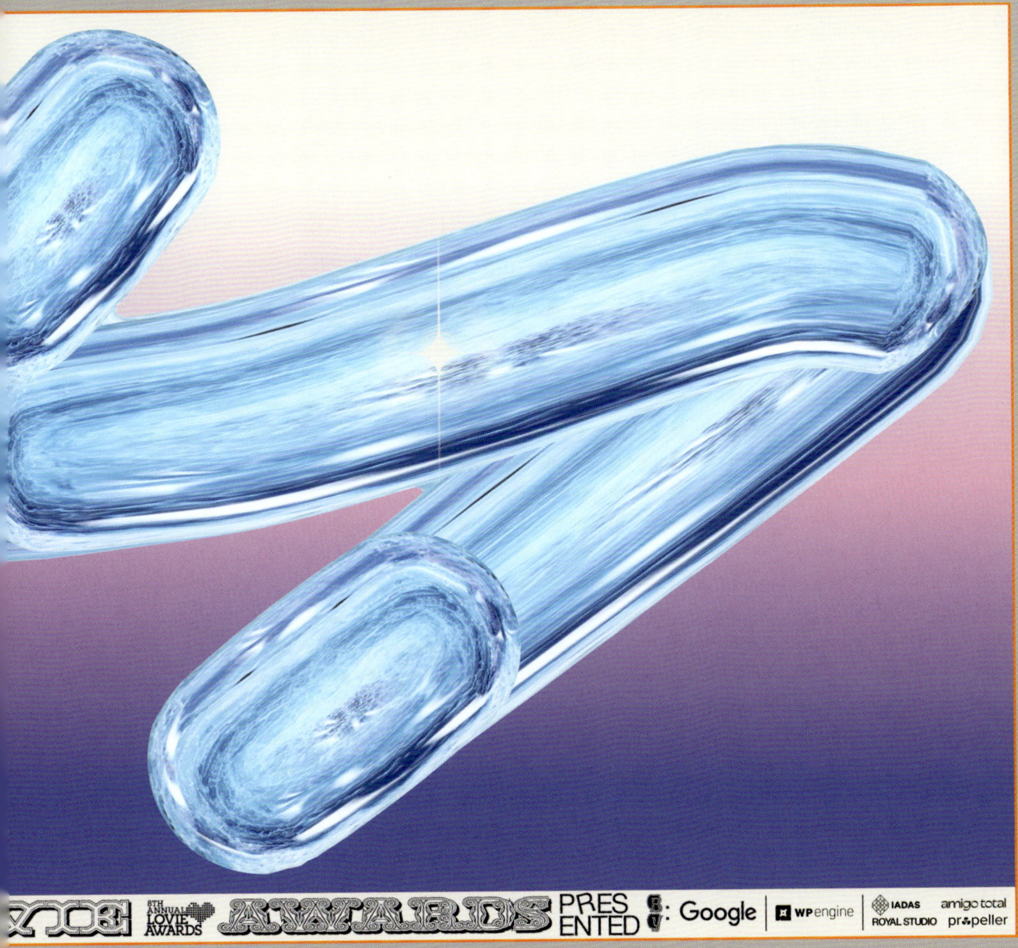
8TH ANNUAL LOVIE AWARDS
AWARDS
PRESENTED BY: Google
WP engine
IADAS
ROYAL STUDIO
amigo total
propeller

09TH ANNUAL
8TH ANNUAL LOVIE AWARDS

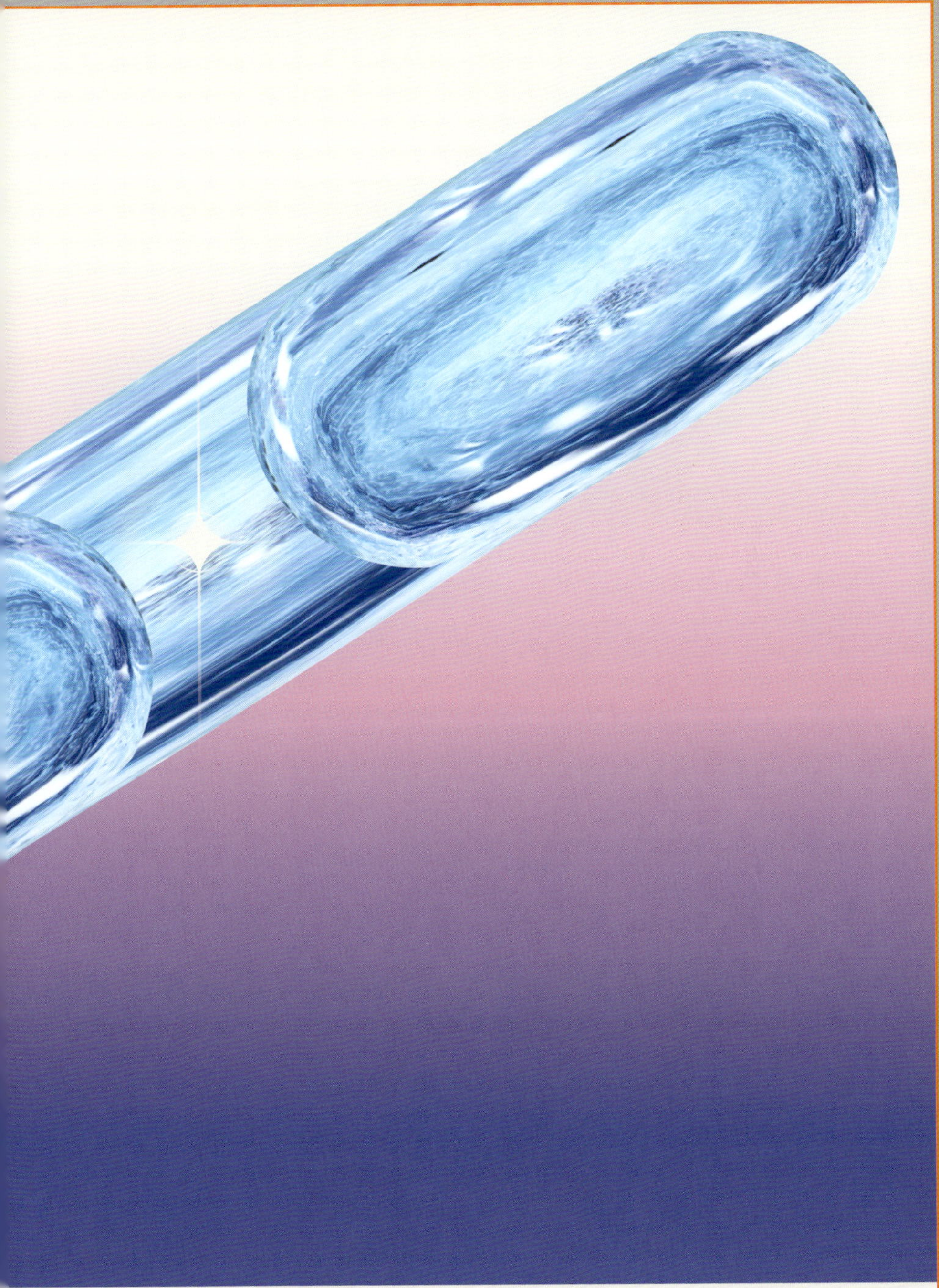

RDS PRESENTED BY: Google | WP engine | IADAS amigo total ROYAL STUDIO propeller

Studio/Designer Everyday Practice Title Gyeonggi Ceramics Biennale 2024 “TOGETHER_ Montaigne’s Cat”

Year 2024 Client Korea Ceramic Foundation

Typeface(s) HARBER, AG Super Black Gothic Condensed, Söhne, Sandoll Gothic Neo Unicode 1

(13)

[3d]→ Floating

: The 2024 Gyeonggi Ceramics Biennale's theme, TOGETHER_ Montaigne’s Cat, was inspired by Richard Sennett's “Together: The Ritual, Pleasure, and Politics of Cooperation”. Everyday Practice brought this theme to life, exploring how “lost co-operation” could be restored in modern society. The logotype, formed from diverse particles and floating graphics in the shape of a cat, symbolised cooperation amidst societal conflicts.

TOGETHER
몽테뉴의 고양이
2024
경기도자비엔날레
Gyeonggi Ceramics Biennale 2024
Montaigne's Cat
이천 · 여주 · 광주 · 경기곳곳
Icheon, Yeoju, Gwangju, and other cities throughout Gyeonggi-do
주최 경기도
주관 한국도자재단
Host Gyeonggi-do Office
Organizer Korea Ceramic Foundation
후원 문화체육관광부, 행정안전부, 외교부, 산업통상자원부, 고용노동부, 한국관광공사
Sponsor Ministry of Culture, Sports and Tourism, Ministry of the Interior and Safety, Ministry of Foreign Affairs, Ministry of Trade, Industry and Energy, Ministry of Employment and Labor, Korea Tourism Organization
2024.9.6.–10.20.
FOR A PERIOD OF 45 DAYS
45
GCB
GYEONGGI CERAMICS BIENNALE
경기도
한국도자재단

(14) [3d]→ Focus

: The 58th Golden Horse Awards visual design marked the first time the film event was treated as a brand. With the theme "Refocus: Adjusting Our Distance to the World", the identity used motion to reflect post-pandemic perspectives. 3D Chinese characters for "Golden Horse", "Trophy", and "58" transformed dynamically, mimicking camera movements to explore focus, clarity, and perception through kinetic typography.

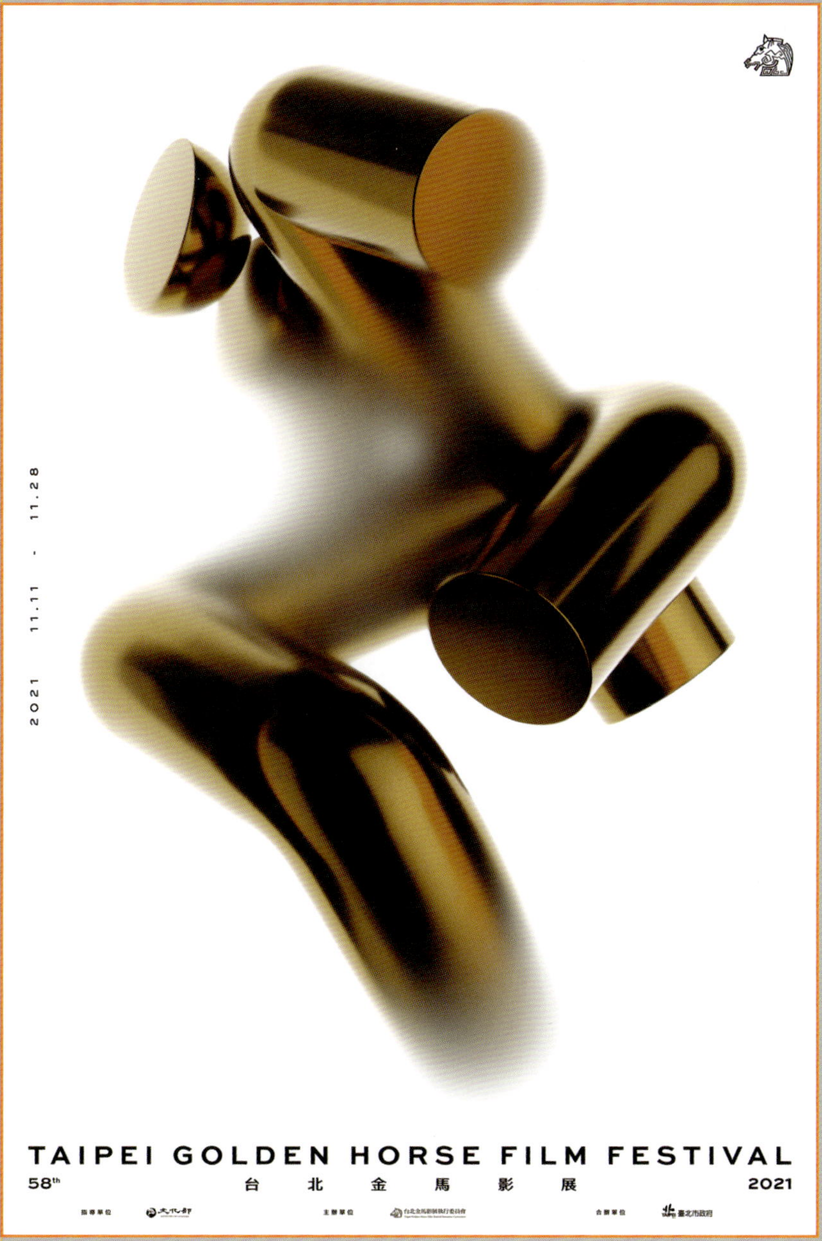

Studio/Designer Bito Title 58th Golden Horse Awards Visual Design
Year 2021 Client Golden Horse Film Festival Executive Committee

2021 11.11 - 11.28
TAIPEI GOLDEN HORSE FILM FESTIVAL
58th
台北金馬影展
2021
指導單位 文化部
主辦單位 台北金馬影展執行委員會
合辦單位 臺北市政府

2021 11.11 - 11.28
TAIPEI GOLDEN HORSE FILM FESTIVAL
58th
台北金馬影展
2021
指導單位
文化部
主辦單位
台北金馬影展執行委員會
合辦單位
臺北市政府

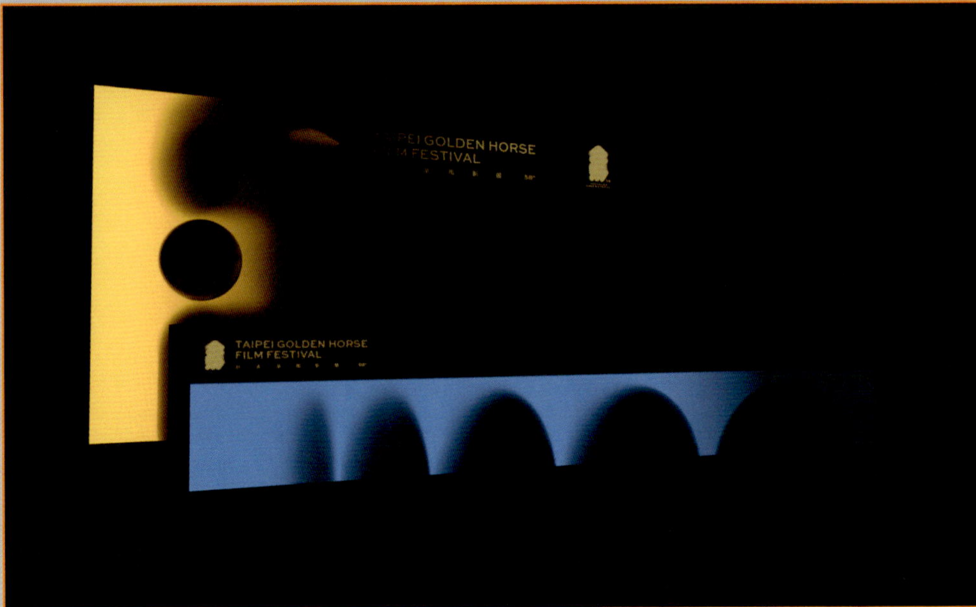
TAIPEI GOLDEN HORSE
FILM FESTIVAL

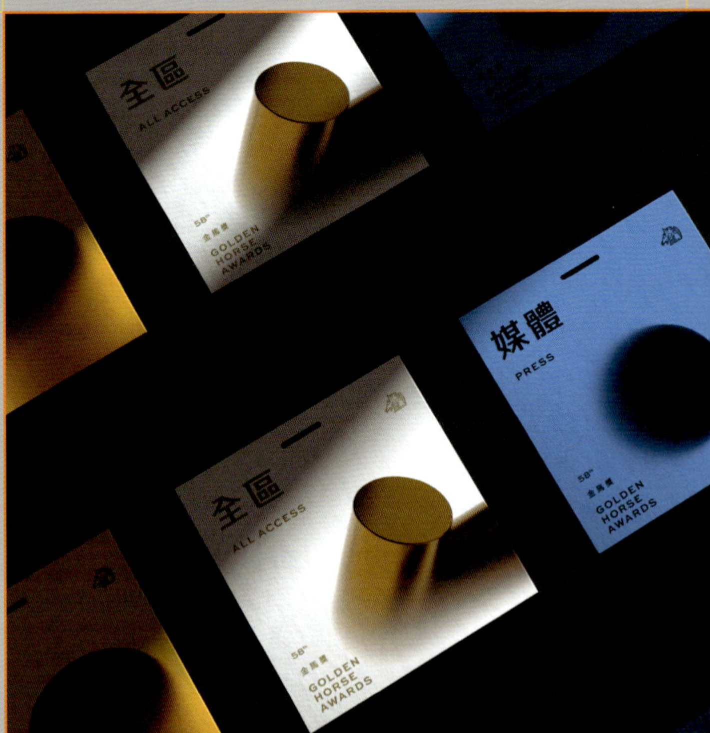
全區
ALL ACCESS
58th
金馬獎
GOLDEN
HORSE
AWARDS
媒體
PRESS

觀影證
THE GOLDEN HORSE
FILM FESTIVAL
工作證
THE GOLDEN HORSE
FILM FESTIVAL

ALL ACCESS
GOLDEN
HORSE
AWARDS
全區
ALL ACCESS
後台

(15)

[3d]→ Post-human

: Independent Designers Collective (ID–C) created the brand identity and promotional material for the Post Human International Standard Poster Exhibition, hosted by the Institute of Technology Telkom Purwokerto. The exhibition examined post-humanism in a post-pandemic world, showcasing 160 artists from 20 countries. Gustav Nordebrink's contribution, Human Tokyo, envisioned a future where technology and humanity are inseparable.

Studio/Designer Independent Designers Collective (ID–C) Title Human Tokyo

Year 2023 Client Institute of Technology Telkom Purwokerto

Typeface(s) Univers Next Pro

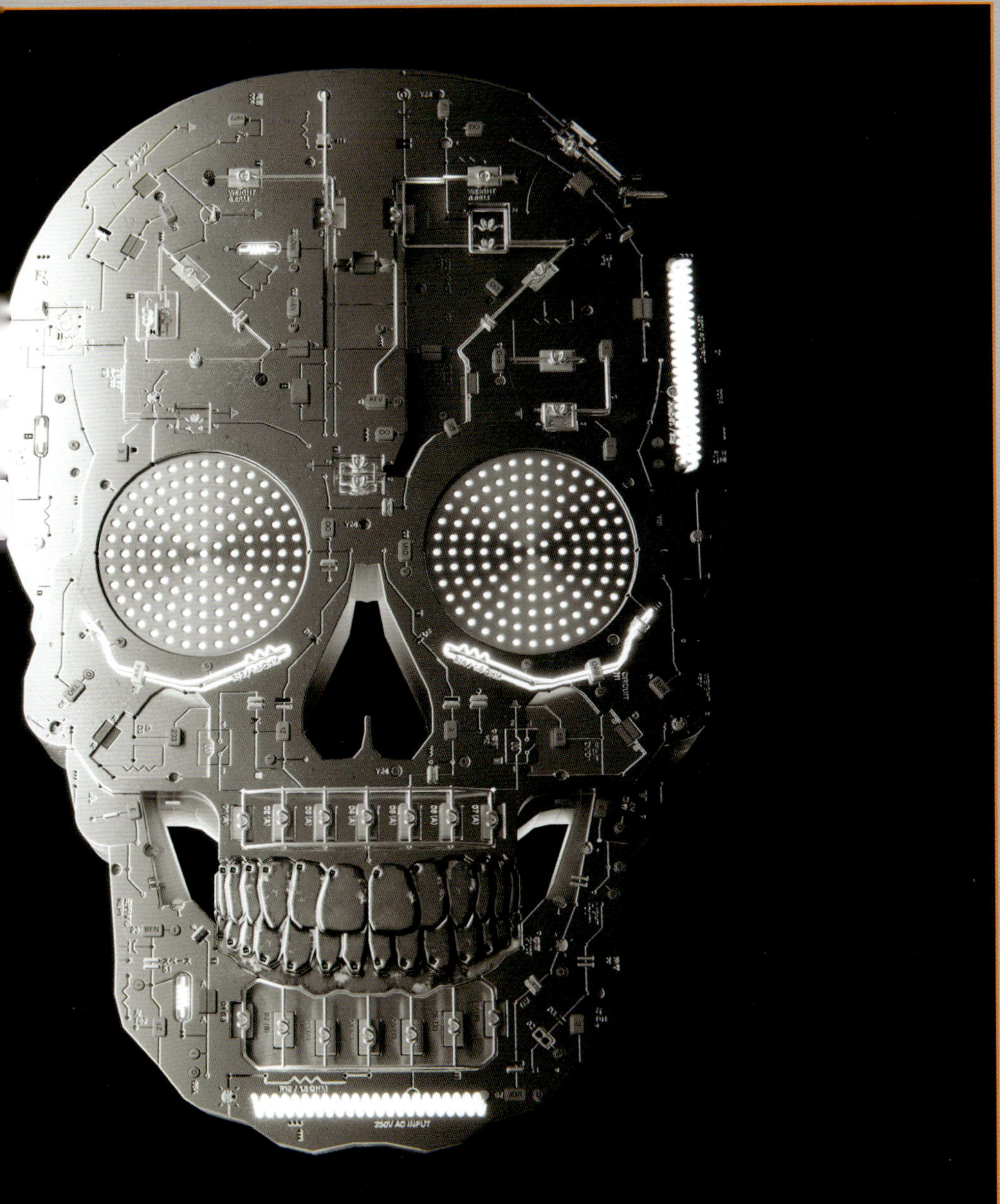

Special Credits

(3D) Human Peng
(Website Development) David Paulsson

DEL
ARA
233

WEIGHT
0.8RM
LOW
UST
AEV
AEV
MID
Y26
D1
D2
R13 / 1.5 OHM

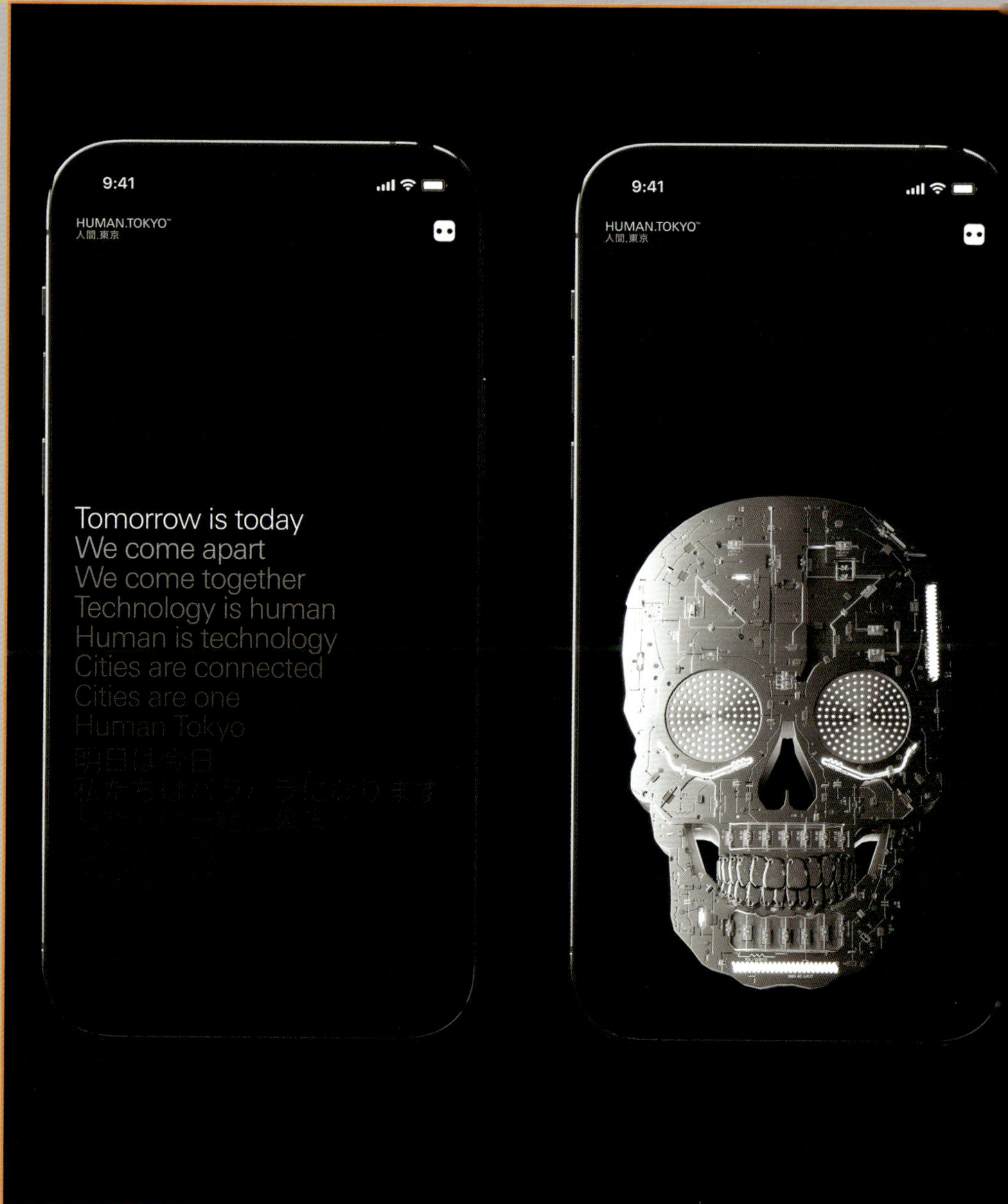
9:41
HUMAN.TOKYO™
人間.東京
Tomorrow is today
We come apart
We come together
Technology is human
Human is technology
Cities are connected
Cities are one
Human Tokyo
明日は今日
私たちはバラバラになります
9:41
HUMAN.TOKYO™
人間.東京

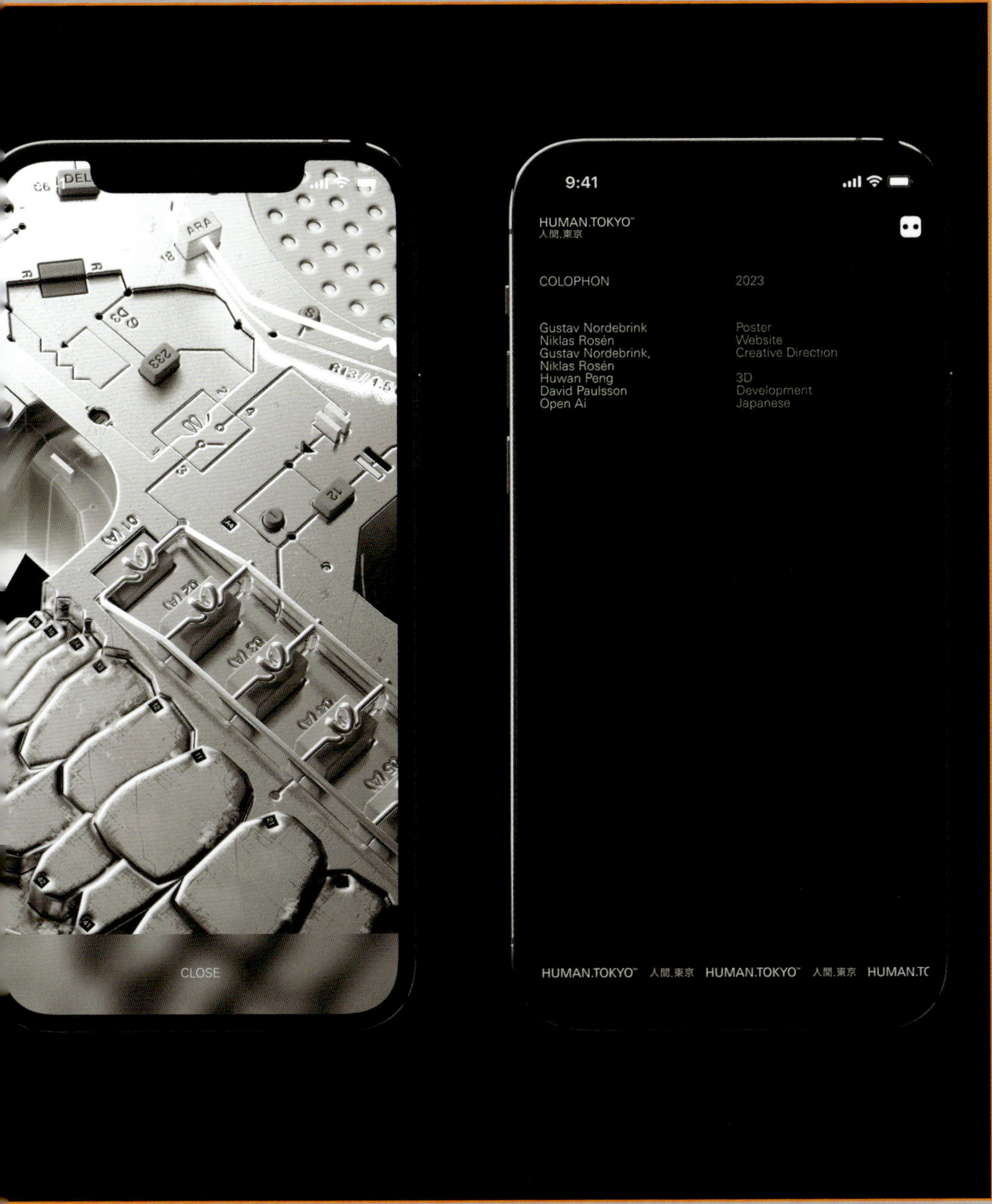
CLOSE
9:41
HUMAN.TOKYO™
人間.東京
COLOPHON
2023
Gustav Nordebrink
Poster
Niklas Rosén
Website
Gustav Nordebrink,
Niklas Rosén
Creative Direction
Huwan Peng
3D
David Paulsson
Development
Open Ai
Japanese
HUMAN.TOKYO™ 人間.東京 HUMAN.TOKYO™ 人間.東京

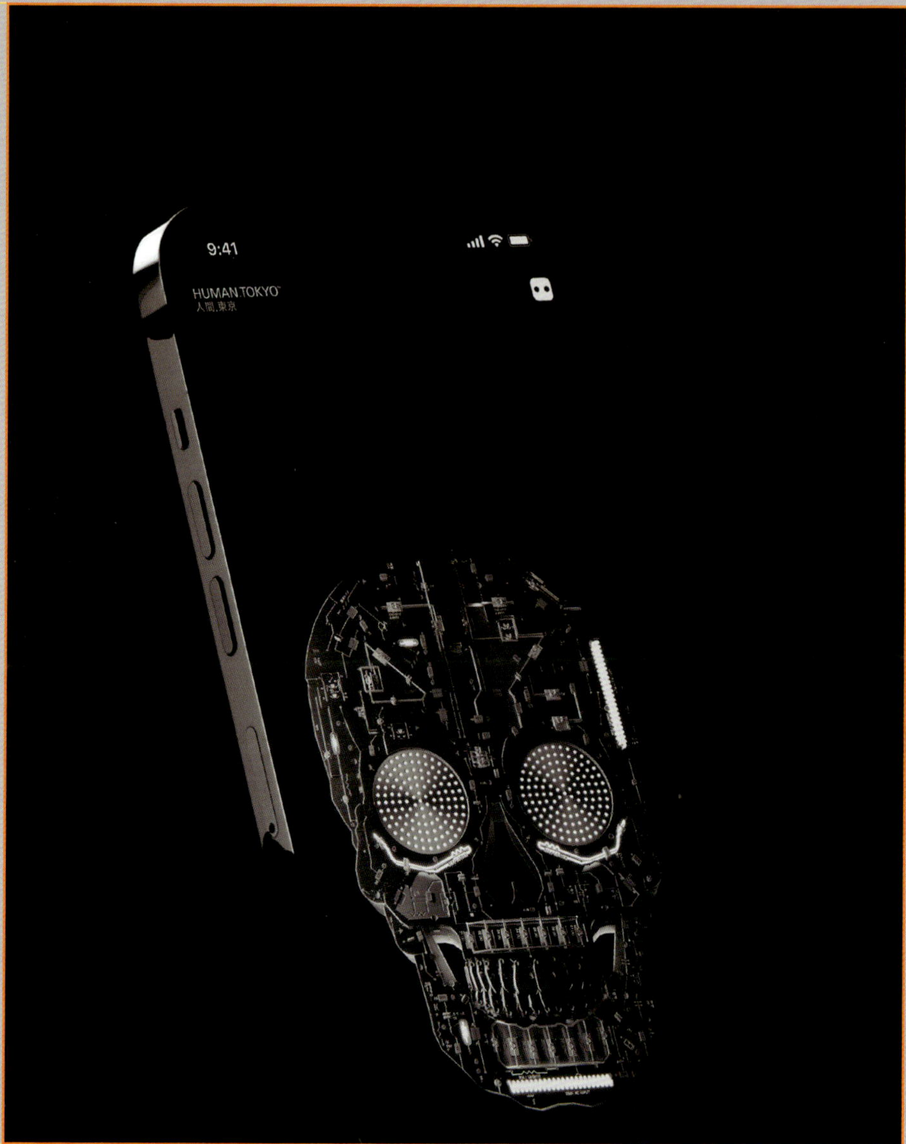
9:41
HUMAN.TOKYO™
人間.東京

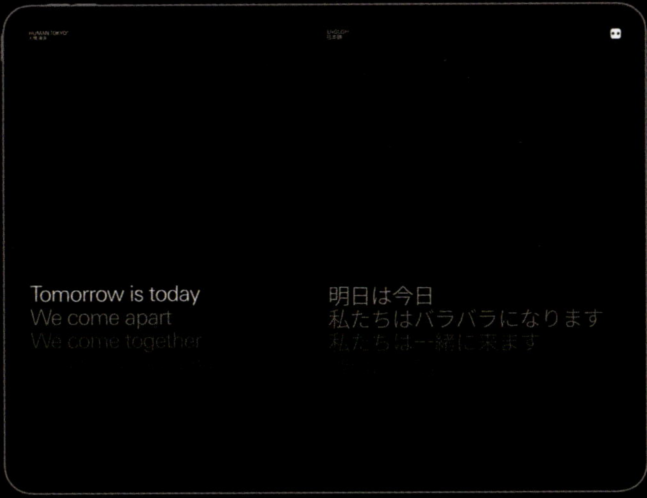
Tomorrow is today
We come apart
We come together
明日は今日
私たちはバラバラになります
私たちは一緒に来ます

左
T02

03 GREY 30

逆行する
REP1

04 GREY 90

LOCKUP

L

HUMA
人間.東

M

HUMAN.
人間.東京

S

HUMAN.TOKY
人間.東京

XS

HUMAN.TOKYO™
人間.東京

TYPEFACE

Univers Next Pro

Light

L

AaBbCcDdE
JjKkLlMmN
SsTtUuVvW
N

012345678

09 MID Y

Regular

L

AaBbCcDd

TOKYO™
KYO™
fGgHhIi
oPpQqRr
XxYyZz
FfGgHhIi
うえお
すせそ
こぬねの
みむめも
あいうえお
スペース
S1
プロトタイプ
001

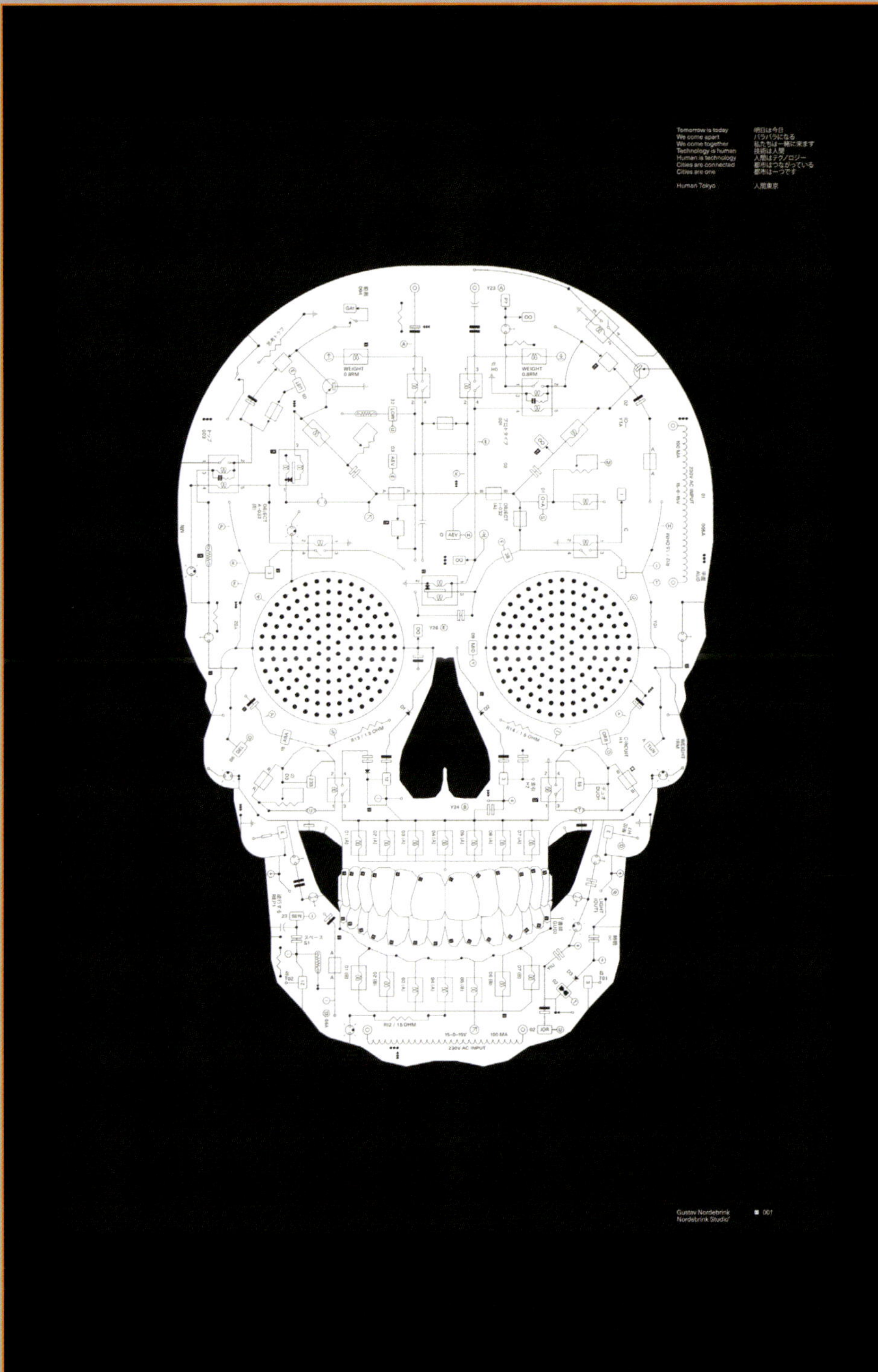
Tomorrow is today
We come apart
We come together
Technology is human
Human is technology
Cities are connected
Cities are one
Human Tokyo
明日は今日
バラバラになる
私たちは一緒に来ます
技術は人間
人間はテクノロジー
都市はつながっている
都市は一つです
人間東京
Gustav Nordebrink
Nordebrink Studio'
001

(16)

[3d]→ Tiles

: The Neubad, a cultural interim use of Lucerne's old municipal indoor swimming pool, marked its opening with a poster designed by Erich Brechbühl. The poster playfully referenced the building's history, using the starting block from the large pool as the perfect symbol to mark the beginning of a new era for the space.

Studio/Designer Erich Brechbühl Title Neubad Start
Year 2013 Client Neubad, Lucerne Typeface(s) Custom

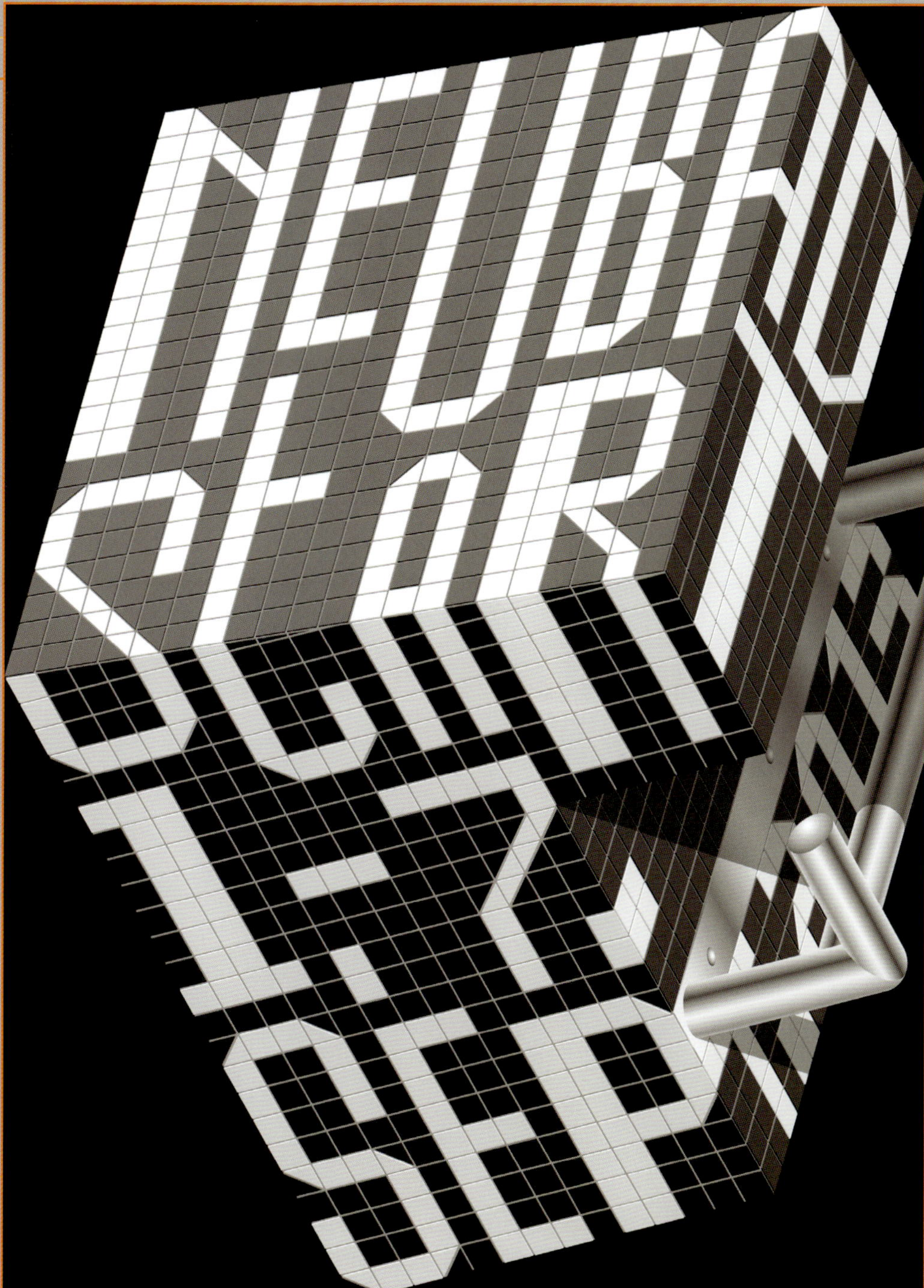

Studio/Designer Aaron Nieh Workshop
Title 2023 KISISF Everything is Connected
Year 2023 Client Bureau of Cultural Affairs, Kaohsiung City Government Typeface(s) Custom, N27

(17) [3d]→ Industrial

: The key visual for the 2023 Kaohsiung International Steel & Iron Sculpture Festival (KISISF) incorporates imagery of steel plate offcuts as its core design elements. By integrating the expression of the thickness and texture of steel plates, geometric stamping, a balanced text layout, and neon colours, it showcases the interdependence of delicacy and rigidity, symbolising the precision and strength of Kaohsiung's legacy steel industry.

高 雄 國 際 鋼 雕 藝 術 節
駁二藝術特區蓬萊區 B4+B3倉庫 & B10倉庫旁
penglai area in the pier-2 art center | warehouse B4+B3 & warehouse B10 aside
10th kaohsiung international
steel & iron sculpture festival
2023 / 11 / 01 —— 12 / 03
everything is connected
高 雄 製 造 中

鋼 雕 藝 術 節
B4+B3倉庫 & B10倉庫旁
r | warehouse B4+B3 & warehouse B10 aside
ng international
steel & iron sculpture festival
2023 / 11 / 01 —— 12 / 03
everything is connected
高 雄 製 造 中

高 雄 國 際 鋼 雕 藝 術 節
駁二藝術特區蓬萊區 B4+B3倉庫 & B10倉庫旁
penglai area in the pier-2 art center | warehouse B4+B3 & warehouse B10 aside
10th kaohsiung international steel & iron sculpture festival
2023 / 11 / 01 —— 12 / 03
everything is connected
高 雄 製 造 中
指導單位 — 文化部
主辦單位 — 高雄市政府文化局
藝文支持 —

高 雄 國 際 鋼 雕 藝 術 節
駁二藝術特區蓬萊區 B4+B3倉庫 & B10倉庫旁
penglai area in the pier-2 art center | warehouse B4+B3 & warehouse B10 aside
10th kaohsiung international
steel & iron sculpture festival
2023 / 11 / 01 —— 12 / 03
everything is connected
高 雄 製 造 中

高 雄 國 際 鋼 雕 藝 術 節
10th kaohsiung international steel & iron sculpture festival
2023 / 11 / 01 —— 12 / 03
everything is connected
高 雄 製 造 中

10th kaohsiung international steel & iron sculpture festival
高 雄 國 際 鋼 雕 藝 術 節
2023 / 11 / 01 —— 12 / 03
everything is connected
高 雄 製 造 中

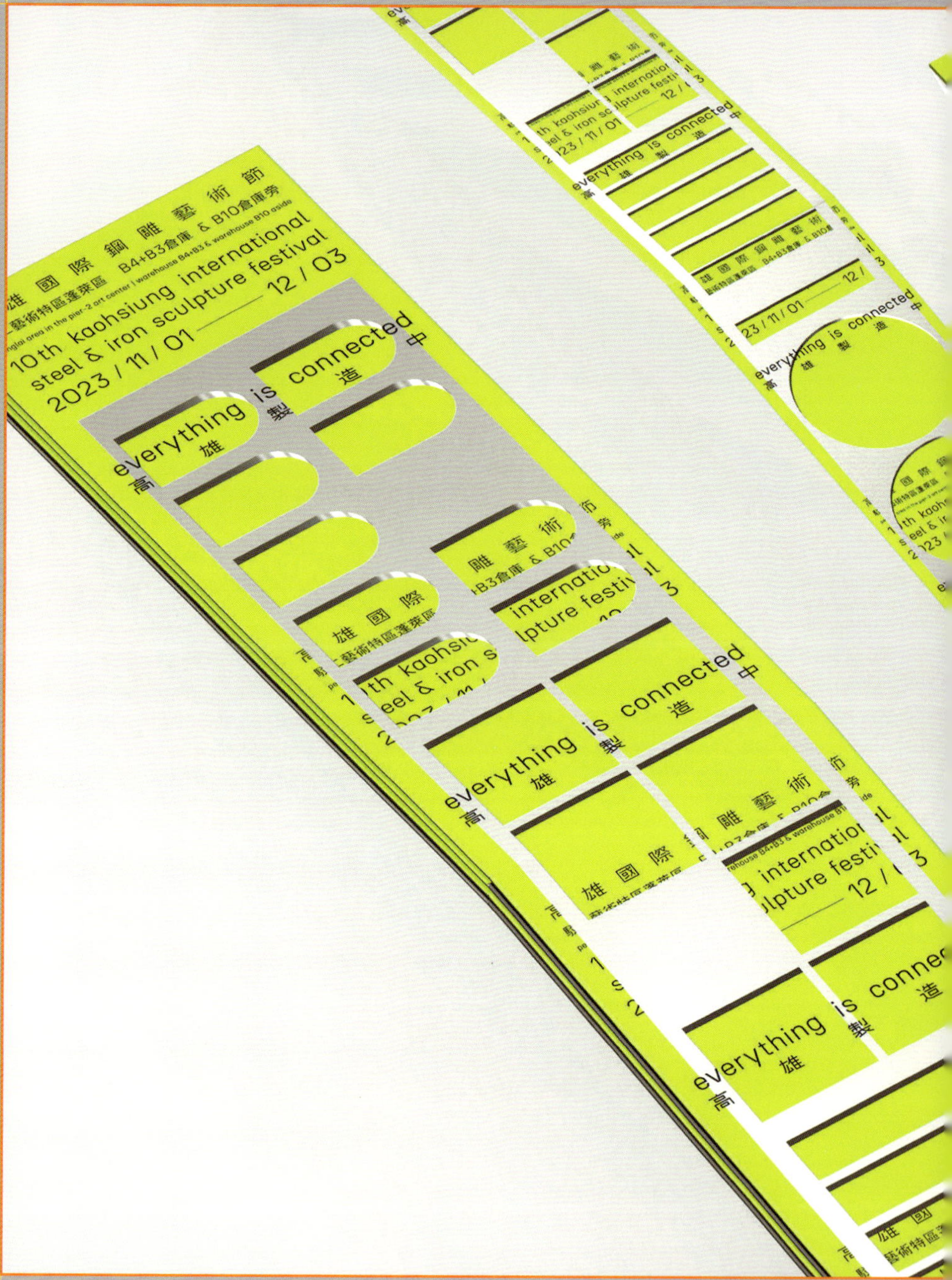
雄國際鋼雕藝術節
藝術特區蓬萊區 B4+B3倉庫 & B10倉庫旁
10th kaohsiung international
steel & iron sculpture festival
2023 / 11 / 01 —— 12 / 03
everything is connected
高雄製造中

Studio/Designer Aaron Nieh Workshop

Title 2024 7th ADA Awards for Emerging Architects

Year 2024 Client Advanced Developers Association / a+tec Quarterly

Typeface(s) N27, PingFang

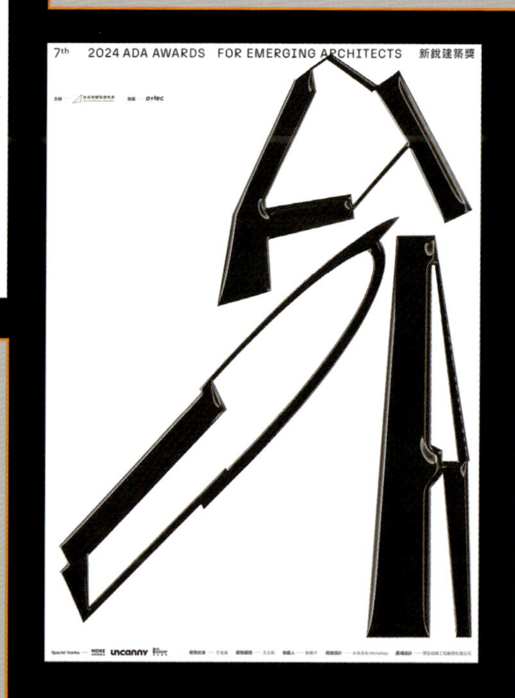

(18) [3d]→ Innovation

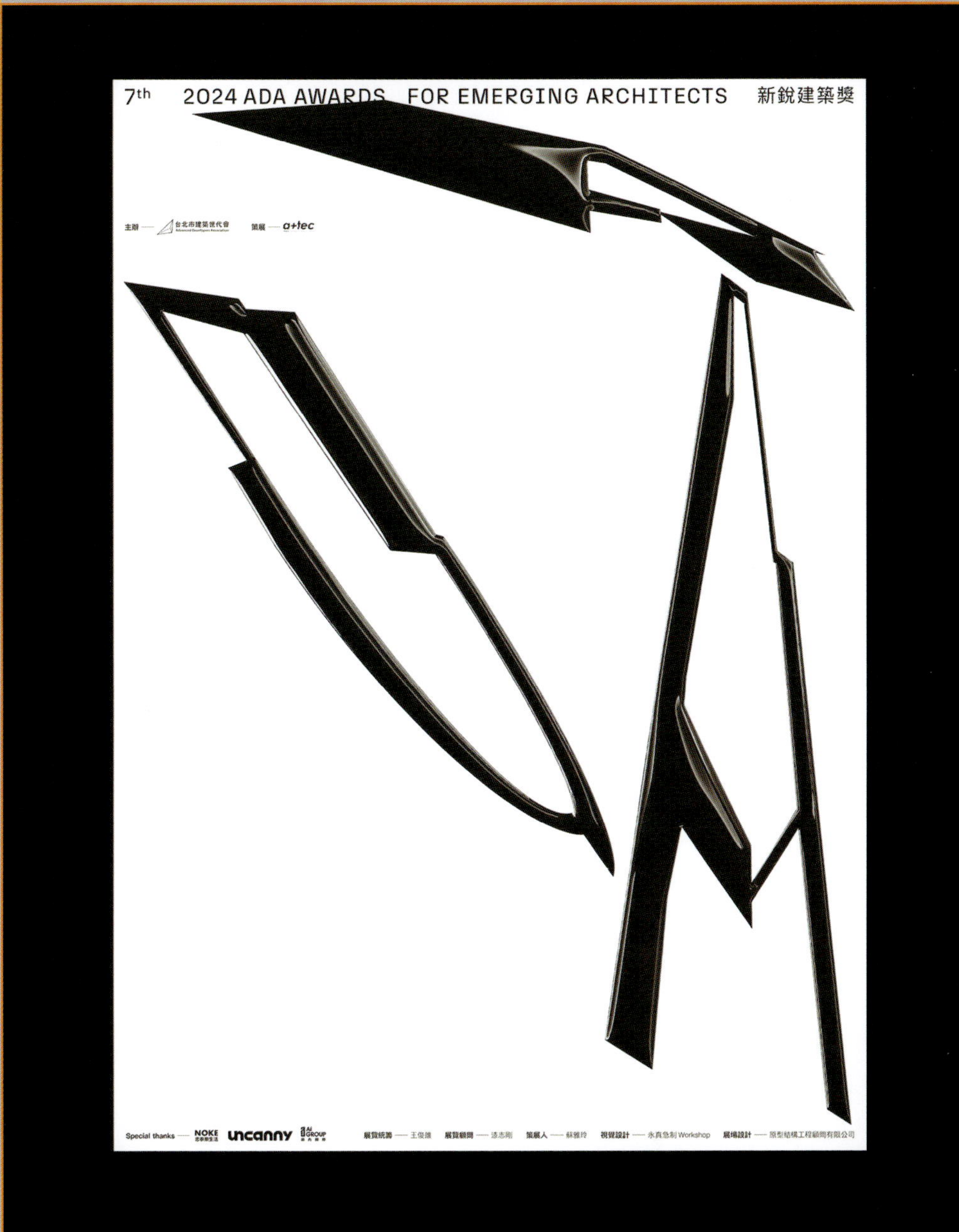

: The key visual for the ADA Awards highlights emerging architects, incorporating ADA typography alongside dynamic geometric forms. With their variations in size, proportion, and angles within the three-dimensional space, the shapes provide an abstract interpretation of the diverse perspectives and possibilities of architecture across different contexts.

7th
2024 ADA AWARDS FOR EMERGING ARCHITECTS 新銳建築獎
主辦 — 台北市建築世代會
策展 — a+tec

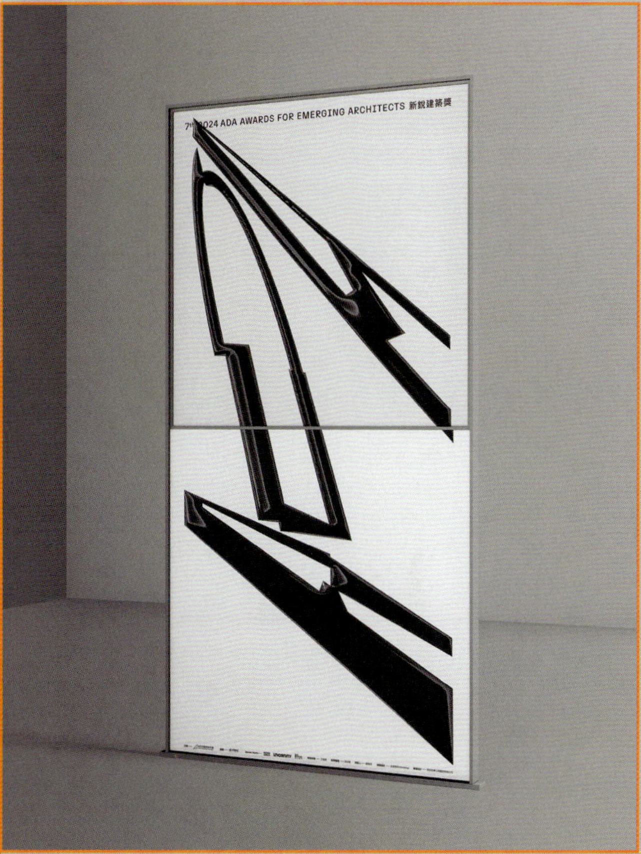
ADA AWARDS FOR EMERGING ARCHITECTS 新銳建築獎

(19)

[3d]→ Details

: Daniel Bornmann's personal poster experiments combine intricate 3D visuals with custom typography. Each piece explores unusual and unexpected compositions, showcasing a hands-on approach to visual storytelling and form-driven design.

Studio/Designer Daniel Bornmann Title NLVC
Year 2024-2025 Client Self-initiated

Foundation Series
FS04 - Now Look Very Closely
Start 0023CET
Finish 0015CET
Friday 14.02.25
Daniel Bornmann
FS 4
LOOK
Very
Closely

(20) [3d]→ Mobile

Studio/Designer High Tide Title AZAK

Year 2025 Client AZAK Typeface(s) FT Aktual

: High Tide developed a new brand identity for AZAK, a company revolutionising mobility by embedding all vehicle components within the wheel. The identity translates AZAK's cutting-edge engineering into a clear, accessible visual language, featuring a high-tech wordmark, modular icon system, and diagrammatic illustrations. The design approach communicates the system's compactness, precision, and ruggedness to both technical and mainstream audiences.

Special Credits

(Strategy / Copywriting) Thomas Pokorn, Mariah Wright
(CGI Creative Direction) Palam Digital

AZAK
Menu
Reinventing the Wheel.
Revolutionizing Mobility.
Explore Now
AZAK
Menu
Collapse and Rebuild
Built for performance. In all aspects.
In all terrains.
AZAK
Menu
No Tools Needed.
Our Quick Connect Technology enables you to connect AZAK wheels to any object, chassis, platform or idea without the need for additional components.

AZAK
Products
Company
Contact
Reinventing the Wheel.
Revolutionizing Mobility.
Explore Now

AZAK

AZAK is a wheel with everything needed to move, scale, cross, climb, reach and do more—right inside of it. It's also a platform to create vehicles that were previously impossible. Everything needed to build a vehicle is in the wheel, making it the most efficient, powerful, and modular mobility system. In functionality, technology, design and range, AZAK goes where others can't.

AZAK.CO

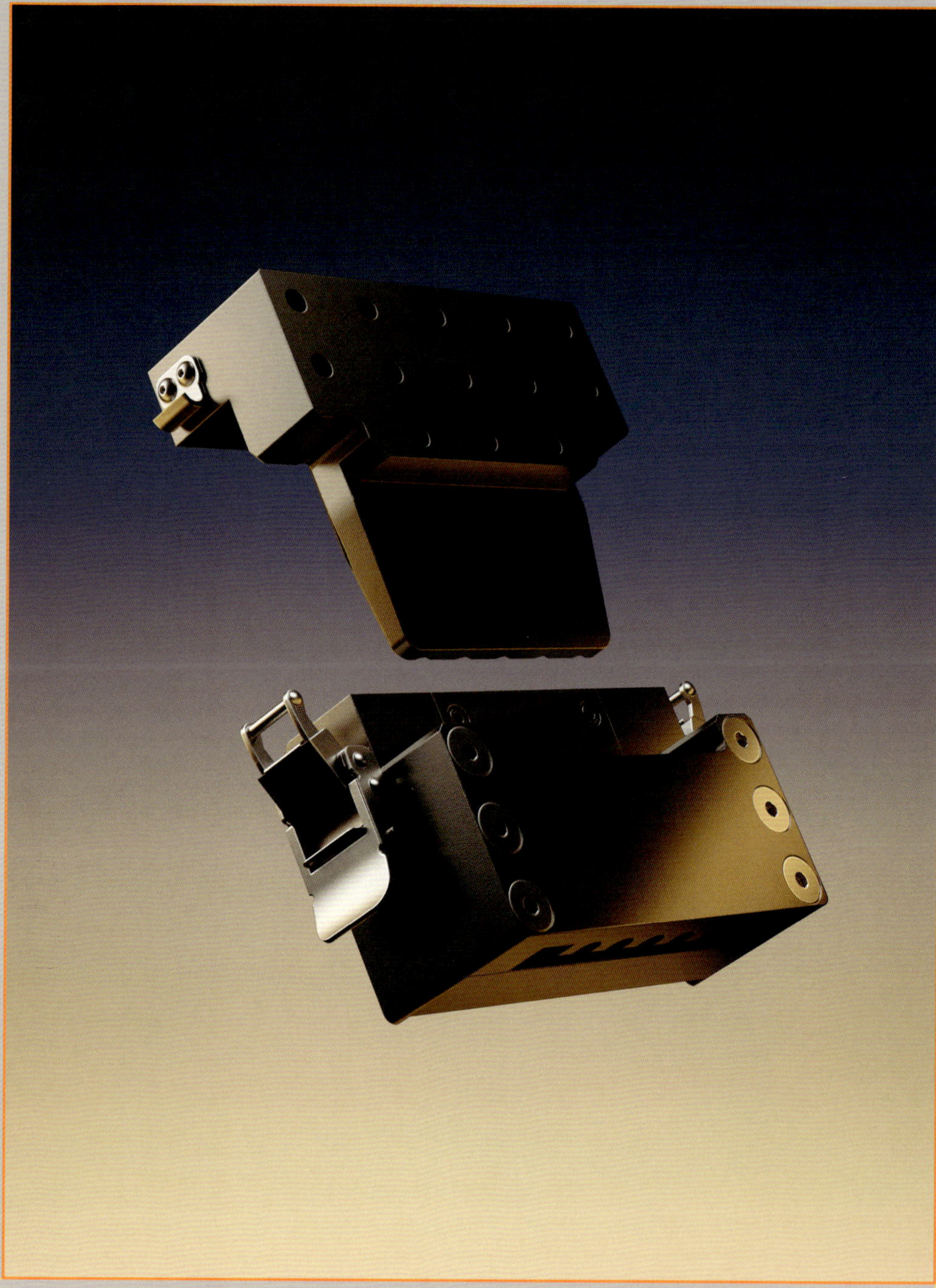

(21) [3d]→

Tactile

: The event poster for NewTab Music reimagines its established visual identity, drawing on familiar textures, forms, and graphic motifs from past releases. Through thoughtful reinterpretation, the elements are transformed into a fresh, cohesive composition that reflects the brand's evolving aesthetic.

Studio/Designer Daniel Bornmann

Title New Tab Music Poster Year 2022 Client New Tab Music

Typeface(s) Dazzed Medium, Simplon Mono Light

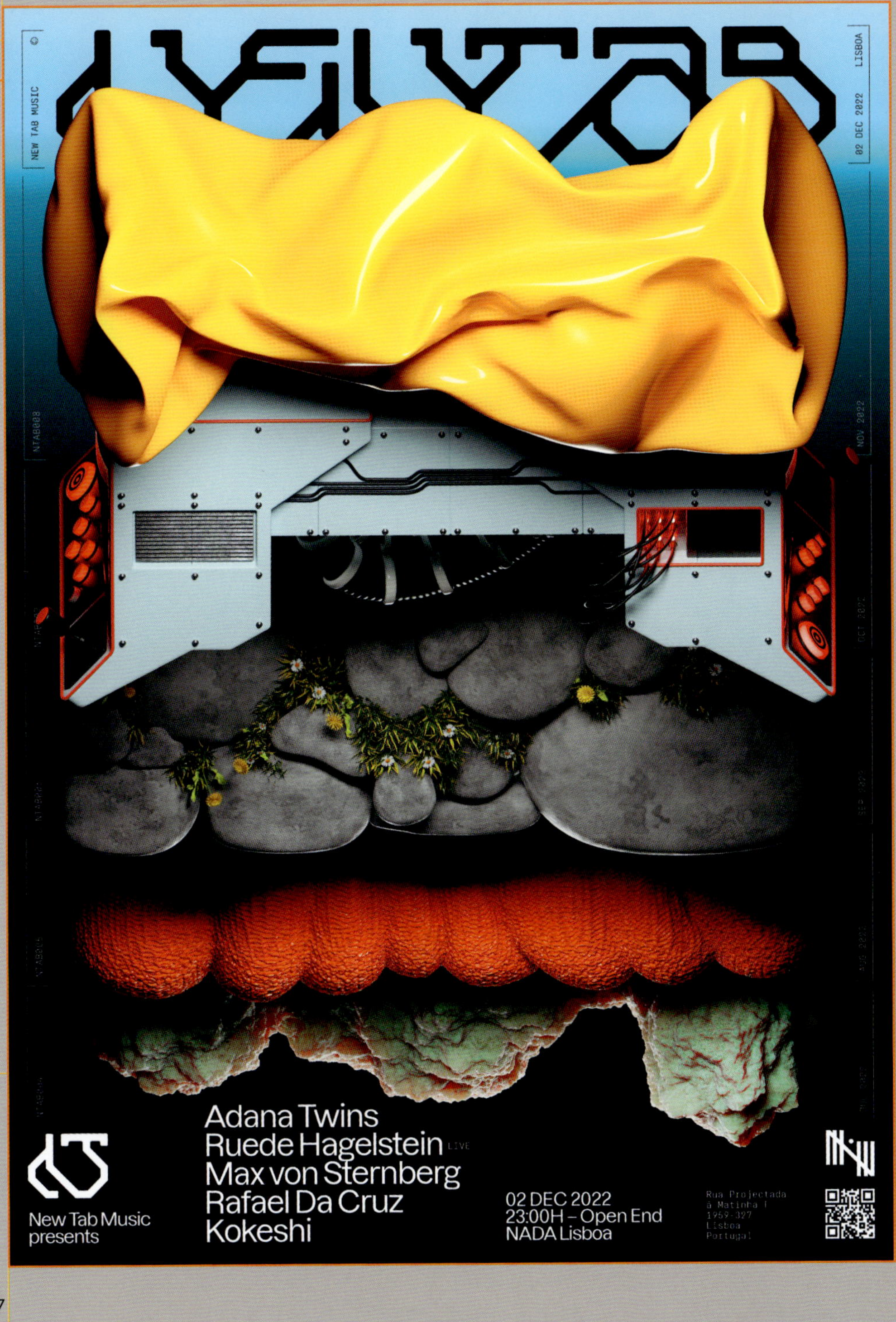
NEW TAB MUSIC
02 DEC 2022
LISBOA
NTAB008
NOV 2022
Adana Twins
Ruede Hagelstein LIVE
Max von Sternberg
Rafael Da Cruz
Kokeshi
New Tab Music
presents
02 DEC 2022
23:00H – Open End
NADA Lisboa
Rua Projectada
à Matinha 1
1959-327
Lisboa
Portugal

Studio/Designer Indego Design Year 2022

Title "FOREST BATH" DINO ARTS AND TOYS EXHIBITION

Client 50% TOY Typeface(s) Plage 2, Teta-Teta

(22)

[3d]→ Forest

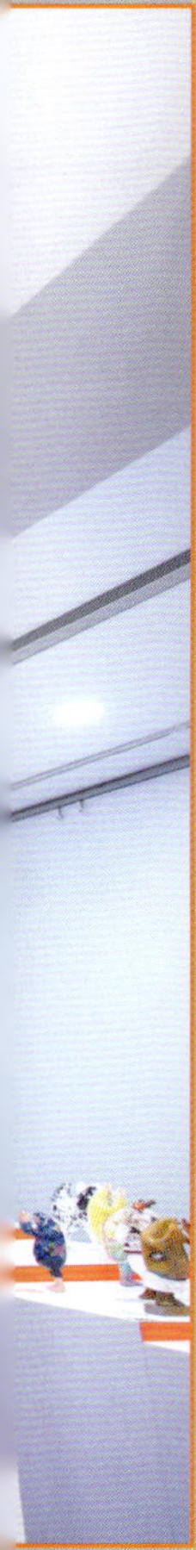

: Indego Design developed the visual identity for Forest Bath, a solo exhibition by Macanese artist Siomeng Chan. Inspired by nature's transition from dawn to sunrise, the team crafted a vibrant visual eco-system centred around Dino, a recurring character in Chan's work. By blending organic typography and shifting natural hues, the project highlighted the dynamic connection between humans and nature.

(SAT - SUN)
01PM - 08PM
FOREST
BATH
DINO ARTS AND TOYS EXHIBITION
(FOREST BATH)
婆仔屋文創空間 - A2展覽廳
ALBERGUE SCM - A2 GALLERY
(OPENING)
2022.11.11/06PM
(MON - FRI)

DINO ARTS AND TOYS EXHIBITION 2022
FOREST
BATH
(FOREST BATH)

DINO ARTS AND TOYS EXHIBITION
(FOREST BATH)
INSTAGRAM MACAOILLUSTRATORSASSOCIATION
50%
INSTAGRAM DINO_BY_SIOMENG
(Exhibition Venue)
ALBERGUE SCM - A2 GALLERY
(OPENING)
2022.11.11/06PM
(MON - FRI)
12PM - 6:30PM
(SAT - SUN)
01PM - 08PM
FOREST

(Exhibition Venue)
ALBERGUE SCM - A2 GALLERY
(MON - FRI)
12PM - 6:30PM
(SAT - SUN)
01PM - 08PM
(OPENING)
2022.11.11/06PM
BATH
INSTAGRAM: DINO_BY_SIOMENG
INSTAGRAM : MACAOILLUSTRATORSASSOCIATION
(FOREST BATH)
DINO ARTS AND TOYS EXHIBITION

DINO ARTS AND TOYS EXHIBITION
(FOREST BATH)
INSTAGRAM : MACAOILLUSTRATORSASSOCIATION
INSTAGRAM : DINO_BY_SIOMENG
50%
50%
50%
50%
(Exhibition Venue)
ALBERGUE SCM - A2 GALLERY
(OPENING)
2022.11.11/06PM
(MON - FRI)
12PM - 6:30PM
(SAT - SUN)
01PM - 08PM
FOREST

(Exhibition Venue)
ALBERGUE SCM - A2 GALLERY
(MON - FRI)
12PM - 6:30PM
(SAT - SUN)
01PM - 08PM
(OPENING)
2022.11.11/06PM
50%
50%
INSTAGRAM DINO_BY_SIOMENG
INSTAGRAM MACAOILLUSTRATORSASSOCIATION
(FOREST BATH)
DINO ARTS AND TOYS EXHIBITION
50%

FOREST
開放時間 Opening Hours :
MON - FRI 12PM-6:30PM SAT - SUN 01PM-08PM
謹定於二〇二二年十一月十一日(星期五)下午六時於澳門婆仔屋文創空間舉行
「"森林浴FOREST BATH" — DINO專題藝術玩具作品展」開幕儀式。
恭請 閣下撥冗 光臨指導　澳門插畫師協會 敬約
Macao Illustrators Association has the pleasure of inviting you to the opening ceremony of
"FOREST BATH : DINO ARTS AND TOYS EXHIBITION",
to be held on the 11th of November, 2022 (Friday), 6:00 p.m. at the Albergue SCM.
展覽日期 Duration of the Exhibition :
11.10 (THU) → 12.10 (SAT) 2022
FOREST BATH
免費入場 Free Admission / 查詢 Information : moillopower@gmail.com
BATH
DINO ARTS AND TOYS EXHIBITION
DINO ARTS AND TOYS EXHIBITION

FOREST
BATH
DINO ARTS AND TOYS EXHIBITION

"DINO"
2022 11.10 (THU) → 12.10 (SAT)
"DINO"
(FOREST BATH)
DINO ARTS AND TOYS EXHIBITION
50%
50%

"DINO"
2022 11.10 (THU) → 12.10 (SAT)
"DINO"
50%
DINO ARTS AND TOYS EXHIBITION
50%

Studio/Designer Indego Design
Title Western Calligraphy Annual Exhibition - Handicraft Art in an Era of Technology Year 2022 Client LAAOM Typeface(s) Custom

[3d]→ High-tech

: For the Western Calligraphy Annual Exhibition, Indego Design delivered a bold, imaginative concept that repositions calligraphy for the digital age. Their futuristic "tool set" reinterpreted classic Western letterforms through a sci-fi lens – merging handcraft with high-tech. The result was a striking visual identity that celebrates calligraphy's enduring and evolving form.

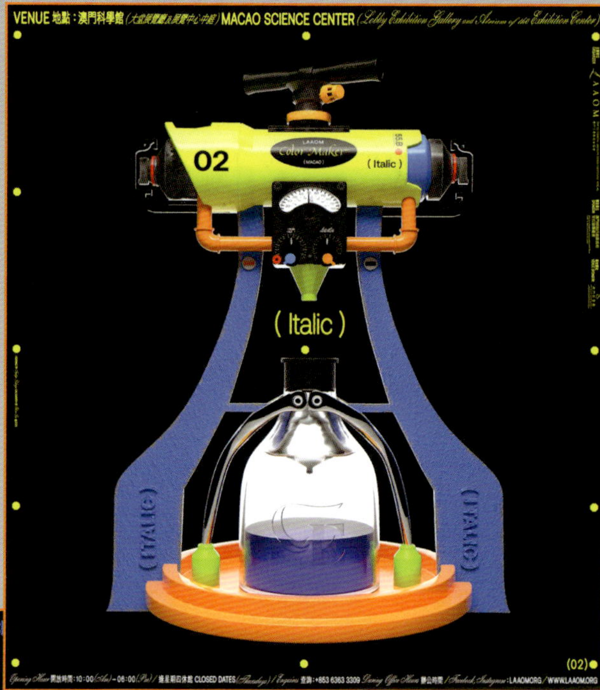
VENUE 地點：澳門科學館(大堂展覽廳及展覽中心中庭) MACAO SCIENCE CENTER (Lobby Exhibition Gallery and Atrium of the Exhibition Center)
02
LAAOM
Color Maker
(MACAO)
(Italic)
(Italic)
(ITALIC)
(ITALIC)
(02)
Opening Hour 開放時間：10:00(Am) – 06:00(Pm) / 逢星期四休館 CLOSED DATES (Thursdays) / Enquiries 查詢：+853 6363 3309 During Office Hours 辦公時間 / Facebook, Instagram：LAAOMORG / WWW.LAAOM.ORG

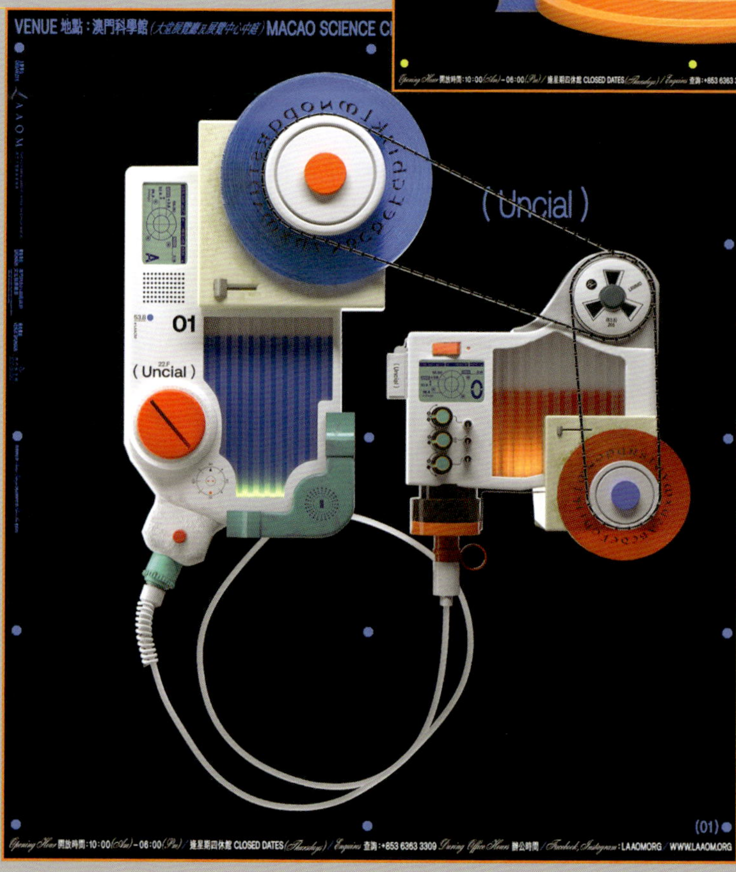
VENUE 地點：澳門科學館(大堂展覽廳及展覽中心中庭) MACAO SCIENCE C
(Uncial)
01
(Uncial)
(01)
Opening Hour 開放時間：10:00(Am) – 06:00(Pm) / 逢星期四休館 CLOSED DATES (Thursdays) / Enquiries 查詢：+853 6363 3309 During Office Hours 辦公時間 / Facebook, Instagram：LAAOMORG / WWW.LAAOM.ORG

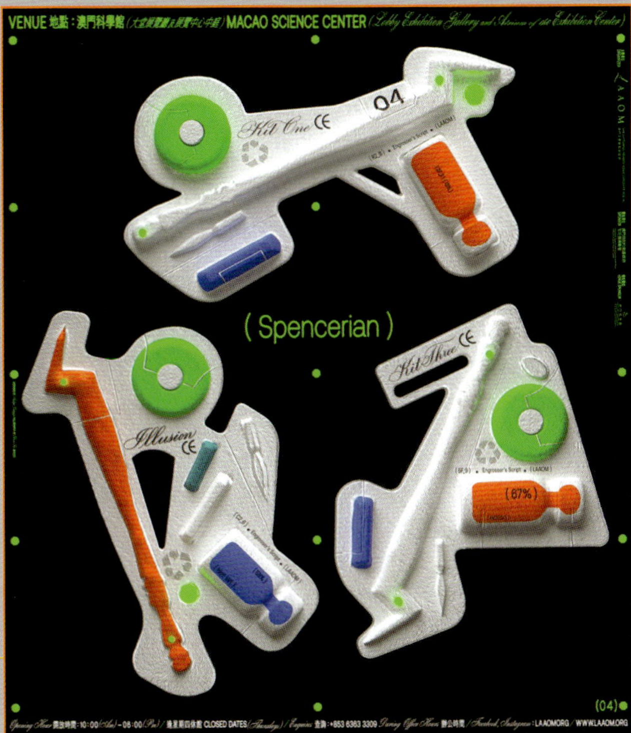
VENUE 地點：澳門科學館 (大堂展覽廳及展覽中心中庭) MACAO SCIENCE CENTER
04
Kit One
Kit Three
Illusion
(67%)
(Spencerian)
(04)
開放時間：10:00 – 06:00 / 逢星期四休館 CLOSED DATES / 查詢：+853 6363 3309 辦公時間 / LAAOMORG / WWW.LAAOM.ORG

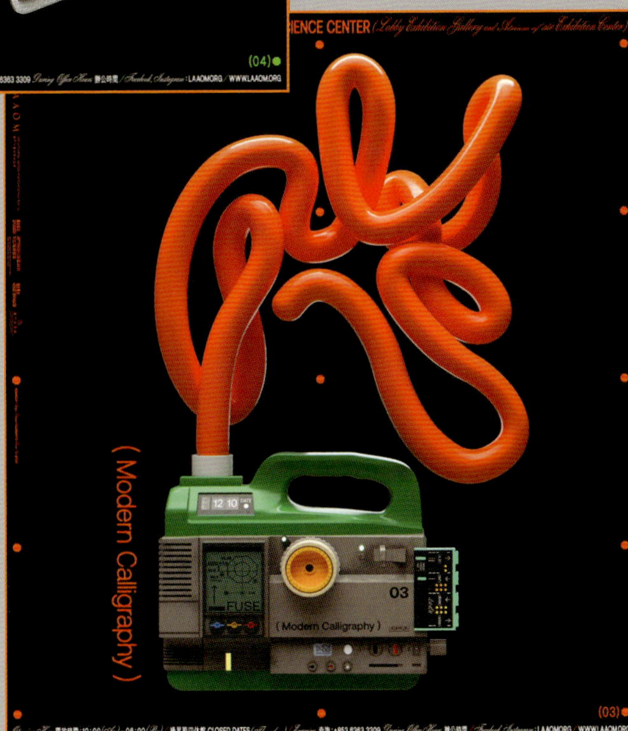
IENCE CENTER
(Modern Calligraphy)
12 10
FUSE
03
(Modern Calligraphy)
(03)
開放時間：10:00 – 06:00 / 逢星期四休館 CLOSED DATES / 查詢：+853 6363 3309 辦公時間 / LAAOMORG / WWW.LAAOM.ORG

LAAOM
THE ANNUAL Exhibition
HANDICRAFT ART IN AN ERA OF TECHNOLOGY
PERIOD 12.10 →01.08
MACAO SCIENCE CENTER
(西洋書法年展—科技時代的工藝)
(01) (Uncial)
(02) (Italic)
(03) (Modern Calligraphy)
(04) (Spencerian)

LAAOM
THE ANNUAL Exhibition
HANDICRAFT ART IN AN ERA OF TECHNOLOGY
PERIOD 12.10 →01.08

PERIOD 12.10 → 01.08
(OPENING 開幕式)
02
(Italic)
(02)
THE ANNUAL Exhibition
HANDICRAFT ART IN AN ERA OF TECHNOLOGY
(西洋書法年展—科技時代的工藝)
AAOM
LAAOM
PERIOD 12.10 → 01.08
VENUE 地點：澳門科學館
MACAO SCIENCE CENTER
(Modern Calligraphy)
(03)
(Spencerian)
(04)
(Uncial)
(01)

Studio/Designer Zuzanna Rogatty Title Pluk de Nacht
Year 2024 Client Pluk de Nacht Open Air Festival
Typeface(s) Custom, Documan

(24) [3d]→ Bounce

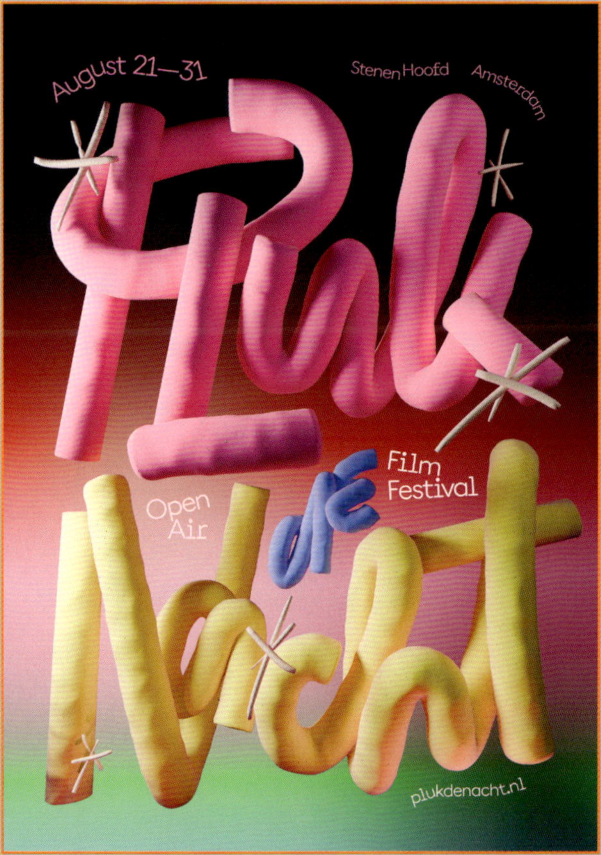

: Zuzanna Rogatty's posters for Pluk de Nacht 2024 bounce with joy and typographic flair. Chunky, 3D letterforms twist like inflatable toys in mid-air, rendered in juicy colours and soft textures. Playful, bold, and full of summer energy, they perfectly capture the spirit of open-air cinema nights in Amsterdam and Utrecht.

August 2—10
Basecamp, Utrecht Nijverheidsweg 16
Pluk de Nacht
Open Air
Film Festival
plukdenacht.nl

Studio/Designer Untitled Macao Title Shenzhen Fringe Art Festival 2023 Year 2023 Client Fringe Art Center Shenzhen Typeface(s) Sharp Grotesk Bold, Neue Haas Grotesk Text Pro, Noto Sans

: Centred on the theme “Fringe Marathon”, the 2023 Shenzhen Fringe Art Festival celebrated creative endurance and non-stop artistic expression. Its identity featured vibrant, sprite-like characters inspired by the diversity of performances. The dynamic figures embodied imagination and guided audiences through a rich, ever-evolving programme — fostering participation, collaboration, and celebration across disciplines.

Special Credits

(Design) Untitled Macao / Intox Design & Communication
(Photography) Rex Chang

14TH SHENZHEN FRINGE FESTIVAL 第十四届深圳湾艺穗节
艺穗大戏
FRINGE STAGE
WWW.SZFRINGE.ORG
南山区新时代文明实践系列活动
FAC
Fringe Art Center Shenzhen
深圳市南山区
NANSHAN DISTRICT, SHENZHEN, CHINA
11.18-22
Sponsor Nanshan District Shenzhen Propaganda Department Nanshan District Culture, Radio, Television, Tourism and Sports Bureau Shenzhen Fringe Festival Committee
Organizer Shenzhen Fringe Art Center
Co-organizer Nantou City

14TH SHENZHEN FRINGE FESTIVAL 第十四届深圳湾艺穗节
FRINGE
OPEN
艺穗在场
WWW
.SZFRINGE
.ORG
南山区新时代文明实践
系列活动
FAC
Fringe Art Center
Shenzhen
深圳市南山区
NANSHAN
DISTRICT,
SHENZHEN,
CHINA
11.17-26
Sponsor Nanshan District Shenzhen Propaganda Department ○ Nanshan District Culture, Radio, Television, Tourism and Sports Bureau ○ Shenzhen Fringe Festival Committee
Organizer ○ Shenzhen Fringe Art Center | Co-organizer ○ ○ Nantou City

14TH SHENZHEN FRINGE FESTIVAL
第十四届深圳湾艺穗节
艺穗町
RIN
E
SHOP
WWW
.SZFRINGE
.ORG
南山区新时代文明实践系列活动
FAC
深圳市南山区
NANSHAN
DISTRICT,
SHENZHEN,
CHINA
11.17-26

14TH SHENZHEN FRINGE F
RI
IN TOW
南山区新时代文明实践系列活动
FAC
Fringe Art Center
深圳市南山区
NANSHAN
DISTRICT,
SHENZHEN,
CHINA
11.17-26

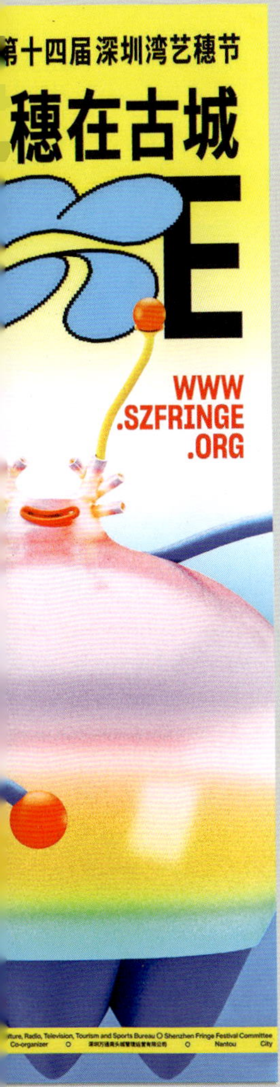
第十四届深圳湾艺穗节
穗在古城
E
WWW
.SZFRINGE
.ORG

14TH SHENZHEN FRINGE FESTIVAL
第十四届深圳湾艺穗节
艺穗巴士
FRINGE
BUS
WWW.
SZFRINGE.
ORG
深圳市南山区
NANSHAN
DISTRICT,
SHENZHEN,
CHINA
11.18

km
42.195
SHENZHEN FRINGE FESTIVAL
Marathon
14TH Shenzhen Fringe Festival

FRINGE
SINCE 2010
(Marathon)
km
42.195
RUN
42.195km
(Marathon)

FRINGE IN TOWN
艺穗在古城
WWW .SZFRINGE .ORG
深圳市南山区 NANSHAN DISTRICT, SHENZHEN, CHINA
11.17-26
第十四届 14TH
FESTIVAL
2023 11.17-26
艺穗大戏 FRINGE STAGE
艺穗在古城 FRINGE IN TOWN
艺穗巴士 FRINGE BUS
艺穗时 FRINGE SHOP
FRINGE STAGE
11.18-22
SINCE 2010
Marathon
42.195 km
MARATHON
艺穗马拉松

11.17-26
MARATHON
艺穗节
WWW
.SZFRINGE
.ORG
深圳市南山区
NANSHAN
DISTRICT
SHENZHEN
艺穗
马拉松
FRINGE
RUN
42.195km
(Marathon)
14TH SHENZHEN FRINGE FESTIVAL
第十四届深圳湾艺穗节
艺穗巴士
BUS
WWW.
SZFRINGE.
ORG
11.18
艺穗在古城
IN TOWN
WWW
.SZFRINGE
.ORG
11.17-26
MARATHON
艺穗
马拉松
艺穗大戏
WWW.
SZFRINGE.
ORG
STAGE
艺穗町
SHO

(26) [3d]→ Bloom

: Initiated by the Macao Designers Association, MDW 2020 showcased the strength of the local design scene. Inspired by the Chinese proverb “a hundred flowers bloom”, the visual identity symbolised the industry’s flourishing. A silvery-grey palette evoked modernity, while classic fonts and 3D floral illustrations blended tradition with innovation, creating a sophisticated, intergenerational aesthetic.

Studio/Designer Untitled Macao Title Macao Design Week 2020

Year 2020 Client Macao Designers Association

Typeface(s) Helvetica, Voyage, Hiragino Mincho Pro

Special Credits

(3D Motion) MIRAGE VISUALS
(Music & Motion) Summer Ha
(Photography) Rex Chang

MACAO DESIGN WEEK 2020
30° DESIGN EXHIBITION
11.16 To 12.16
WWW.MACAUDESIGNERS.ORG
TELEPHONE 電話: +853 28520335
FREE ADMISSION 免費入場
OPENING HOURS 開放時間
10 A.M. - 7 P.M.
OPENING CEREMONY 展覽開幕
11/20 (FRI) 6 P.M.
2020
澳門設計周
DESIGN WEEK
MACAO
CONTEMPORARY
ART CENTER
NAVY YARD NO.1
RUA DE S.
TIAGO
DA BARRA
澳門
當代
藝術中心
海事工房1號
澳門媽閣
上街
FACEBOOK:
MACAUDESIGNWEEK

N30°
EXHIBITION
11.16 To
12.16
MACAO
CONTEMPORARY
ART CENTER
NAVY YARD NO.1
RUA DE S.
TIAGO
DA BARRA
澳門
當代
藝術中心
海事工房1號
澳門媽閣
上街
MACAU
DESIGNERS
ASSOCIATION
澳門設計師協會
FREE
ADMISSION
免費入場
OPENING HOURS
開放時間
10 A.M. - 7 P.M.
OPENING CEREMONY
開幕典禮
11/20 (FRI) 6 P.M.
2020
澳門設計周
MACAO DESIGN WEEK
FACEBOOK:
MACAUDESIGNWEEK
MACAU
DESIGNERS
ASSOCIATION
澳門設計師協會
11.21
20:00
21:30
MACAO DESIGN WEEK 2020
MACAO DESIGN WEEK 2020
MACAO DESIGN WEEK 2020
MACAO DESIGN WEEK 2020
MACAO DESIGN WEEK 2020
MACAO DESIGN WEEK 2020
澳門
設計周
2020

MACAO DESIGN WEEK
2020
澳門
設計周
11.16 To
12.16
FACEBOOK :
MACAUDESIGNWEEK
MACAU DESIGNERS
ASSOCIATION
澳門設計師協會

MACAO DESIGN
WEEK
2020
澳門
設計周
11.16 To
12.16
FACEBOOK :
MACAUDESIGNWEEK
MACAU
DESIGNERS
ASSOCIATION
澳門設計師協會

VANESSA LEONG 梁妍慧
AIFY LEI 李研珊
STEVEN WU 吳俊
LAM KA HOU 林家豪
DAN FERREIRA 李潮藝
MACAO
DESIGN
WEEK 2020
FACEBOOK :
MACAUDESIGNWEEK
N30°
DESIGN
EXHIBITION

MACAO DESIGN WEEK 2020
JINN NG / STEVEN WU / SAM KIN HANG / JAY LEI / AIFY LEI /
CHEOK LEI / DAN FERREIRA / LAM KA HOU / LAM WAI KENG /
LAM IEONG KUN / SI NGA IAN / UNA TONG / CHEONG KA KIT /
VANESSA LEONG / LEONG KIN & LOU KA CHOI / KEIKA LEONG /
SIOMENG CHAN / CHAN IAT HOU / WONG SIN KEI / KAY TUNG /
TRAMY LUI / TINA LOI / LAO CHON HONG / ADDIE, DENG XIAOHUA /
WAKKA CHEANG / SIO KAI TONG / MELISSA LONG /
THOMAS MCZ / RAYMOND NOGUEIRA & KID LEI
澳門
設計周
FACEBOOK :
MACAUDESIGNWEEK
11.16 To
12.16
N30° DESIGN
EXHIBITION
MACAU DESIGNERS
ASSOCIATION
澳門設計師協會

MACAU
DESIGNERS
ASSOCIATION
澳門設計師協會
MACAO
澳門
設計周
MACAO DESIGN WEEK 2020
MACAO DESIGN WEEK 2020
PASS
MACAO DESIGN WEEK 2020
PASS
MACAO
DESIGNERS.ORG
+853 28520335

(27)

[3d]→ Textile

Studio/Designer Toby Ng Design

Title PolyU School of Fashion & Textiles

Year 2023 Client PolyU School of Fashion & Textiles

Typeface(s) TWK Everett

: Toby Ng Design reimagined PolyU's 65-year-old Institute of Textiles and Clothing as the future-facing School of Fashion & Textiles. The identity featured upward-moving, intertwined strands symbolising collaboration, growth and transformation from ITC to SFT. The cross-section became a mannequin-like emblem clad in varied materials, reflecting interdisciplinarity and expansive possibilities in fashion education.

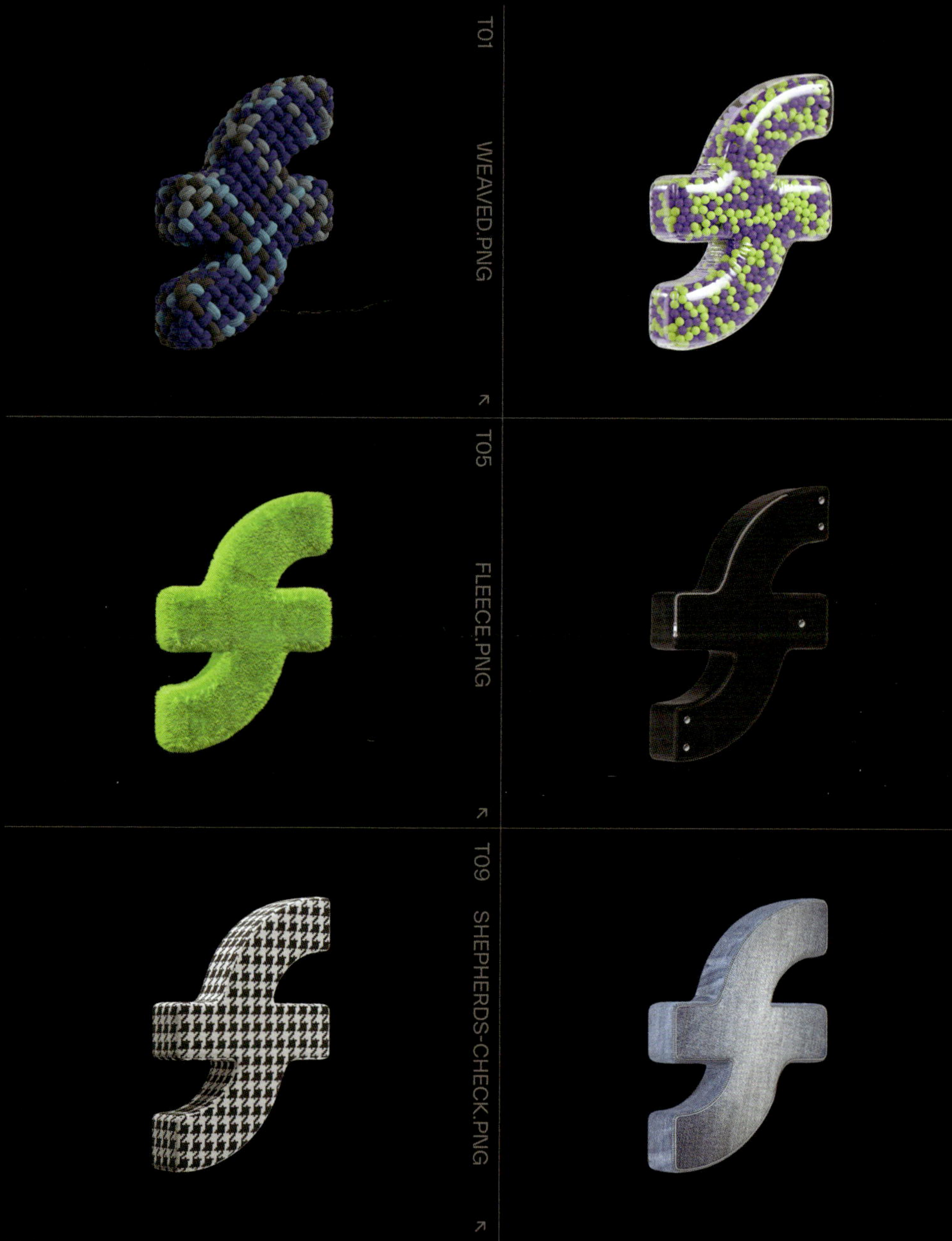
T01
WEAVED.PNG
T05
FLEECE.PNG
T09
SHEPHERDS-CHECK.PNG

T04 SMOCKED.PNG ↖

T08 PLEATED.PNG ↖

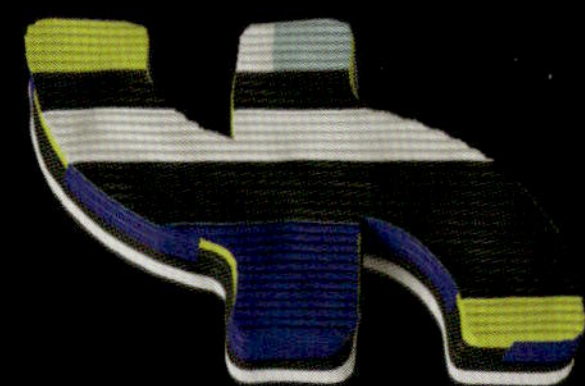

T12 SYNTHETIC.PNGT ↖

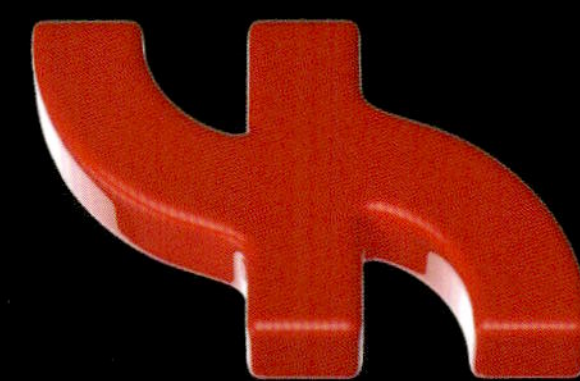

T03 DOWN.PNG ↖

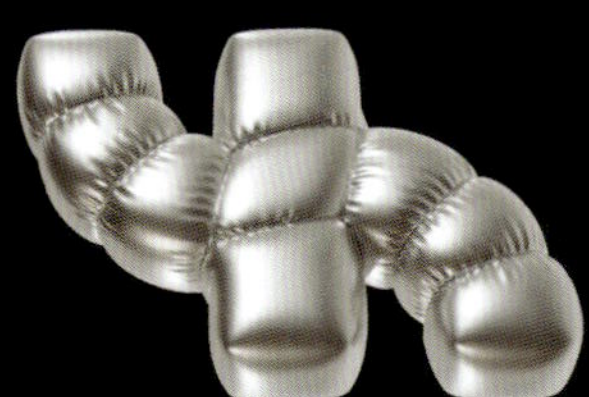

T07 SPIRELLI.PNG ↖

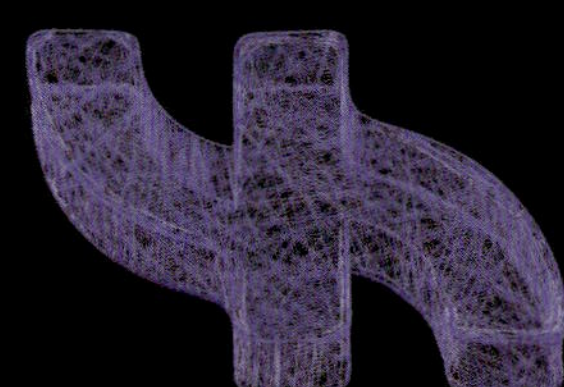

T11 QUILTED.PNG ↖

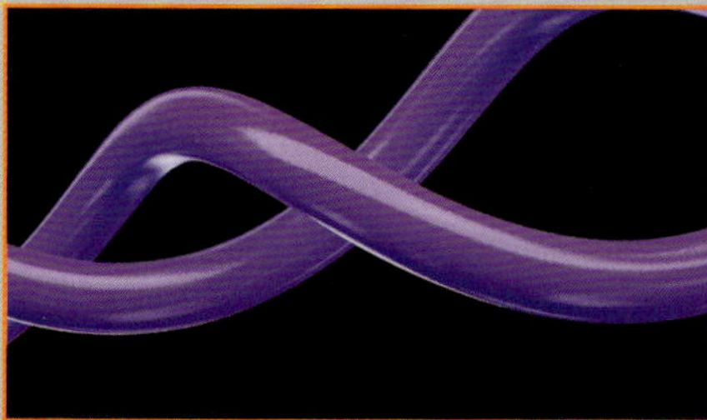

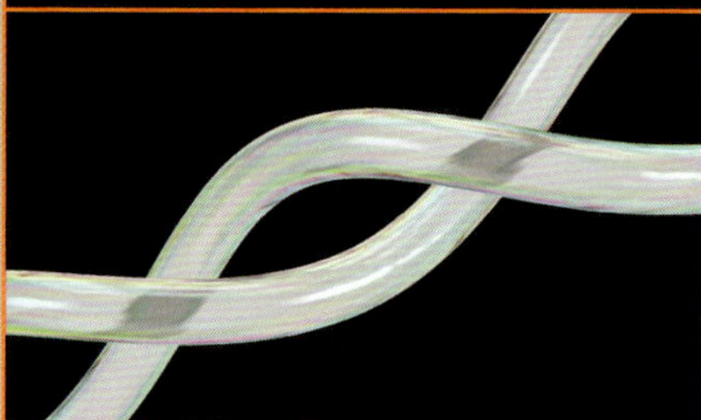

SCHOOL OF FASHION
AND TEXTILES
MODERNISING A
HISTORY OF RESEARCH
AND INNOVATION
FASHIONING
THE NEXT
INTO A FASHION SCHOOL
FOR THE FUTURE.

OF FASHION
TILES
MODERNISING A
HISTORY OF RESEARCH
AND INNOVATION
FASHIONING
THE NEXT
SCHOOL OF FASHION
AND TEXTILES

(28) [3d]→ Balloon

: "Welcome to Paradise" by Erich Brechbühl captures theatrical immortality through elegantly subversive poster design. Created for a 2016 production exploring two eternal women's annual encounters, his work balances the profound with the playful – transforming narrative complexity into accessible visual intrigue with infinitely inflating and deflating letterforms. The poster's design philosophy mirrors the play's cyclical nature, where repetition becomes revelation.

Studio/Designer Erich Brechbühl Title Welcome to Paradise
Year 2016 Client Sonah Theater Typeface(s) Custom

SONAH THEATER
PRODUKTIONEN
REGIE:
JULIEN SCHMUTZ
SPIEL:
URSULA HILDEBRAND
ANNE JENNY
WWW.SONAH-
THEATER.CH

(29)

Studio/Designer Bito Title 2023 Romantic Route 3 Art Festival

Year 2023 Client Hakka Affairs Council

[3d]→ # Roadtrip

: The 2023 Romantic Route 3 Art Festival celebrated Hakka culture through the theme "Falabidbog", a vibrant traditional term that challenges conservative stereotypes. Drawing from local elements, the team created whimsical character designs that blur the line between reality and fantasy – evoking the spirit of "a road trip you can take with you" and spotlighting the rich diversity of contemporary Hakka identity.

3
漫台③線藝術季
mantic Route 3

浪漫台③線藝術季
2023.6.24-8.27 花啦嗶啵
Romantic Route 3 Falabidbog

浪漫台③線藝術季
2023.6.24-8.27 花啦嗶啵
Romantic Route 3 Falabidbog

浪漫台③線藝術季
2023.6.24-8.27 花啦嗶啵
Romantic Route 3 Falabidbog

3.6.24-8.27 花啦嗶啵
antic Route 3 Falabidbog
浪漫台③線藝術季
2023.6.24-8.27 花啦嗶啵
Romantic Route 3 Falabidbog
浪漫台③線藝術季
3.6.24-8.27 花啦嗶啵
antic Route 3 Falabidbog
浪漫台③線藝術季
2023.6.24-8.27 花啦嗶啵
Romantic Route 3 Falabidbog
浪漫台③線

TAIPEI DESIGN AWARD 2023
TDA
臺北
設計
獎
TAIPEI DESIGN
AWARD 2023

(30)

[3d]→ Pulse

TDA
臺北
設計
獎
TAIPEI DESIGN
AWARD 2023
TAIPEI DESIGN AWARD 2023

Studio/Designer Whitelight Motion Title Taipei Design Award 2023
Year 2023 Client Taipei City Government Department of Economic Development, China Productivity Center

: Whitelight Motion developed "The Geometry of Heartbeats" as the theme for TDA 2023, capturing the emotional pulse of great design. By transforming the TDA cube into rhythmic, soundwave-inspired visuals, they illustrated design's role in everyday resonance. The ceremony's motion graphics dynamically unveiled winning entries, reflecting how creativity fuels connection, exchange, and urban vitality.

Special Credits

(Key Visual Design) Yi Hua Hsu
(Motion Design) Kyle Jhuang
(Music & Sound Design Production) Audio Textural

TDA
臺北設計獎
TAIPEI DESIGN
AWARD 2023
TAIPEI DESIGN

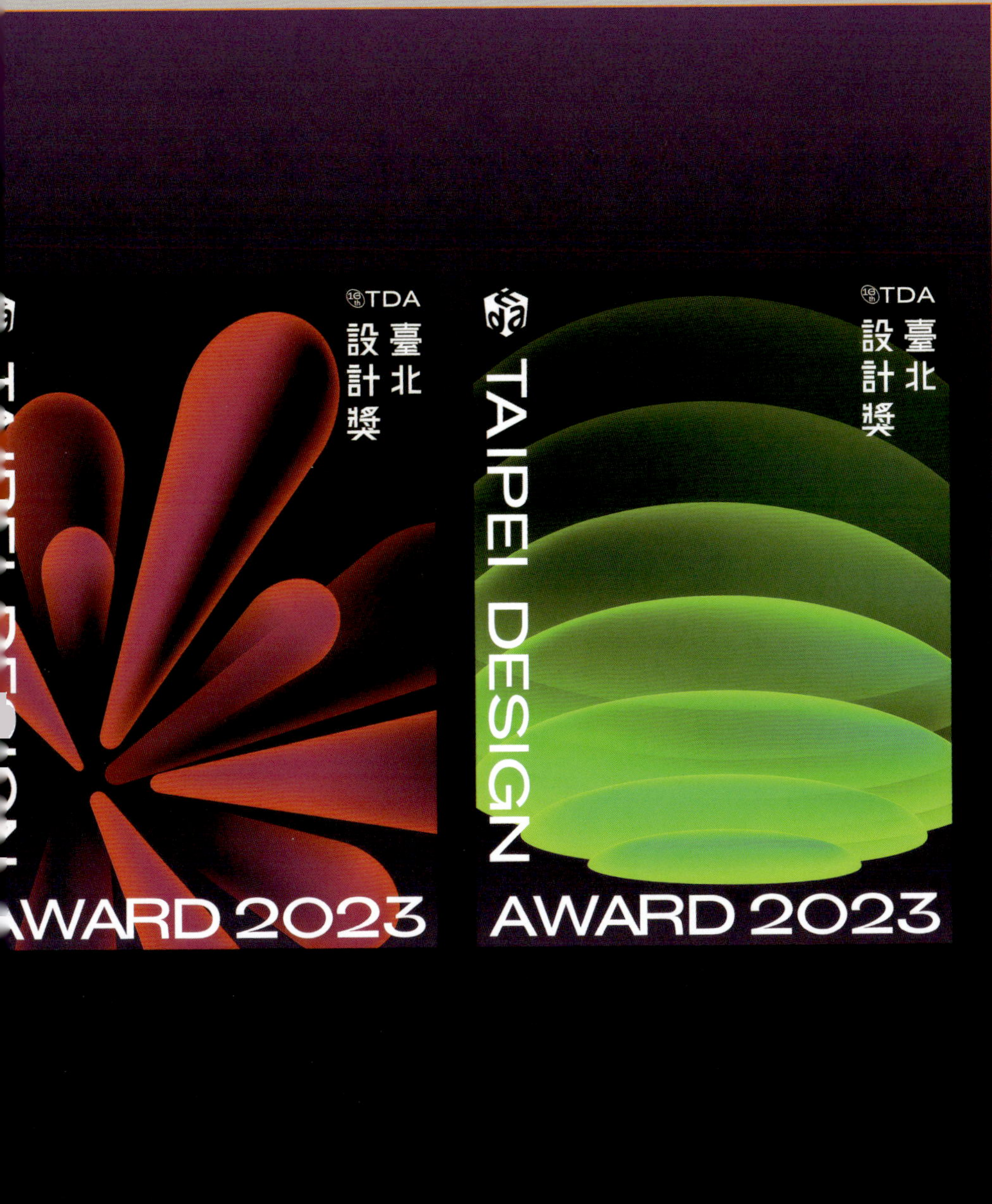
TDA
臺北設計獎
AWARD 2023
TDA
臺北設計獎
TAIPEI DESIGN
AWARD 2023

公共空間設計類

PUBLIC SPACE DESIGN

工業設計類

INDUSTRIAL DESIGN

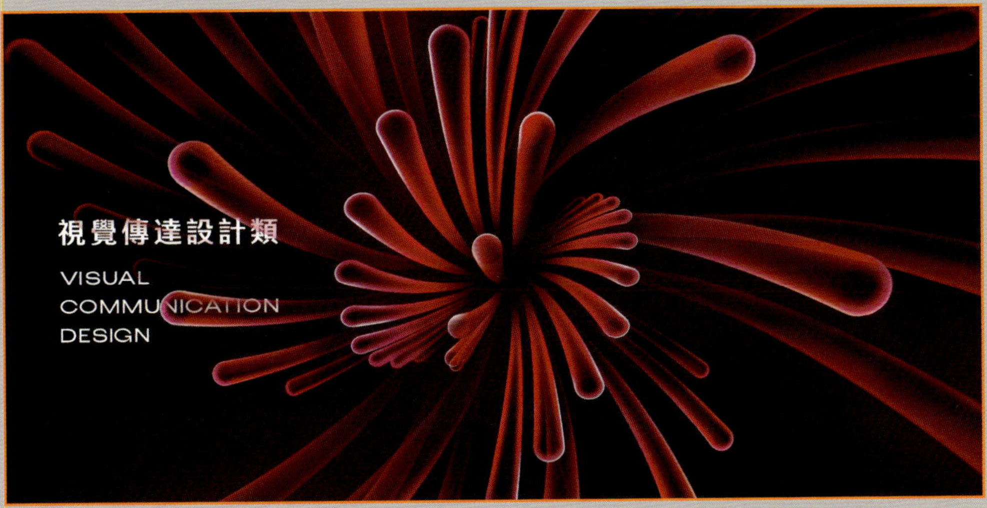
視覺傳達設計類
VISUAL
COMMUNICATION
DESIGN

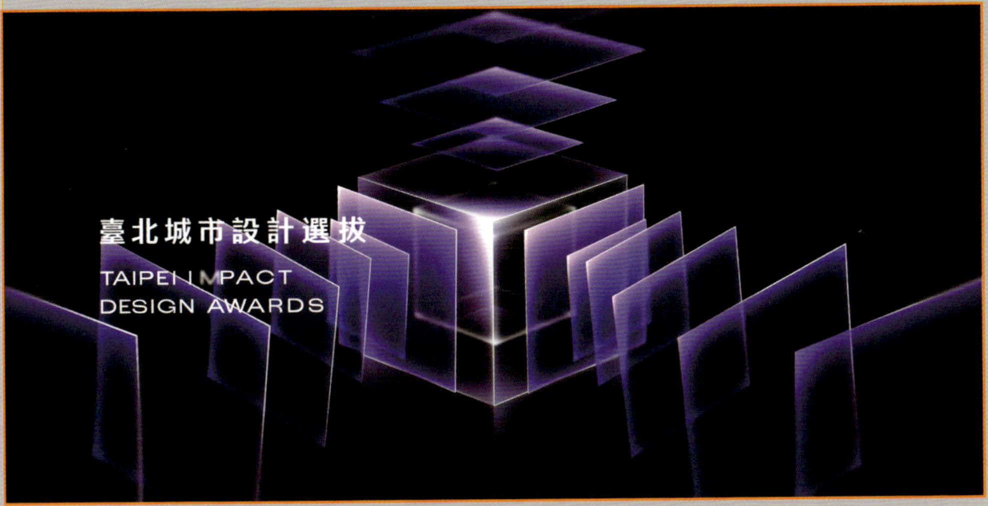
臺北城市設計選拔
TAIPEI IMPACT
DESIGN AWARDS

TDA
臺北
設計獎
TAIPEI DESIGN
AWARD 2023
tda 2hr
Comment

TDA
臺北
設計獎
TAIPEI DESIGN
AWARD 2023
工作證
STAFF
媒體證
MEDIA
貴賓證
VIP

TDA
臺北設計獎
TAIPEI DESIGN
AWARD 2023

TAIPEI DESIGN AWARD
TDA
臺北設計獎

(31)

Studio/Designer Whitelight Motion

Title 34th Golden Melody Awards & Festival Year 2023

Client Bureau of Audiovisual and Music Industry Development, MOC., YOUNG HOPE ENTERTAINMENT CO., LTD.

Typeface(s) TearsFont by justfont

: The identity for the 34th Golden Melody Awards centres on the theme “permeating boundaries”, reflecting the fluid and transformative nature of music. The visuals and logotype express how sound dissolves barriers, using liquid forms to symbolise emotional and cultural exchange, while the design celebrates music’s soft power and its role in fostering connection, creativity, and mutual influence across Asia and beyond.

Special Credits

(Key Visual Design) Wild Design, Tung Teng Liao
(Nominee Video Motion Design) CLIFFS STUDIO, COMPUTERFACE Ltd., C-Grass.tv, AGE Creative

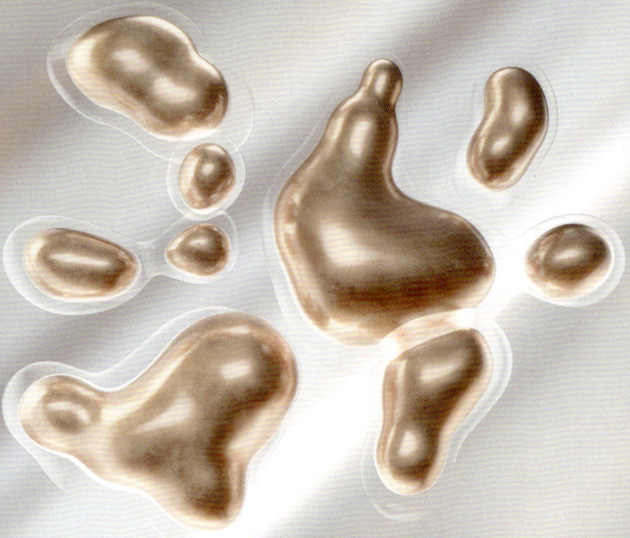

GMMA

金曲獎

GMA
金曲獎

GMA

GMA
金曲獎
GOLDEN MELODY
AWARDS & FESTIVAL
2023

金曲獎
GOLDEN MELODY
AWARDS & FESTIVAL
2023

歌手獎
34th GOLDEN MELODY AWARDS CEREMONY
演唱類・個人獎
最佳作詞人獎
入圍名單
第34屆
金曲獎頒獎典禮
入圍名單
34th
GOLDEN MELODY
AWARDS CEREMONY
演唱類・出版獎
年度專輯獎
入圍名單

演奏類最佳
作曲
獎
BEST
INSTRUMENTAL
COMPOSER

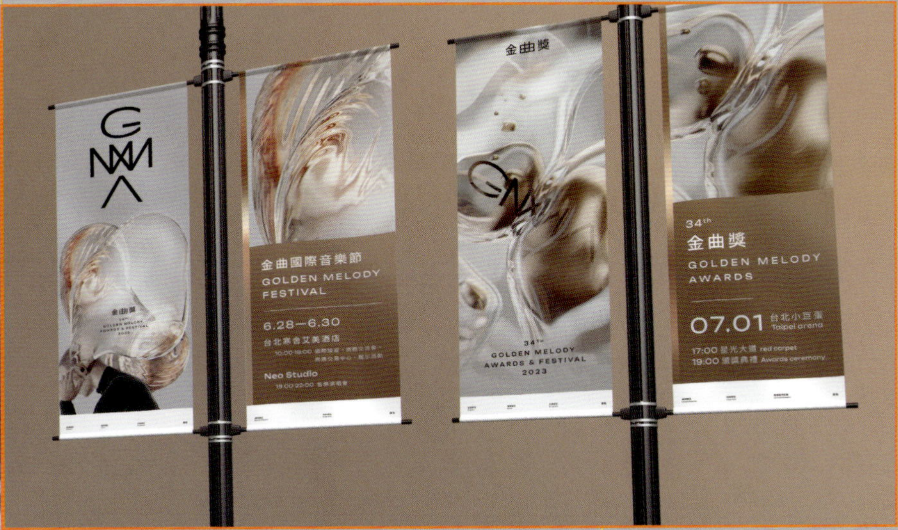
金曲國際音樂節
GOLDEN MELODY
FESTIVAL
6.28—6.30
台北寒舍艾美酒店
Neo Studio
金曲獎
34th
GOLDEN MELODY
AWARDS & FESTIVAL
2023
34th
金曲獎
GOLDEN MELODY
AWARDS
07.01 台北小巨蛋
Taipei arena
17:00 星光大道 red carpet
19:00 頒獎典禮 Awards ceremony

最華男

B

ARIN MALE SINGER

佳語獎

手

最佳台語

B E S T T A I W A N E S

女歌手獎

FEMALE SINGER

(32)

[3d]→

Imperfect

: BÜRO UFHO's GIF Fest III identity for GIFFEST's largest edition at Singapore's National Design Centre celebrates imperfection through playful 3D animation. The inflatable mascot and balloon-inspired type morph from "Imperfect" to "I'M PERFECT" across a massive LED wall, welcoming visitors and showcasing 3D's storytelling potential in brand and festival design.

Studio/Designer BÜRO UFHO Title GIF Fest III Year 2023
Client GIF Fest Typeface(s) Fixture

EYEYAH!
GIFFEST

GIFFEST

: Toby Ng Design crafted a refined new identity for The Shaw Prize, embodying clarity and prestige. At its centre was a universal 'S' radiating within a circle, inspired by natural laws and the cosmos — symbolising discovery and scientific excellence. The system, adaptable across digital platforms, ceremonies, medals, certificates, and packaging, reinforced global recognition and coherence for the award.

Studio/Designer Toby Ng Design Title The Shaw Prize
Year 2023 Client The Shaw Prize Typeface(s) Garda Nova No.2, Signifier

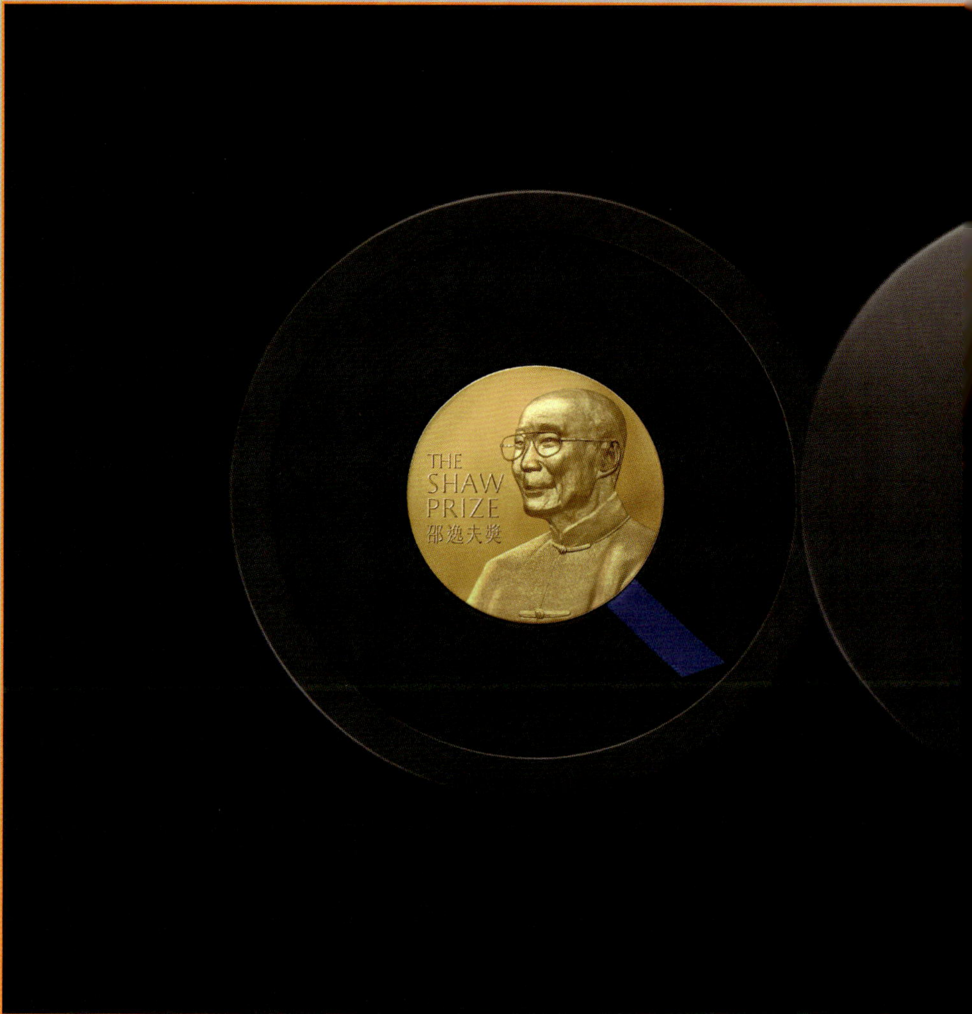
THE
SHAW
PRIZE
邵逸夫獎

THE
SHAW
PRIZE
邵逸夫獎

THE
SHAW
PRIZE
邵逸夫獎

SHAW
LECTURE
In Astronomy
November 13, 2023
Lee Shau Kee Campus, HKUST
Enquiries
+852 3943 7356
enquiries@cuhk.edu.hk
Registration
cuhk.edu.hk/
events/shaw-prize-lecture-2023
In Partnership with
THE HONG KONG UNIVERSITY OF SCIENCE AND TECHNOLOGY
SHAW
LECTURE
In Life Science &
Medicine
November 13, 2023
Cheung Kung Hai Conference Centre, HKUMed
Enquiries
+852 391709305
enquiries@hku.edu.hk
Registration
www.med.hku.hk/
events/shawprize-lecture/2023

SHAW
LECTURE
In Mathematical
Sciences
November 13, 2023
Lecture Theatre, Shaw College, CUHK
Enquiries
+852 3943 7356
enquiries@cuhk.edu.hk
Registration
cuhk.edu.hk/
events/shaw-prize-lecture-2023
In Partnership with

Projects (34-83)

[3d]→

Graphics / Renders / Visuals

(pp.224-515)

(34)

[3d]→ Retro

Studio/Designer Ayumi Tan

Title Art Block Year 2024

Client Self-initiated

: “Art Block” by Ayumi Tan is a playful series that reimagines retro electronics as deconstructed block forms. Prompted by a bout of creative block, the project explores “block” both as a mental hurdle and a visual concept. Through dismantling nostalgic devices into smaller components, Tan transforms a creative challenge into a structured, tongue-in-cheek reflection on form and memory.

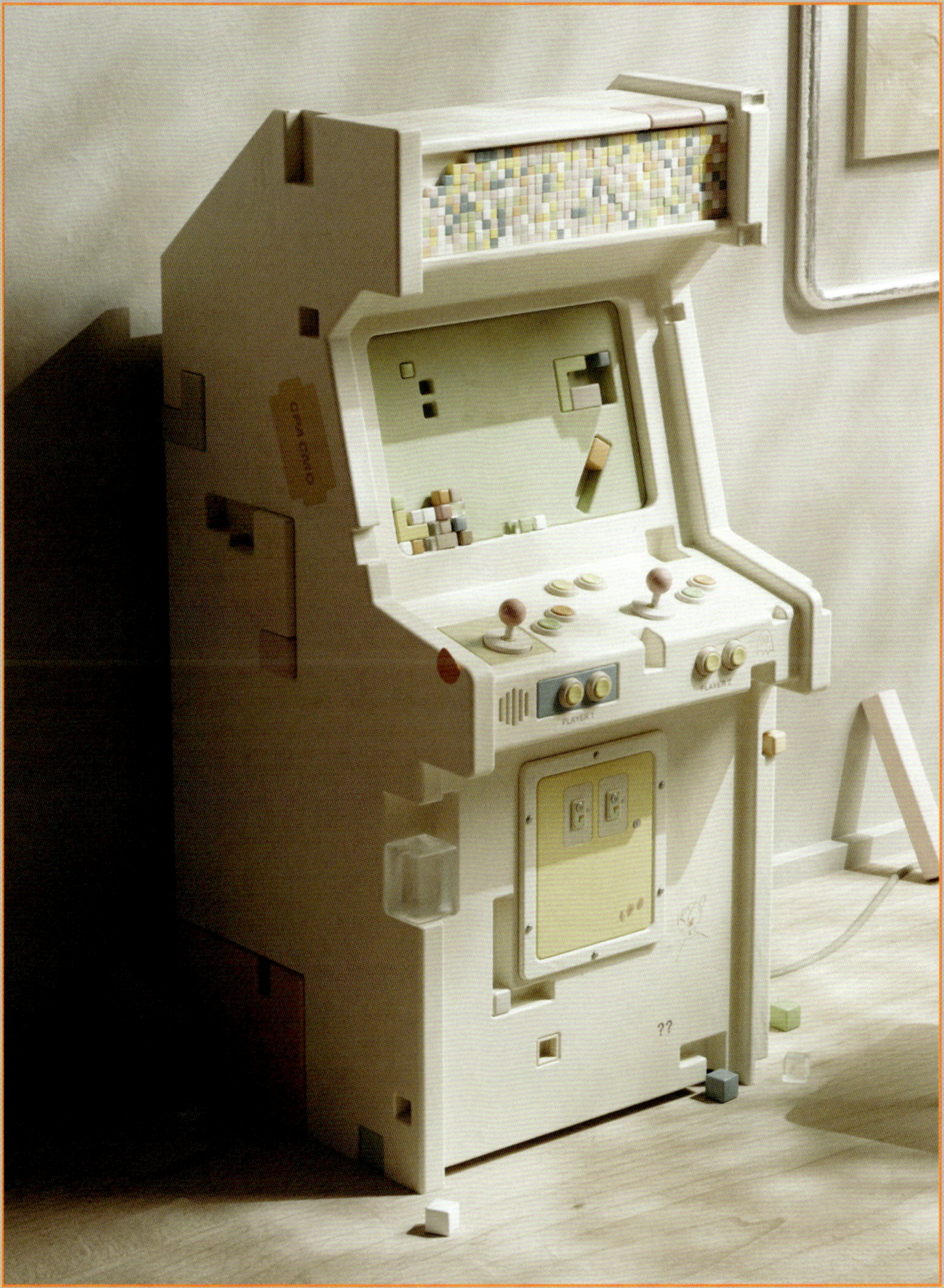
PLAYER 1
??

PLAYER 1

Studio/Designer Anna Fay Title Latent Type Year 2023
Client Self-initiated Typeface(s) Diatype (Dinamo Typefaces)

(35)

[3d]→ Latent

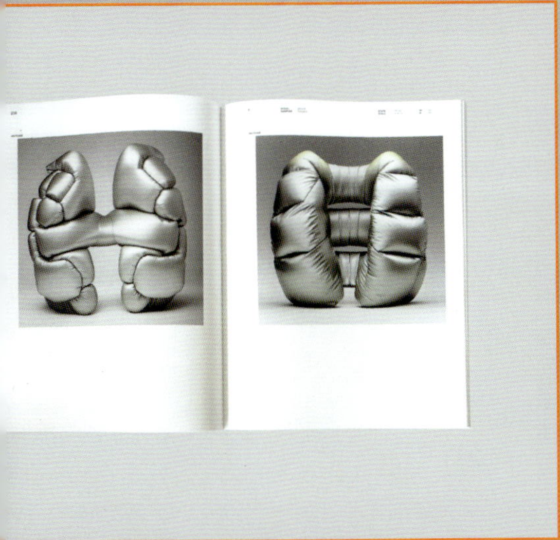

: Latent Type examines the creative potential of AI image-generation tools in typography. Focusing on Text-to-Image models, the project explores how these tools can be used to generate intricate 3D letterforms, despite their current limitations. It also reflects on the evolving relationship between human and machine intelligence in design, raising important questions about authorship, process, and responsibility.

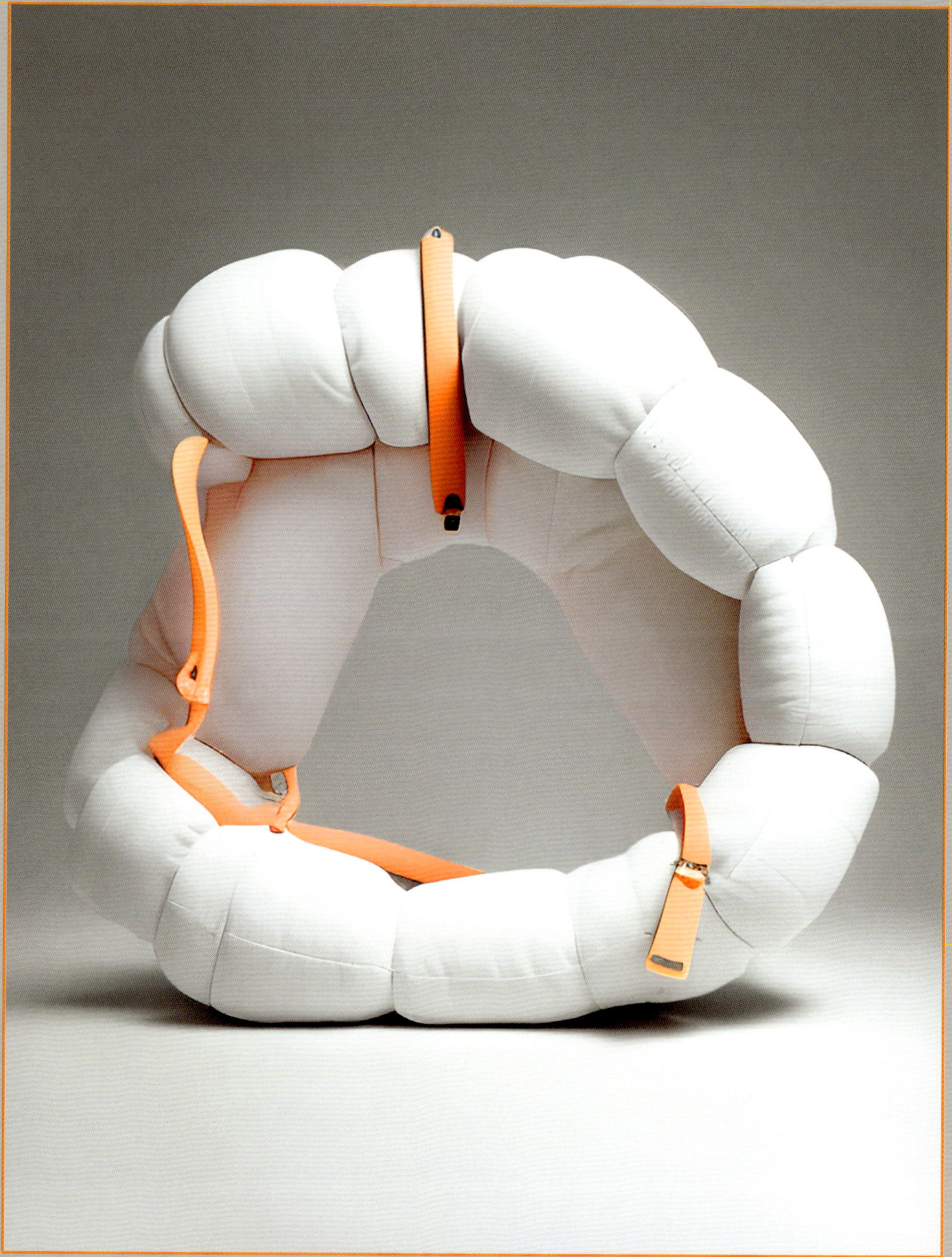

Studio/Designer Facultative Works

Title Visual Universe for Surr.App Year 2021-2024

Client Surr.App Artyom Ignatyev / Denis Sharypin

Typeface(s) Custom

: Facultative Works designed a futuristic visual universe for Surr.App, blending device designs, 3D modelling, rendering, and video and sound design. A modular device, made up of five module types – displays, handles, connectors, multifunctional modules, and keyboards – served as the key communication tool. Each module type featured ten variations, creating a dynamic and versatile vision of a potential future.

(36)

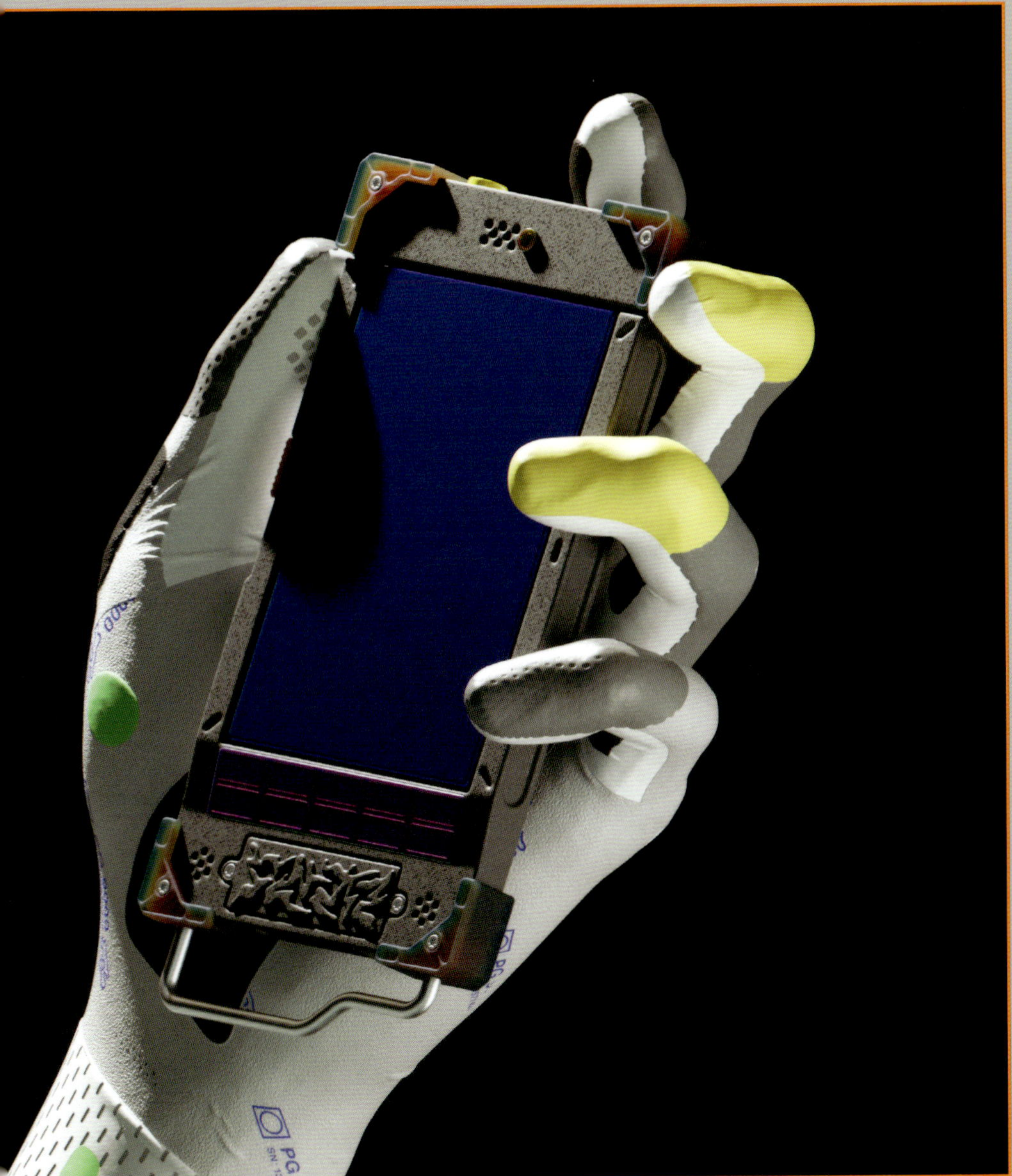

[3d]→Display

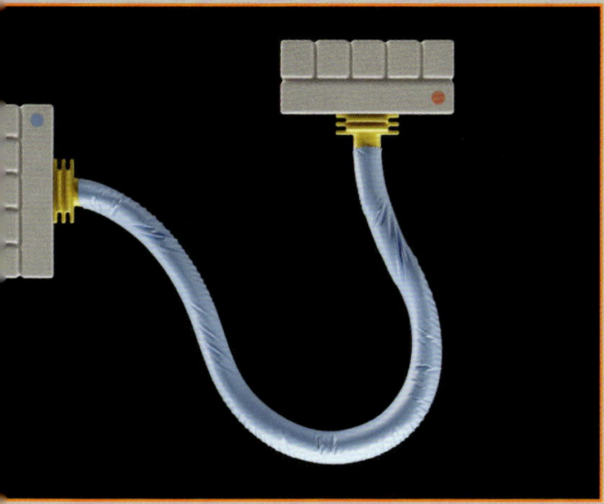

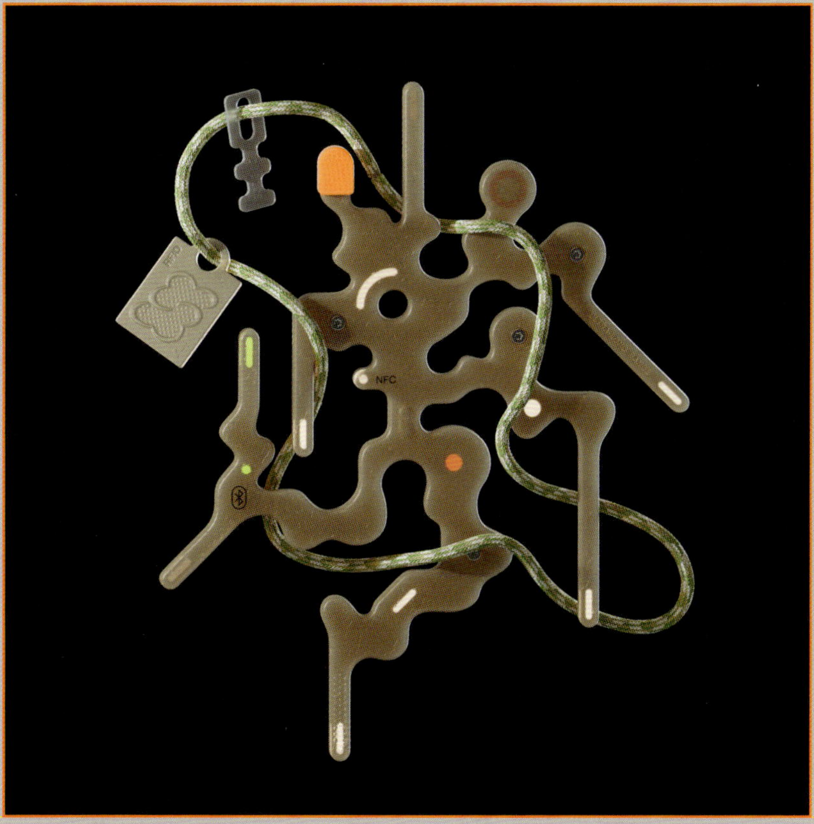
NFC

BEST BEFORE: 03.07.2028
Calories 400
Total Carb 27g
Sugars 27g
Riboflavin Vit B2 1.7mg
Niacin Vvvit B3 20mg
Vitamin B6 2mg
Vitamin B12 6mcg
Sodium 180mg
Taurine 1000mg
Panax Ginseng 200mg
Energy Blend 2500mg
L-Caritine Glucose Caffeine Guarana
Inositol Glucuronolactone Maltodextrin

DOI: 06.58.05.675

SN:530968502398

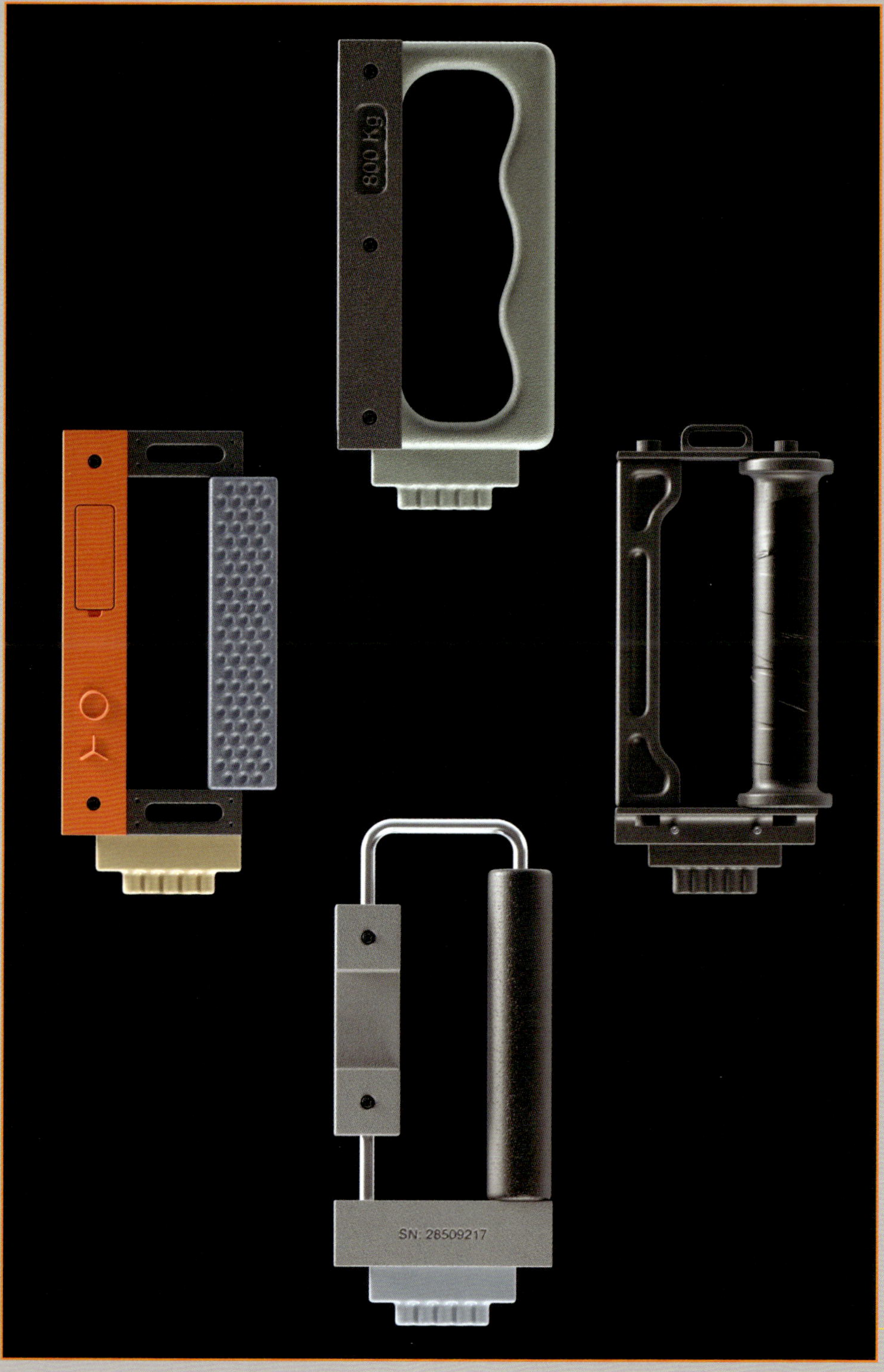
800 Kg
SN: 28509217

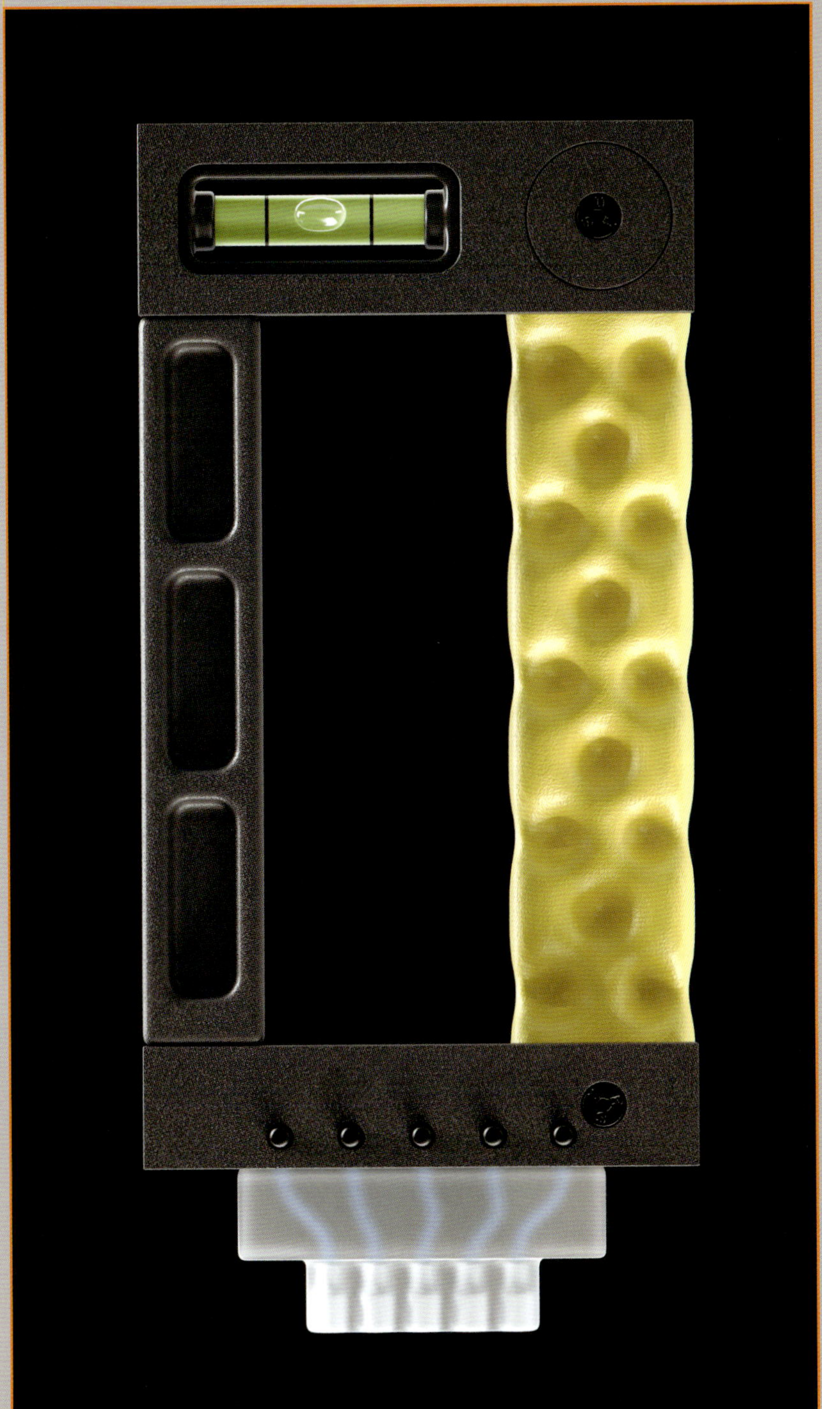

Section (A)
Section (B)

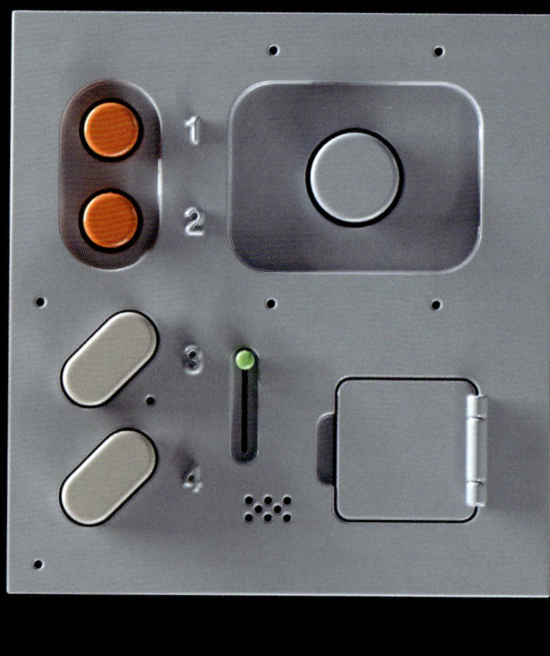
1
2
3
4

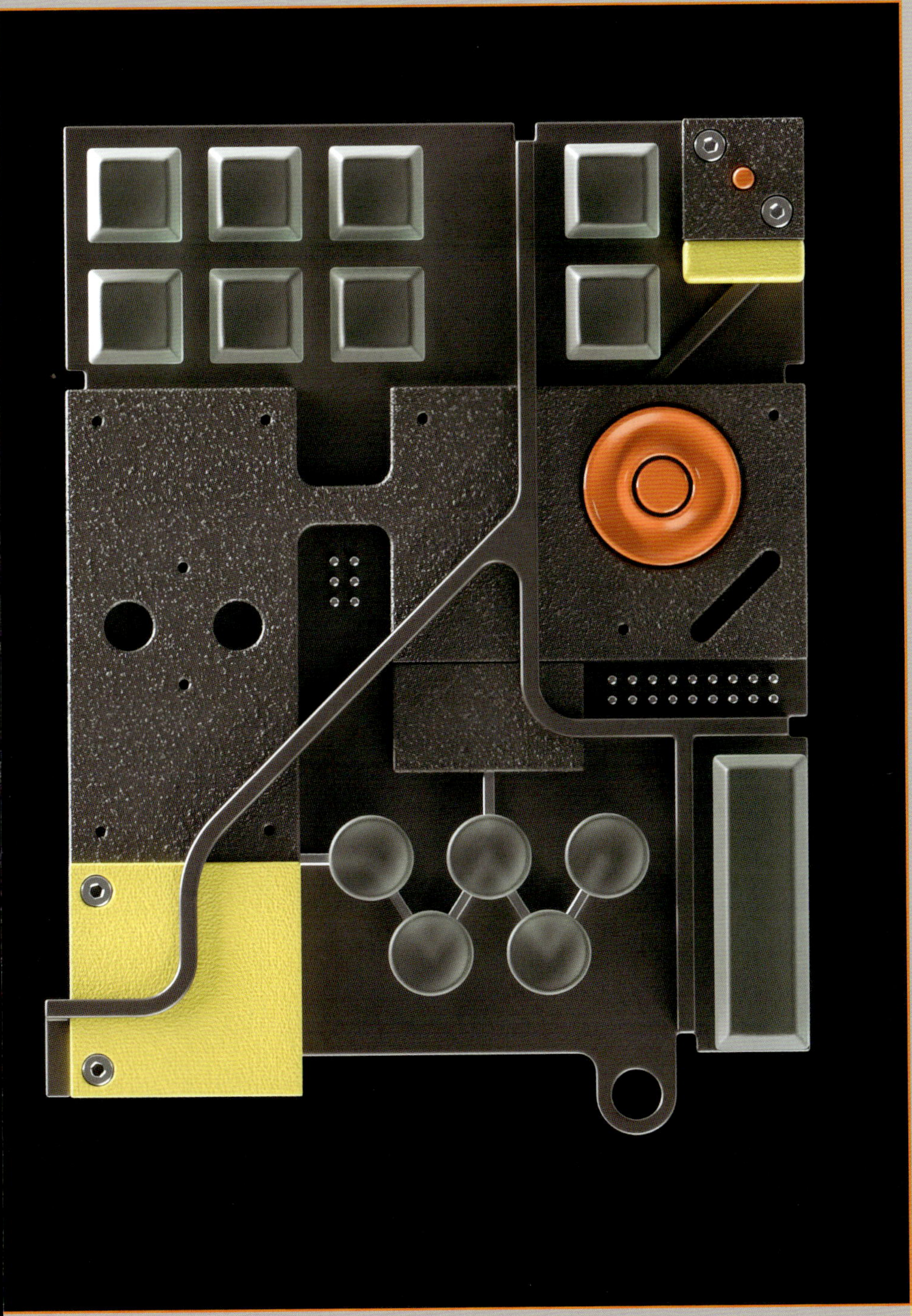

MAGNETIC FIELD
N
S

LOW GRAVITY

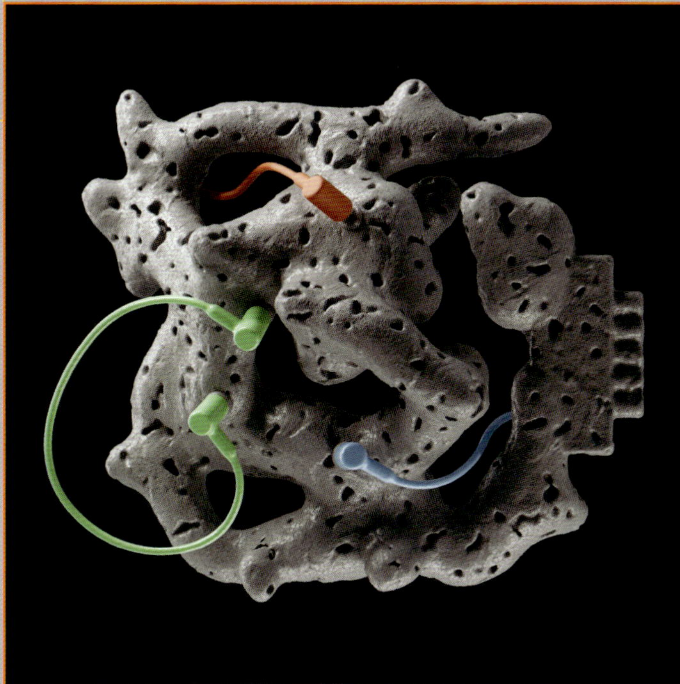

16:24
40%
32°C
WARNING
Do not operate without a face mask

Studio/Designer Facultative Works Title 3D Visuals for P.Y.E Optics

Year 2018 - Ongoing Client P.Y.E Optics

: Facultative Works has been working with P.Y.E Optics, an innovative eyewear brand, for almost a decade, creating a diverse range of designs together. From eye-catching illustrations and optician cabinet walls to business cards, client cards, microfibre cloths, bags, and the online store interface, their collaboration shows how eyewear can be both precise and creatively bold, blending style with functionality in every piece.

F.Y.E

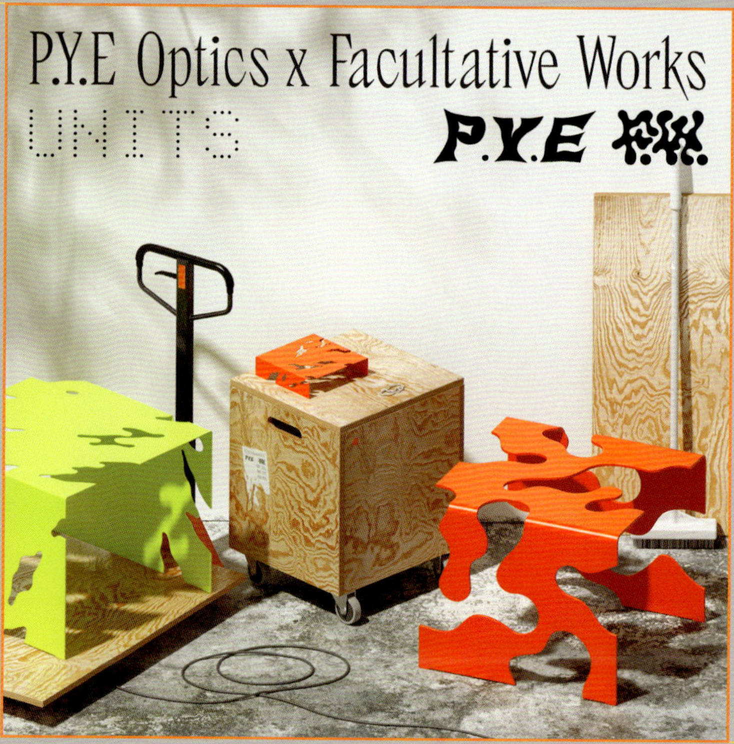
P.Y.E Optics x Facultative Works
UNITS
P.Y.E

P.Y.E Optics x
RAL 3026
RAL 7047
RAL 1026

MacGuffin
The Life of Things
Nº 8
UNITS-3
UNITS-1
UNITS-2

(38)

[3d]→

Continuum

Studio/Designer Sawdust
Title Continuum Year 2021–2024
Client Dalbin

: Continuum explores the shifting flow between pattern configurations through form, light, and shadow. While shapes appear distinct at opposite ends, they blend subtly when placed in sequence. The transient viewing experience challenges perception, making the fluid transition between arrangements the focal point of the piece.

(39)

[3d]→ Force

Studio/Designer Dennis Hoelscher

Title [J]uggernaut – A Massive Inexorable Force

Year 2024 Client Self-initiated

: Dennis Hoelscher's sculptural letterform explores pressure and control through physical distortion. As part of a series, the piece contrasts inflated sections with areas restrained by pins, creating a dynamic tension between expansion and containment.

Studio/Designer Fonts From Folch Franc Studio Folch
Title Acid Grotesk Soft Year 2025 Client Self-initiated
Typeface(s) Acid Grotesk Soft

(40) [3d]→ Baseball

: Acid Grotesk Soft by Fonts From Folch transforms typographic rebellion into tactile poetry. The typeface presentation employs baseball iconography as a metaphor, where hard-hitting geometric forms soften into plush, sculptural letterforms. The monochromatic packaging contrasts with vibrant blue dimensional type, creating a playful dialogue between industrial precision and organic comfort that redefines contemporary type specimen design.

Special Credit

This project is a collaboration between Fonts From Folch, Franc Studio and Folch.

(41)

[3d]→

Fruit

: Joseph Töreki's "Tutti Frutti" explores the hyperreal aesthetics of fruit, inspired by Japan's meticulously cultivated produce. Encountering seemingly artificial perfection, he examines the tension between realism and abstraction. His work questions authenticity, revealing how digital tools achieve flawlessness that nature rarely can. Tutti Frutti highlights a paradox: the simpler something appears, the more precision it requires.

Studio/Designer Joseph Töreki

Title Tutti Frutti Year 2024 Client Self-initiated

(42)

[3d]→ Rust

Studio/Designer Vincent Wagner

Title Xtal Year 2024 Client Self-initiated

: "Xtal" is an abstract study of material and form, sculpted in virtual reality. While the text is inspired by the Aphex Twin track of the same name, the final piece carries no direct reference to the music or the potential meanings of its title.

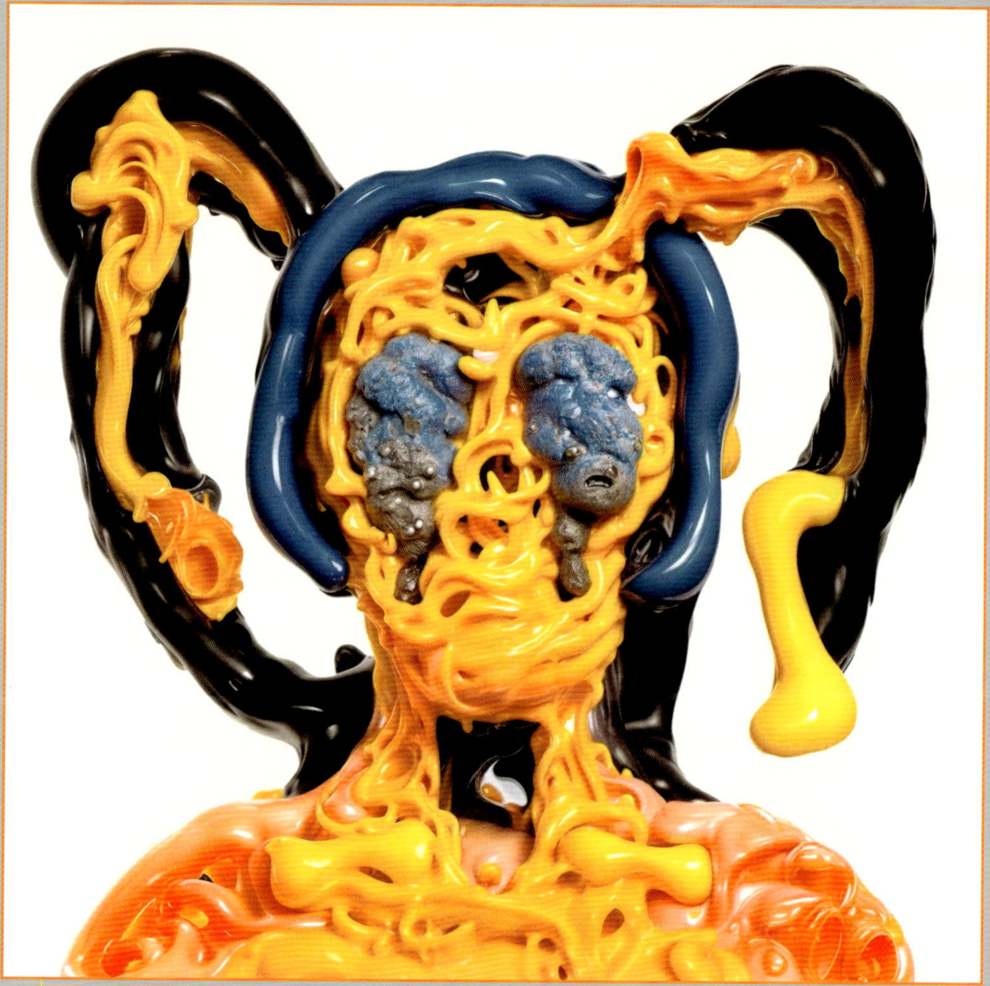

(43)

[3d]→ Nodes

Studio/Designer Dennis Hoelscher

Title ERWERB Year 2024

Client Self-initiated

: Dennis Hoelscher experimented with Blender's Geometry Nodes, combining brush techniques and cloth simulation to explore sculptural typography and motion-driven forms. Utilising node-based procedural logic and dynamic deformation, his work played with visual texture and fluidity in three dimensions.

Studio/Designer Sawdust

Title Relaxed Year 2023 Client Self-initiated

(44)

[3d]→ Relaxed

: “Relaxed” is an ongoing study of three-dimensional typographic forms, with a particular interest in light, shadow, and texture.

Title Wassergeist Year 2021

(45)

[3d]→

Monolithic

Studio/Designer Kopfgestaltung

Client Self-initiated

Title Zeitlos / Timeless Year 2021

Title Meister der Maschinen / Master of Machines Year 2023

Title Rebel Year 2022

Title Unheil Year 2024

Title Steingeist Year 2022

Title Illusion Year 2023

Title Sie / Her Year 2021

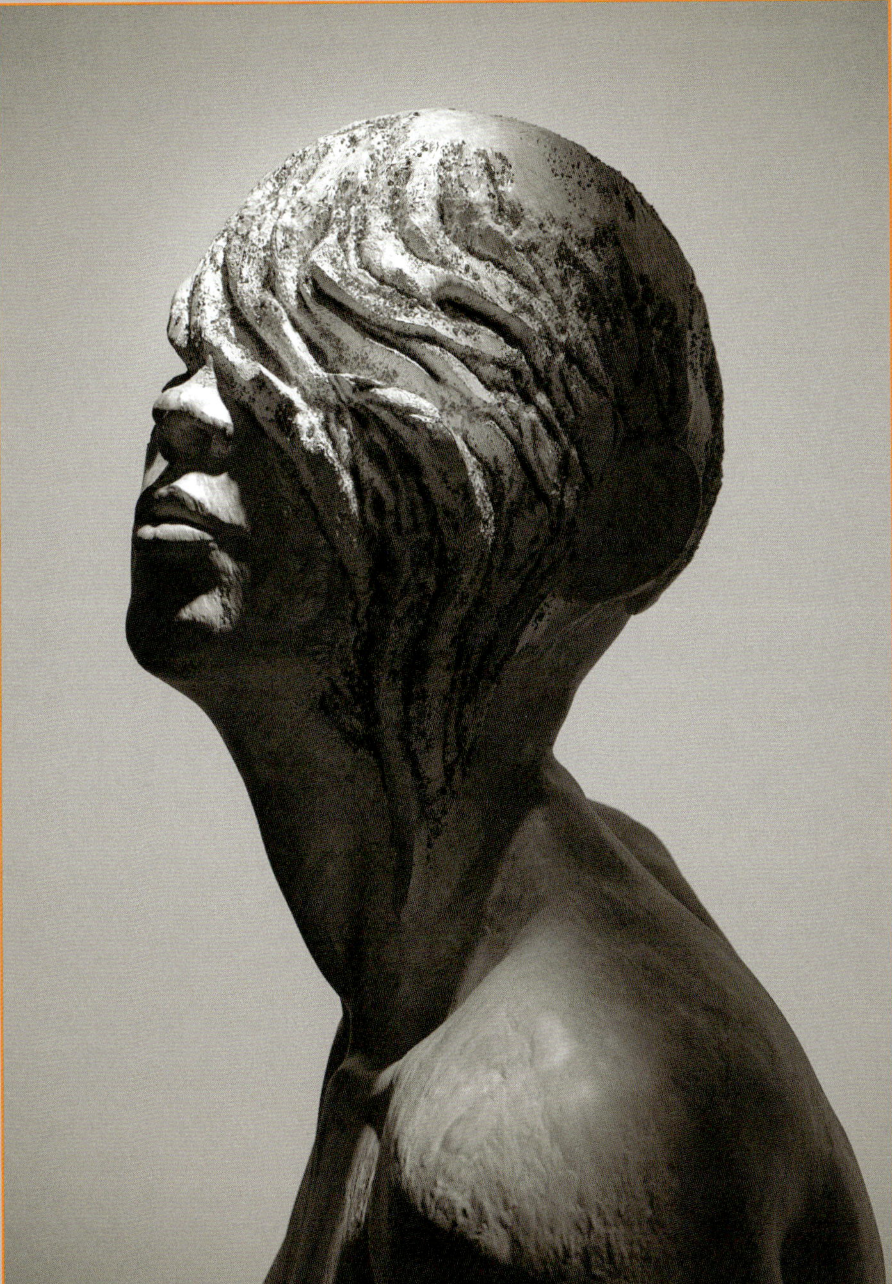

Studio/Designer Maximillen Vert

Title Plastic Flowers Year 2024 Client Self-initiated

(46) [3d]→ Flowers

: "Plastic Flowers" by Maximilien Vert is a 3D art project that recreates plastic flowers with striking realism. Through intricate textures, shapes, and lighting, the work brings artificial yet elegant compositions to life. Exploring the contrast between nature and the synthetic, it highlights the beauty in detail and imitation, showcasing Vert's dedication to advancing digital art using procedural techniques.

17

Studio/Designer Melvin Le Riboter

Title "M" Motorola Identity Year 2022

Client Motorola

(47)

[3d]→ M

:	Melvin Le Riboter reimagined Motorola's iconic "M" as a refined, minimalist symbol, transforming it into a flexible design element that adapts across media. Serving as both logo and canvas, the identity plays with light, depth, and motion – offering a fresh, futuristic take that reflects Motorola's technological edge while preserving its recognisability.

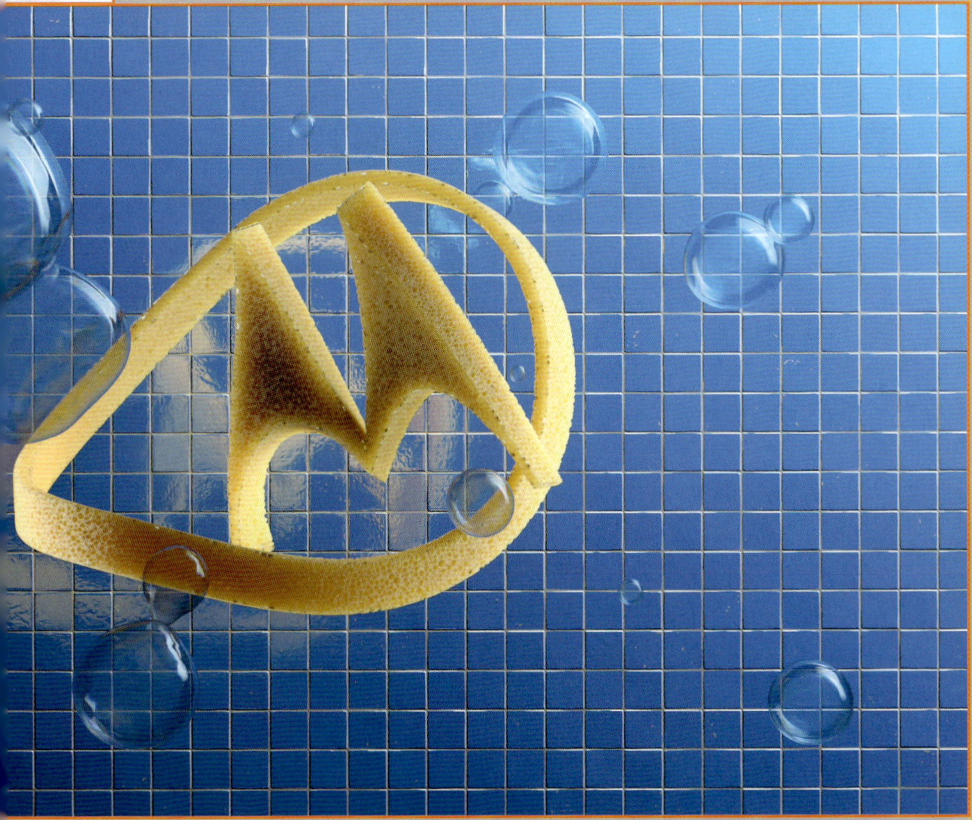

Studio/Designer Kitasavi

Title Boofy – We, The Talentless Cover Art

Year 2025 Client Boofy

Typeface(s) Eskapade Fraktur

(48)

[3d]→ Bulbous

: The cover art for We, The Talentless by Boofy features a chaotic yet controlled 3D structure of bulbous, pierced, and metallic forms. Juxtaposing glossy and gritty textures, the composition evokes a sense of tension and distortion. It visually echoes the EP's sound – fragmented, rhythmic, and sculptural – balancing aggression with a touch of playful intricacy.

Boofy
We, The Talentless

: The cover art for GRiZ – Saxoriddim reimagines a saxophone as a vibrant 3D sculpture. Bold colours, glossy textures and fluid, surreal forms mirror the dynamic energy of the track. Merging digital polish with abstract expression, the artwork reflects the distorted rhythm and playful spirit of GRiZ's music in a visually striking, contemporary style.

(49) [3d]→ Distortion

Studio/Designer Kitasavi

Title GRiZ – Saxoriddim Cover Art Year 2025

Client GRiZ Typeface(s) Neue Haas Grotesk Display Pro (75 Bold)

GRiZ Saxoriddim

Studio/Designer Kitasavi Title Neana – Fantasy Pulse Cover Art
Year 2024 Client Neana Typeface(s) Carbon (Bold)

(50) [3d]→ Fantasy

: Kitasavi's album artwork captures the emotional terrain of Neana's debut release through a surreal 3D landscape. High-gloss typography merges with fluid forms and layered textures, blending digital nostalgia with fantasy aesthetics. The composition explores themes of memory and transformation, where raw and elastic surfaces create a dreamlike tension between harmony and distortion.

Special Credit

(Sound) Zing Audio

: Melvin Le Riboter's "Future Travel" reimagines the joy of travel through a surreal, futuristic lens, placing Floyd's signature suitcase at the centre of a bold visual journey. With retro wheels, glossy surfaces, and standout colours, the suitcase becomes a character in its own right. The playful animation blends unexpected motion and dreamlike landscapes, echoing the brand's irreverent, expressive spirit.

[3d]→

Travel

Studio/Designer Melvin Le Riboter

Title FUTURE TRAVEL Year 2022 Client FLOYD

FLOYD

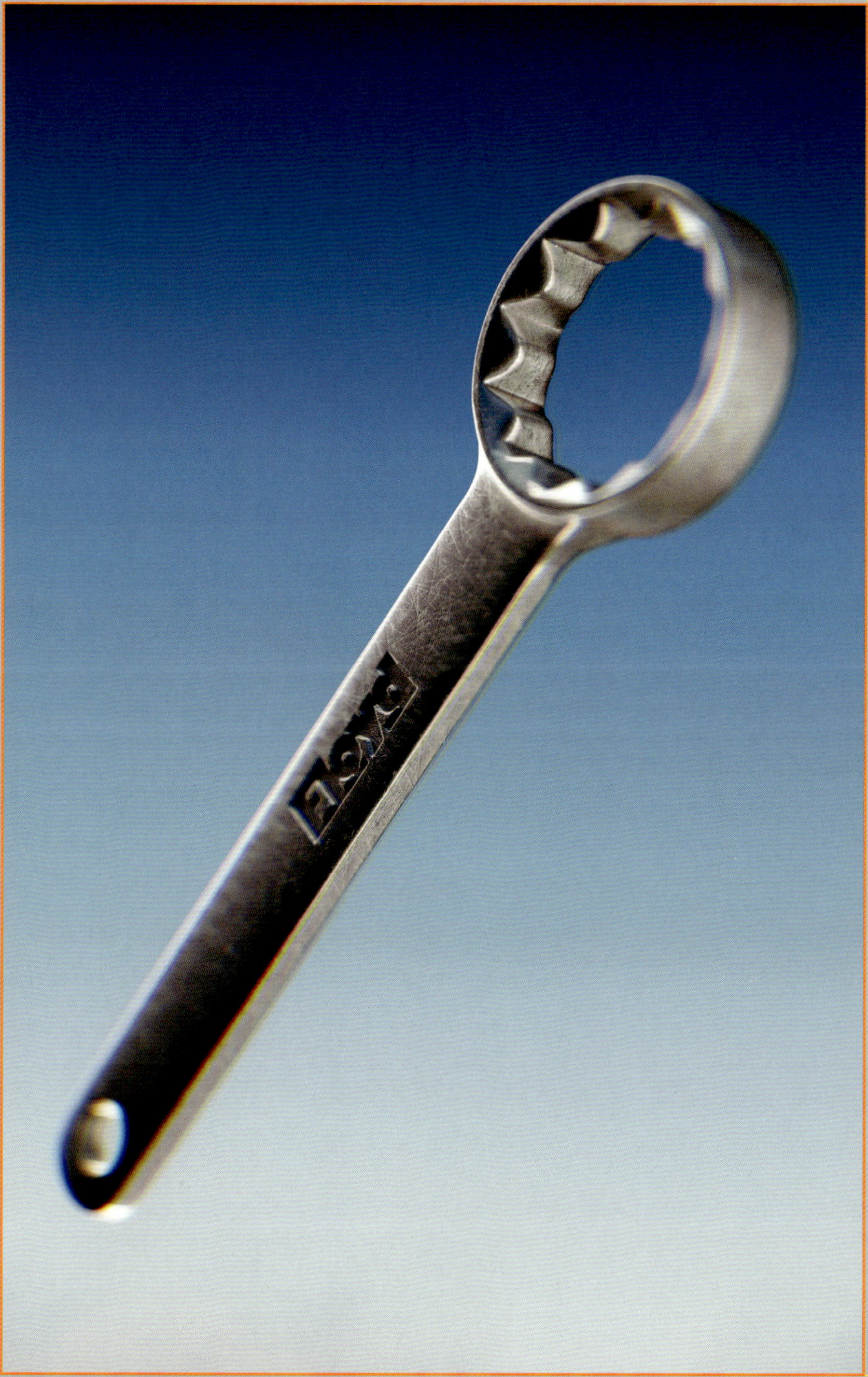

: Studio Dumbar/DEPT® partnered with Utah Jazz to evolve their motion identity for the 50th season. Inspired by sport energy and jazz rhythms, the design focused on four pillars: Rhythmic Momentum, Physical Juxtapositions, Sudden Dimensionality, and Continuous Flow. Featuring reactive typography, metallic 3D patterns, and basketballs made from Utah's natural materials, it heightened game-day excitement and pushed motion design's limits.

(52) [3d]→Jazz

Studio/Designer Studio Dumbar/DEPT®

Title Utah Jazz 50th Season Year 2023 Client Utah Jazz

Typeface(s) "Plaak" custom-made by 205TF

TAKE
NOTE

LET'S
GO
JAZZ

MAKE NOISE
MAKE NOISE

JAZZ BASKE
50
ESTD 19

(53)

Studio/Designer Dada Projects

Title Her Rise Year 2022 Client Nike

: For Nike's "Her Rise" event, Dada Projects crafted refined motion assets, including an interactive face filter, stage visuals, and a film inspired by athletic motifs. As a female-led studio, they embraced a "work-in-progress" aesthetic to reflect the ongoing journey of womxn in sport – celebrating resilience, progress, and empowerment through elegant design and fluid motion.

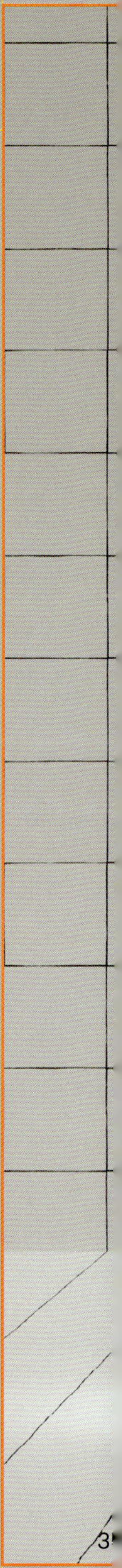

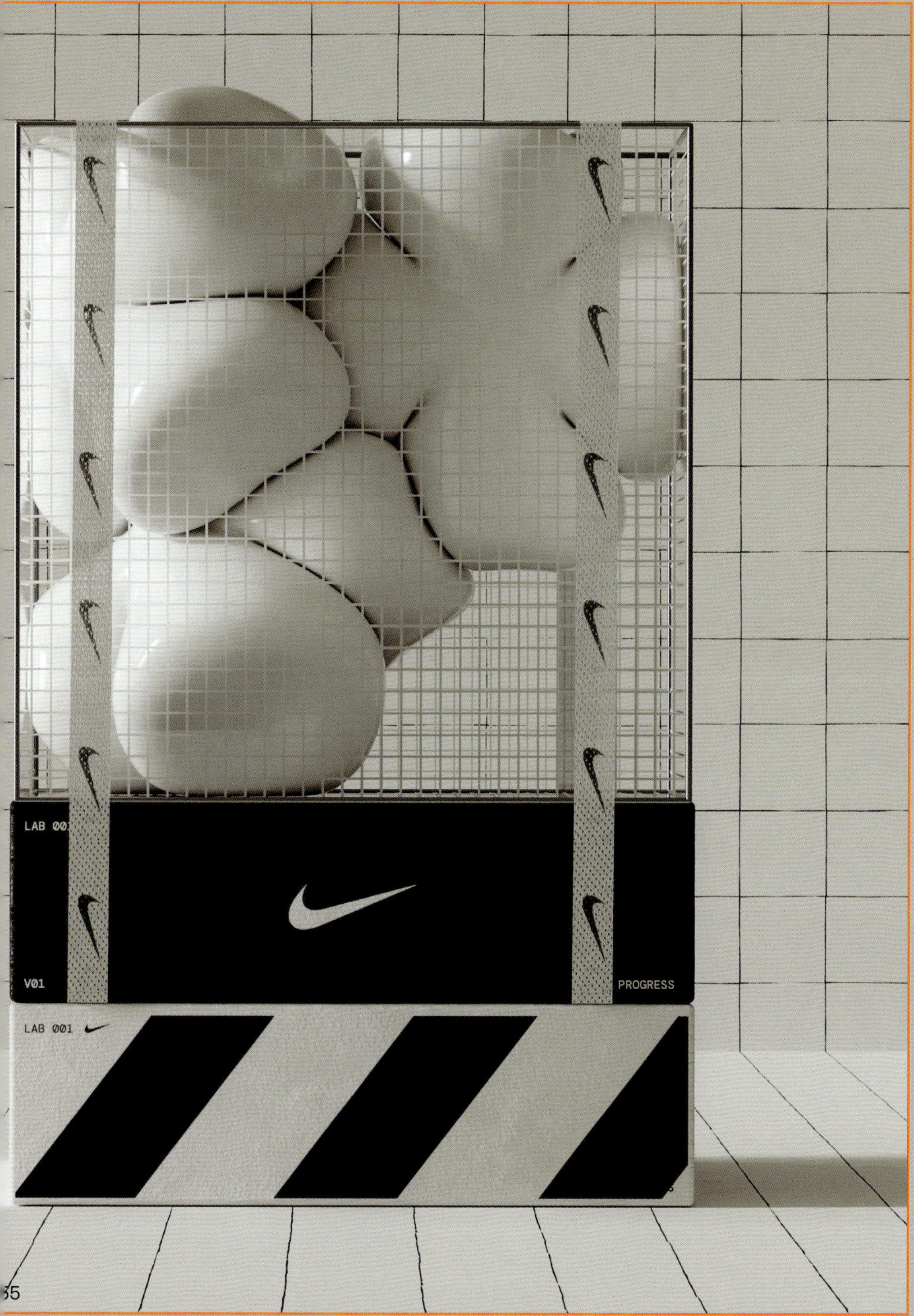
V01
PROGRESS
LAB 001

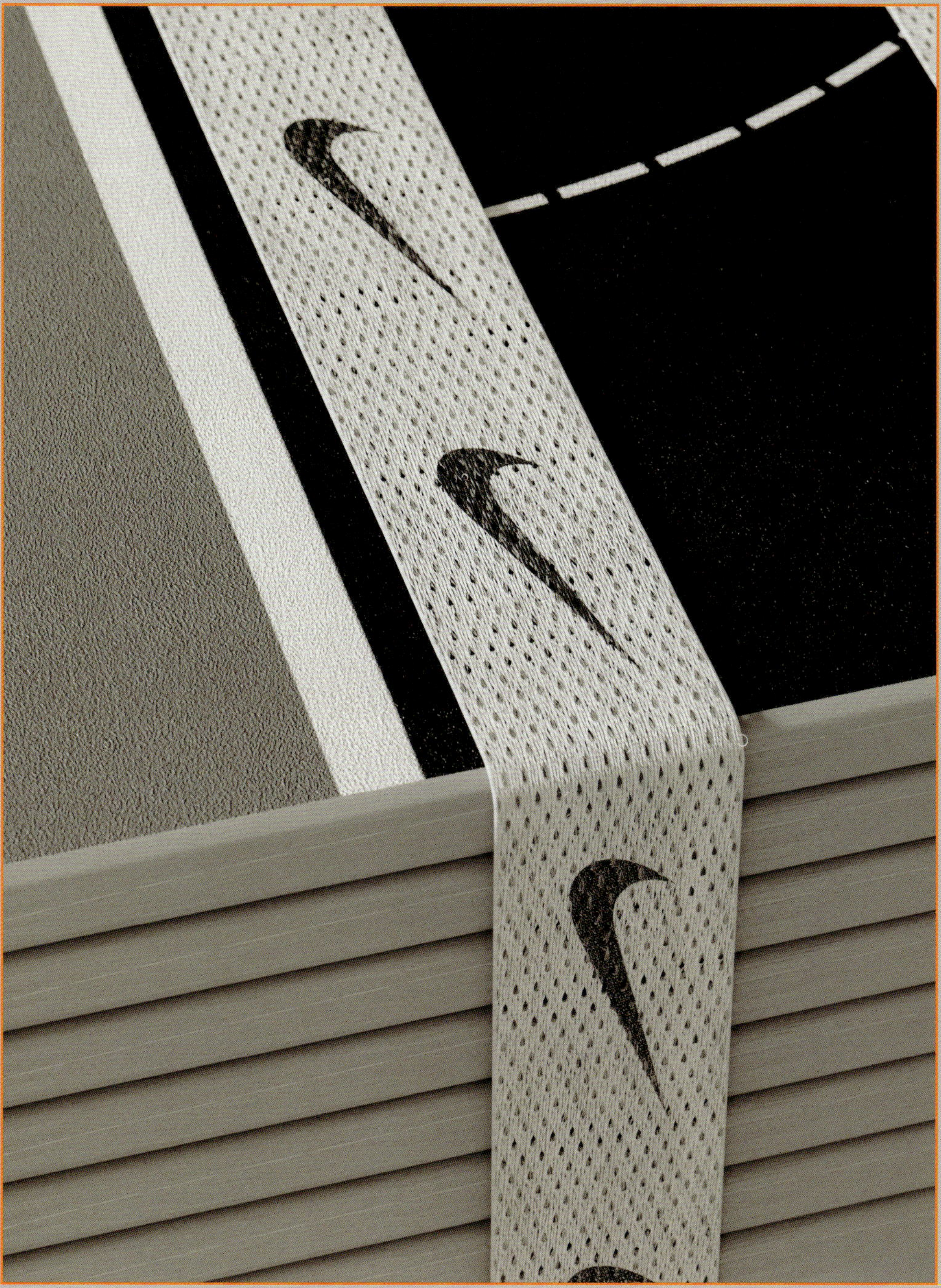

LAB 001
V01
IN PROGRESS
113.5 m/s
37.9838° N, 23.7275° E
v001
254MPH

50

Studio/Designer Dada Projects

Title Patek Philosophies Year 2024

Client Patek Philippe

(54) [3d]→ Intricate

: Dada Projects created a CGI mood film for Patek Philippe that explores the artistry behind watchmaking. Highlighting the five-step process from sketch to metal prototype, the film focuses on the precision and craftsmanship involved. With refined visuals and slow-motion sequences, it celebrates each stage of creation, offering a poetic look at the meticulous design ethos of the iconic luxury brand.

Special Credit Leagas Delaney

: Doris Lin's “Playground” transforms nostalgic childhood memories into surreal digital landscapes. Her 2024 personal project reimagines playground equipment – banana seesaws, whimsical characters with goggles – through dreamlike 3D visualisation. Ultimately, the work celebrates universal play experiences while questioning boundaries between memory and imagination, creating fantastical environments where every surface becomes a playground.

(55) [3d]→ Playground

Studio/Designer Doris Lin Title The Playground

Year 2022 Client Self-initiated

Special Credits (Agency) Publicis
(Audio) Zelig Sound

: FutureDeluxe partnered with Publicis to visually articulate Heineken's sustainability messaging without relying on clichéd imagery. Using Heineken's green bottle as a central motif, they crafted bold, abstract visuals – both motion and static – that communicated each environmental initiative with clarity and sophistication. The resulting modular assets formed the core of a global campaign, highlighting Heineken's ongoing efforts to become more environmentally conscious.

Studio/Designer FutureDeluxe
Title Heineken Sustainability
Year 2021 Client Heineken

(56)

[3d]→ Bottle

Heineken
HEINEKEN ORIGINAL
Heineken
PURE MALT LAGER

ORIGINAL

Heineken
ORIGINAL

Heineken
PURE MALT

Studio/Designer COLORS AND THE KIDS Title Trafo
Year 2024 Client Self-initiated

(57)

: "Trafo" immerses viewers in a landscape of constant change, where feathers drift on air currents and mechanical shapes glide over shifting surfaces. The evolving visuals, paired with a dynamic soundtrack, invite close observation, with each transformation offering subtle clues and deeper meanings.

[3d]→ Feathers

Studio/Designer Kevin Jaeger

Title Habibi Flower Bouquet Year 2023

Client Habibi UG

(58) [3d]→ Bouquet

: Kevin Jaeger created a poetic animation for Hamburg-based clothing brand Habibi, using a flower bouquet as a metaphor for migration. The piece visualises how diverse cultures come together to form something new – like flowers forming a vibrant arrangement. These elements then transform into colourful threads that weave the Habibi logo, symbolising identity, connection, and the beauty of cultural fusion.

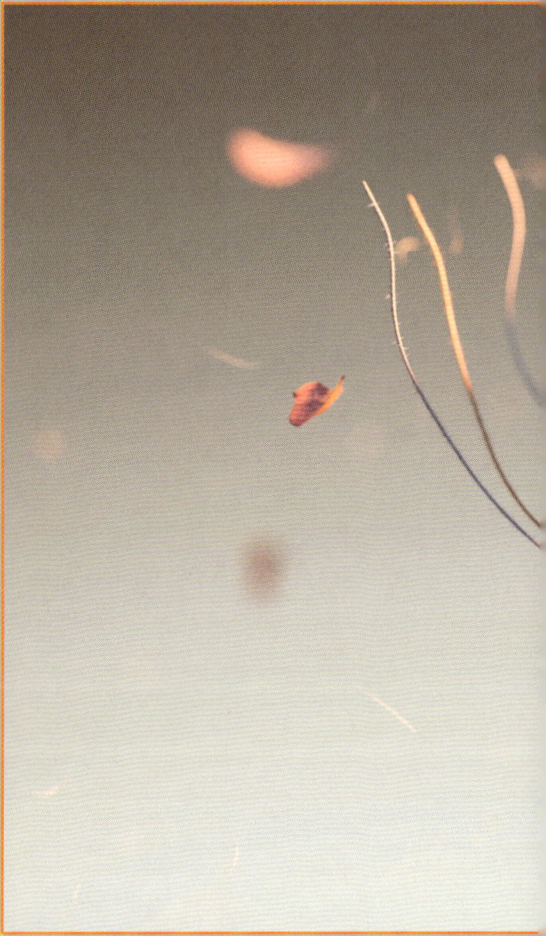

Studio/Designer Tina Touli

Title Shifting Symphonies Year 2023

Client Videocitta Typeface(s) Heading Now

: "Shifting Symphonies" is a kinetic typography series exploring transition – from Yin Yang's balance to the explosive Big Bang, and the rhythms of coming and going. Aligned with Videocittà's festival theme, it highlights change as essential, urging balance and accelerating digital transformation toward a sustainable future.

(59)

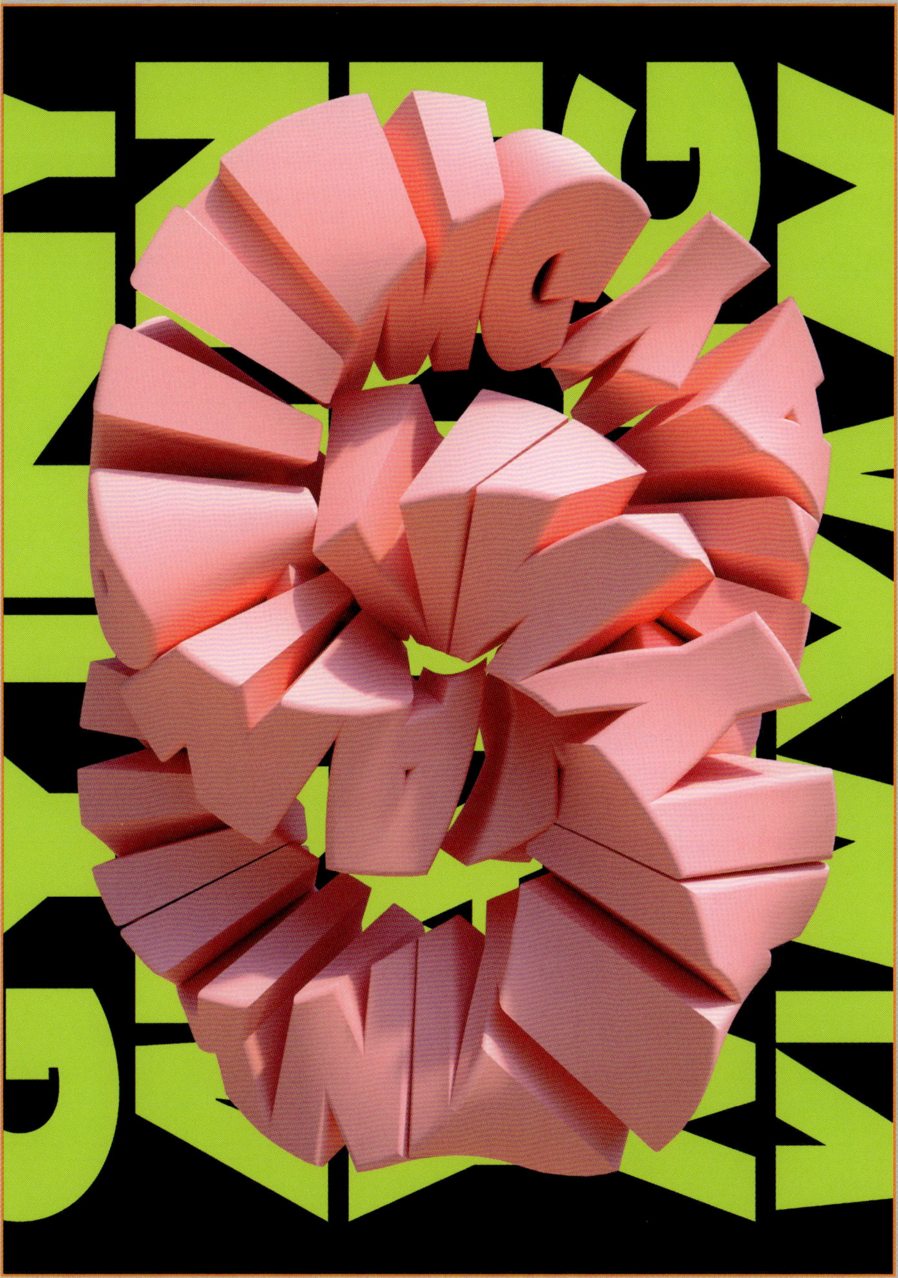

[3d]→Shift

1 01111111

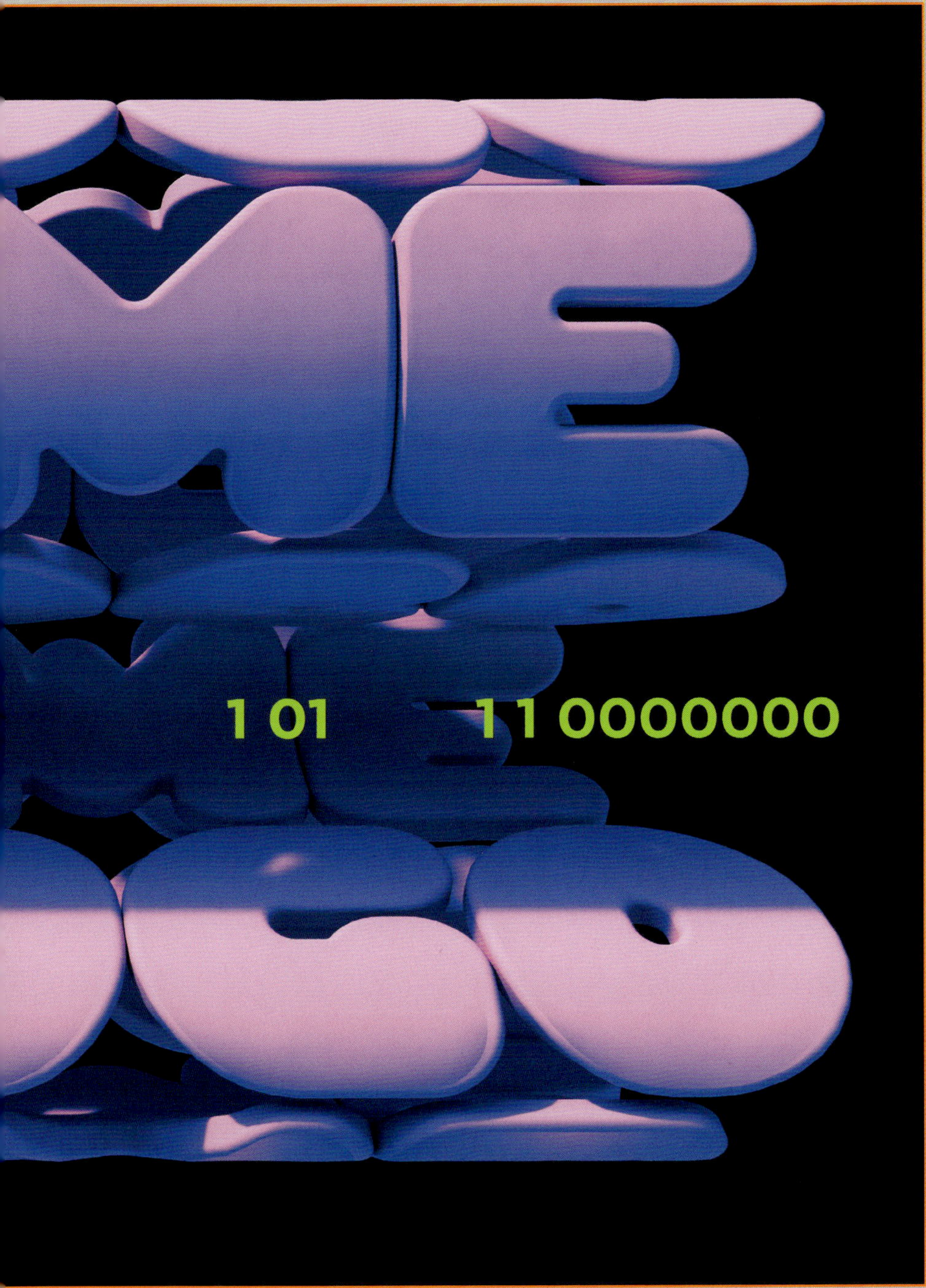
1 01 11 0000000

(60)

Studio/Designer SMLXL Title A Generation Without Tools

Year 2024 Client La Vanguardia

Special Credits

(Art Direction) Rosa Mundet / La Vanguardia
(Photography) Kiwi Bravo

[3d]→Pictogram

: SMLXL created a striking visual for La Vanguardia's article “A Generation Without Tools”, which explores systemic shortcomings in education. It features a solitary stop sign against an open sky bears a pictogram of a graduate digging – cap on, shovel in hand. The minimalist 3D design delivers a sharp metaphor: ambition stalled, and young people left to navigate their futures unequipped.

Studio/Designer Builders Club

Title #SoYou Year 2022 Client Samsung

Special Credits

(Agency) Barbarian NYC, Additional
(Post Production) Okay Studios

(61)

[3d]→ Personalised

: For Samsung's Galaxy Z Flip launch, Builders Club collaborated with Barbarian to create the #SoYou campaign, drawing on Gen Z culture and social media aesthetics. Featuring AR and VFX-driven visuals, the project highlights personalisation through custom colours and style. From live-action shoots to final delivery, the studio handled full production — delivering a sleek, fashion-forward take on the smartphone upgrade experience.

05

(62)

[3d]→ Sticker

Studio/Designer Studio Nari

Title Netflix Stickers Year 2024

Client Netflix

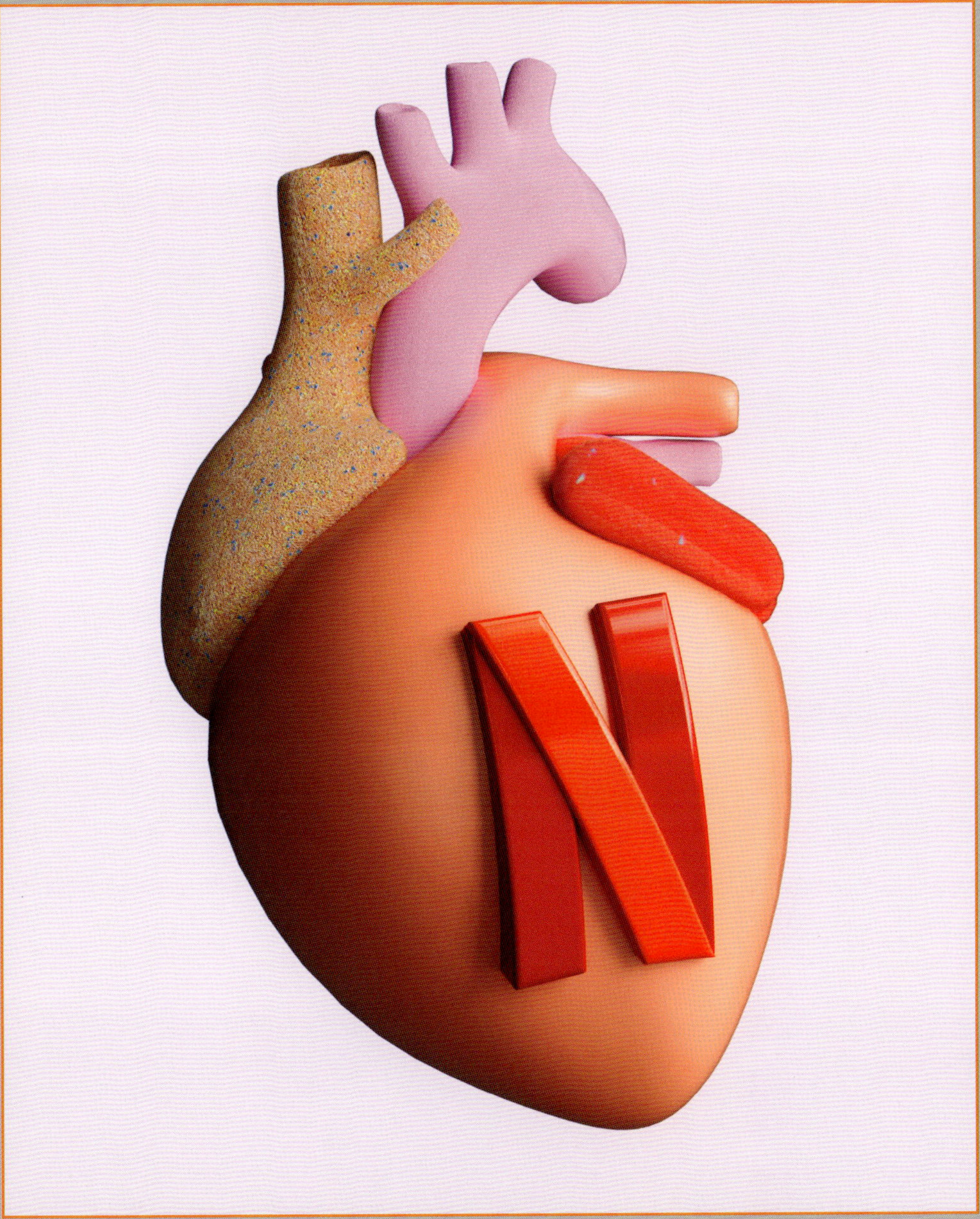

: Studio Nari collaborated with Netflix to reimagine their social media sticker collection, infusing it with digital energy and innovation. The result is a versatile, expressive set of dynamic, age-agnostic 3D animations. Exploring textures and lighting, three distinct styles emerged: hyper-real chromatic finishes, surreal takes on Netflix's dopamine hit, and bold, tactile forms with strong visual impact.

Fan Favourite

Double Like

Next Episod

(63)

[3d]→ Generative

: Charcoal explores how unconventional, sculptural tools shape type design, prioritising atmosphere and abstraction over legibility. Created using 3D software, the project investigates a generative, parametric approach that reintroduces type to three-dimensional space, enabling the creation of infinite character variations through dynamic virtual systems.

Studio/Designer Sass Scimirö Title Charcoal 3D

Year 2022 – Ongoing Client Self-initiated

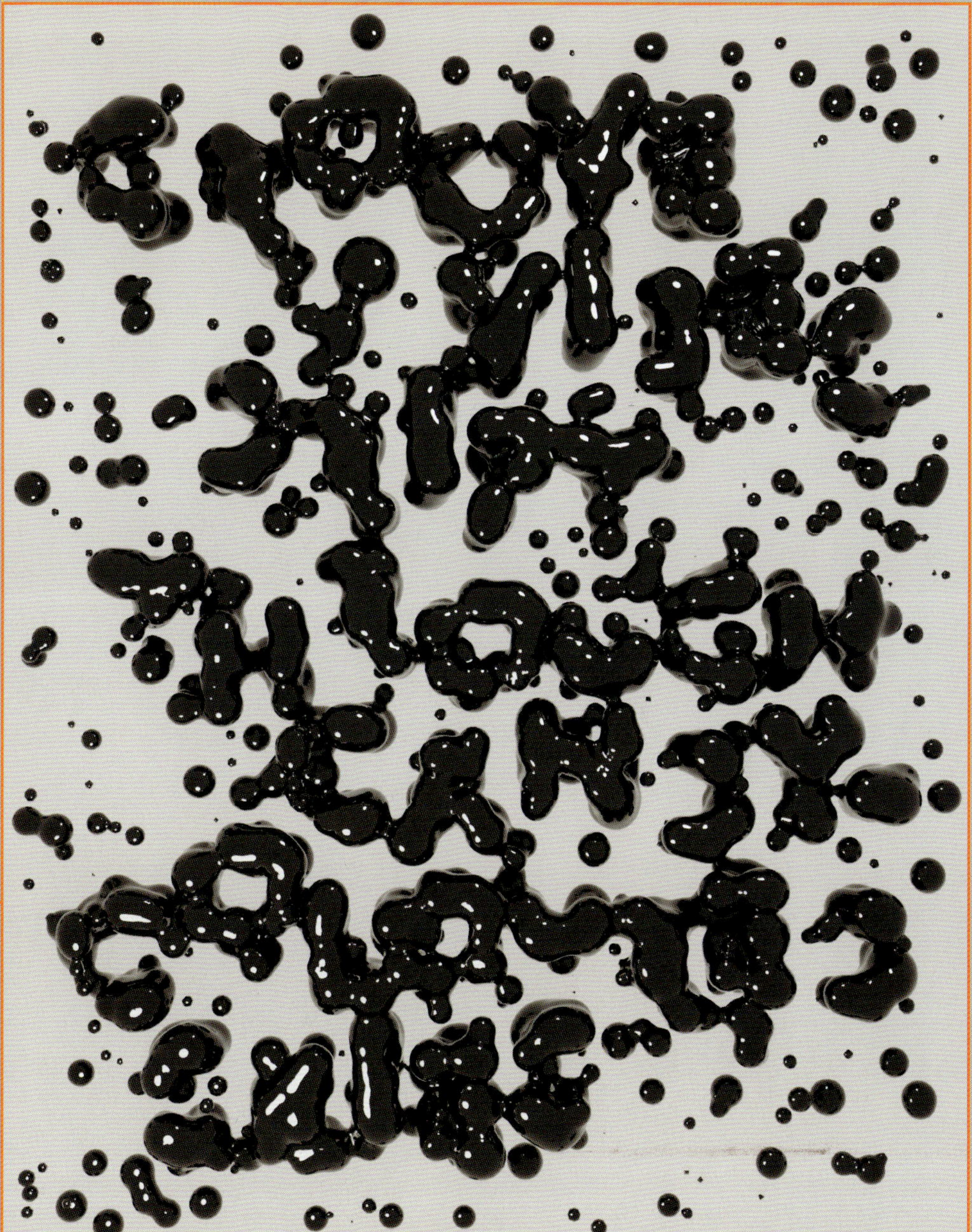

*

CHARCOAL

ELEMENTS: 100	SEED: 0

FRAME	1	25	50	75	100	125

GLYPH

M

A

N

I

F

E

S

T

O

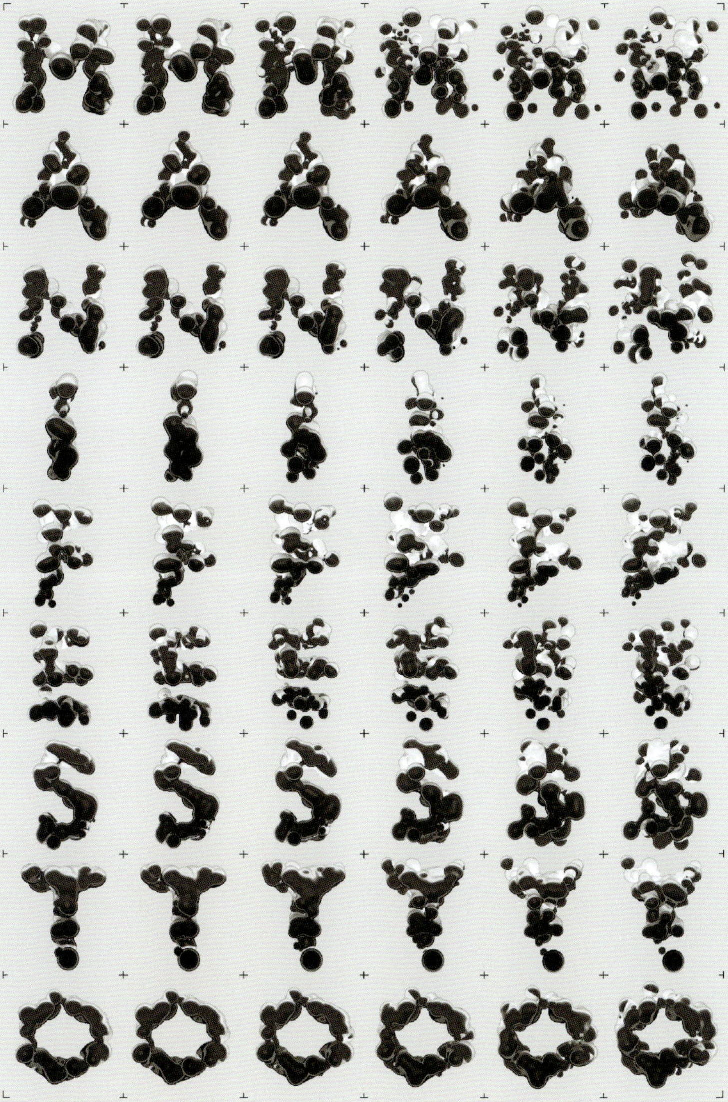

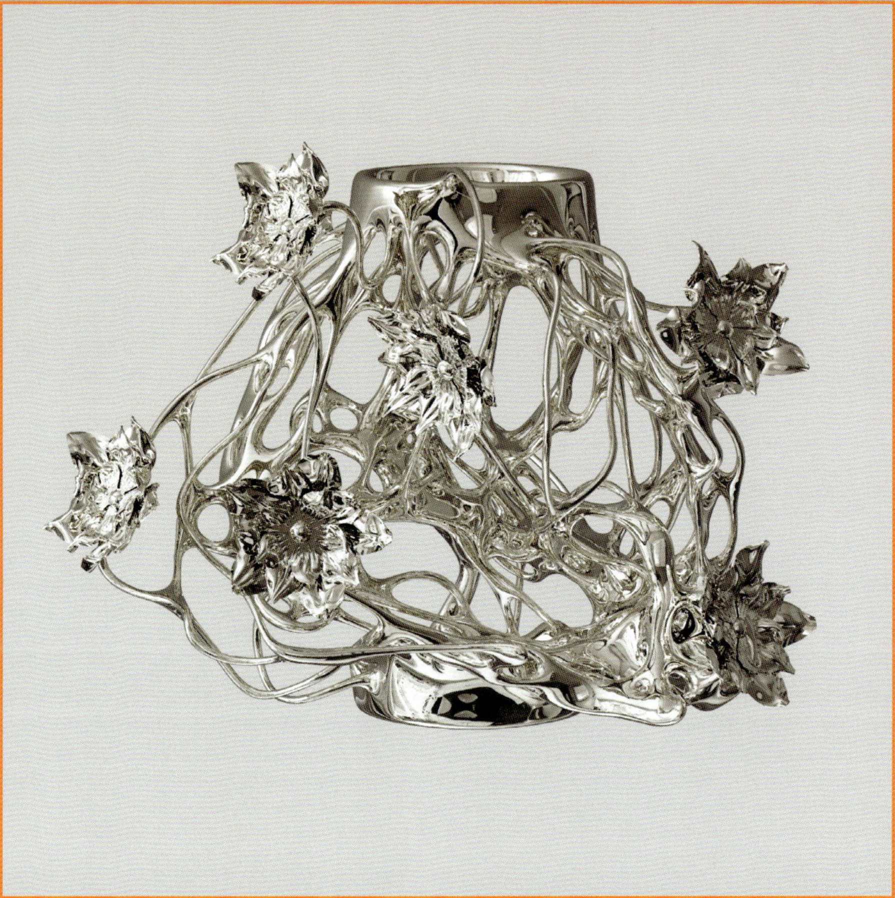

(64)

[3d]→ Organic

Studio/Designer Vladyslav Kuchaiev

Title Organic Structures Year 2024 Client Self-initiated

: Inspired by nature's fluidity, "Organic Structures" uses computational design to reimagine organic forms through unexpected combinations and refined visual language. The resulting compositions blur the line between natural and artificial, evoking wonder while challenging conventional aesthetic boundaries.

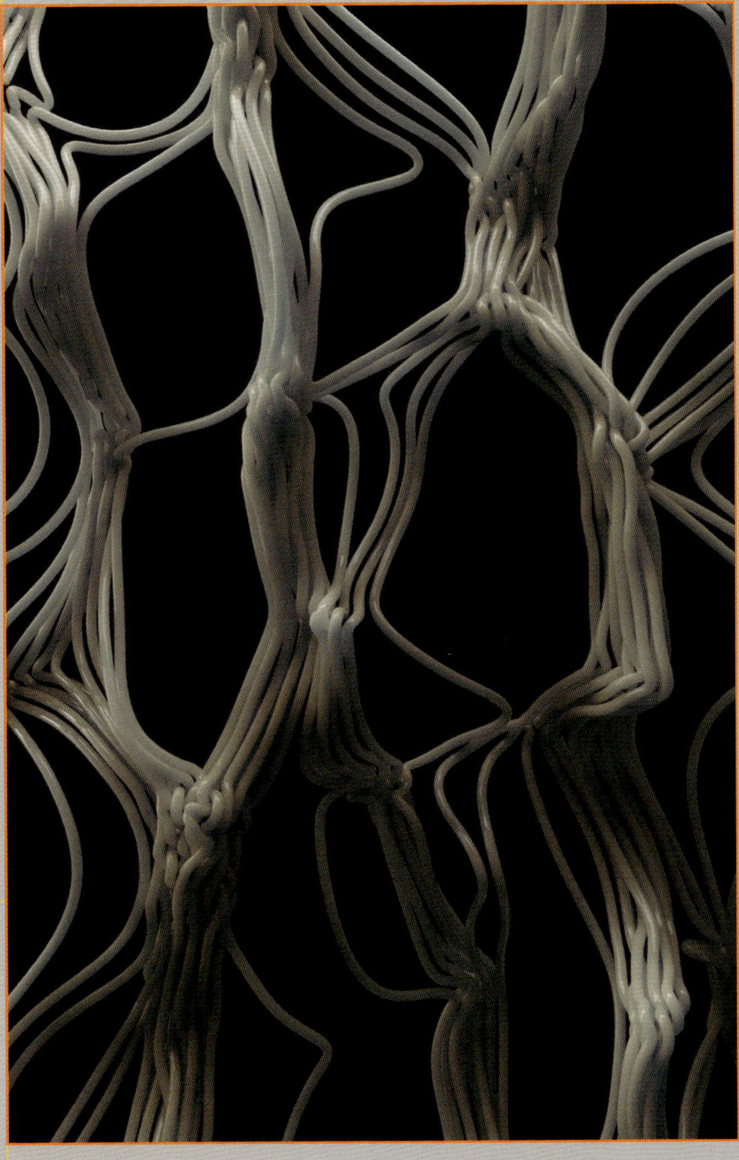

: For Adobe, Get It Studio was commissioned to create a 3D typographic sculpture using the word “FORM”, transforming 2D designs into a dynamic 3D space. By experimenting with materials and textures, they achieved hyper-realistic renders. Each letter was designed in an abstract style, inspired by everyday household objects like headphones, sofas, candles, vases, and toaster knobs.

(65)

[3d]→ Form

Studio/Designer Get It Studio Title Adobe Substance from 2D to 3D
Year 2023 Client Adobe Typeface(s) Inspired by Maxi Font

Special Credits

(Agency) It's Nice That
(Production) Lucy Orr
(Creative Direction) Karl Toomey
(Content & Creation Strategy) Carrie Gotch

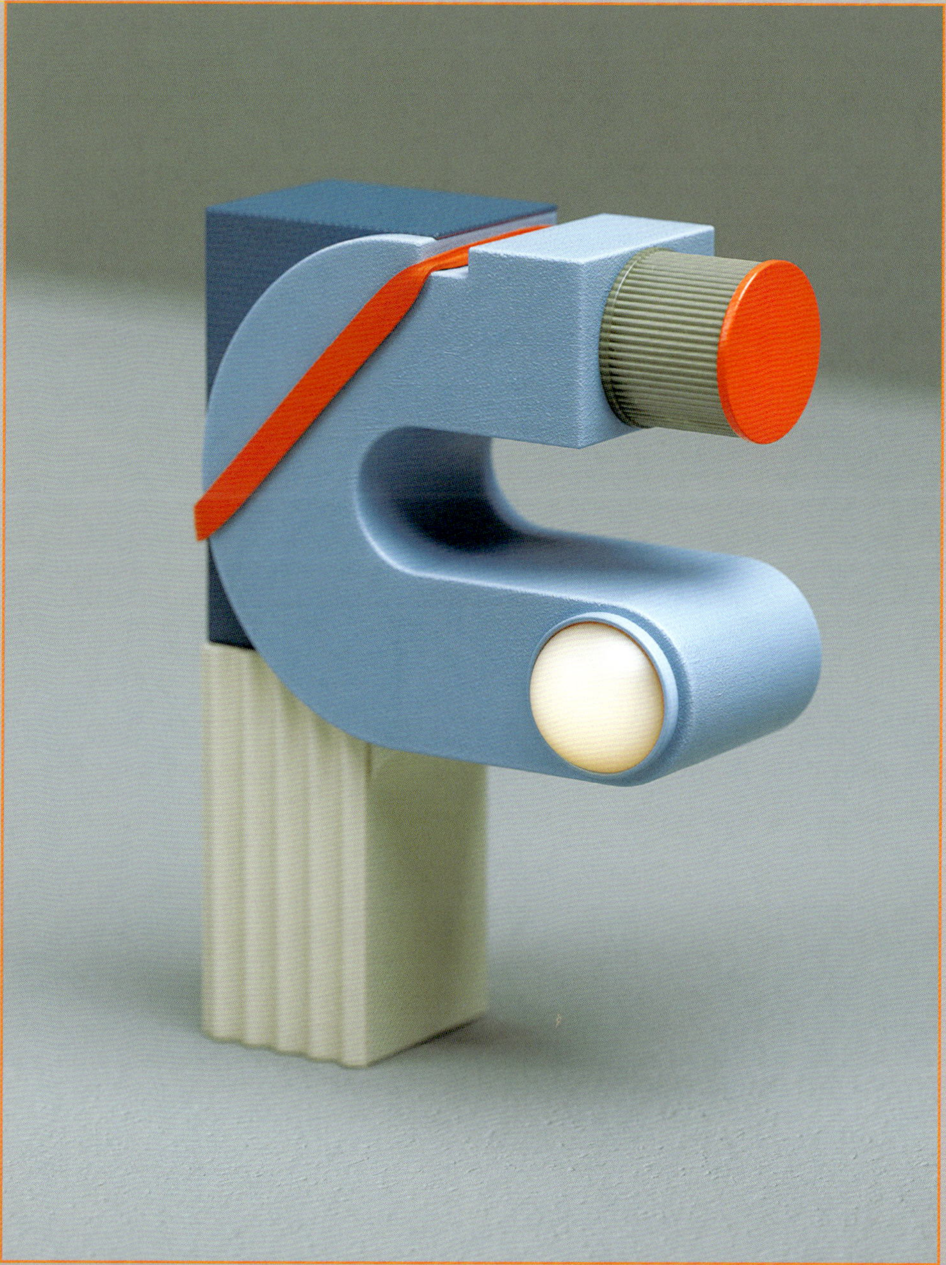

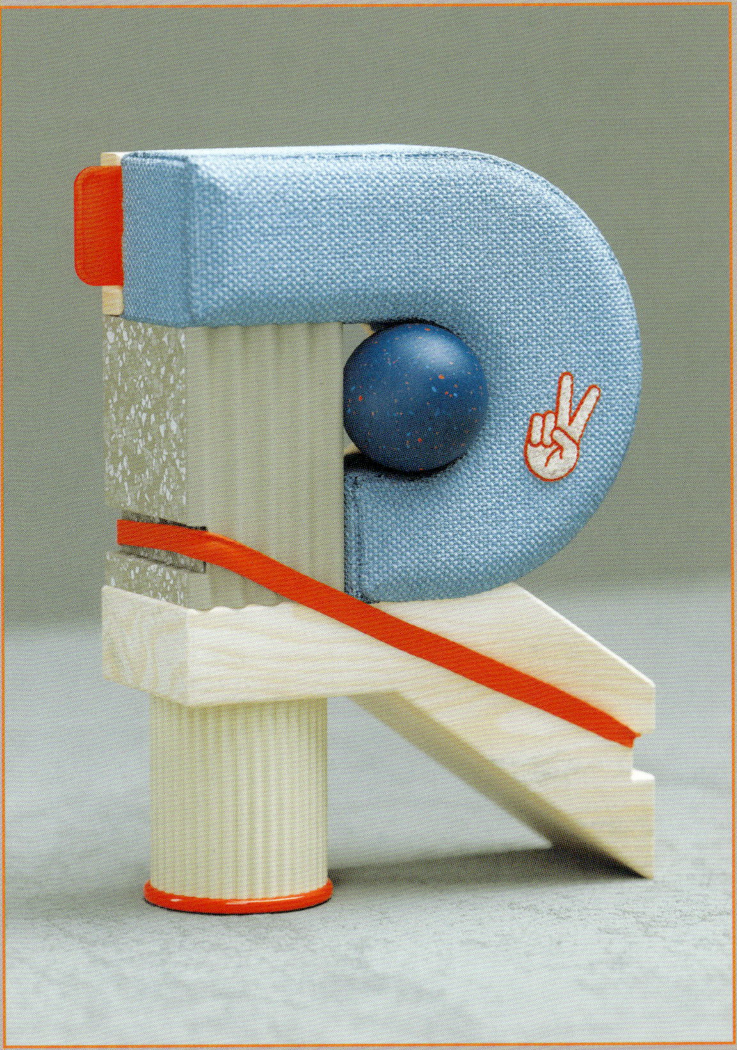

(66) [3d]→ Explosive

Studio/Designer Abra.network

Title This is the New SanDisk Year 2025

Client SanDisk Typeface(s) Obviously Wide

Special Credits

(Agency) ELA Advertising
(Music & Sound Design) Giovanni Dubini
(Motion Toolkit) Daisy Chain Studio
(Logo Sound Design) offgrid studio

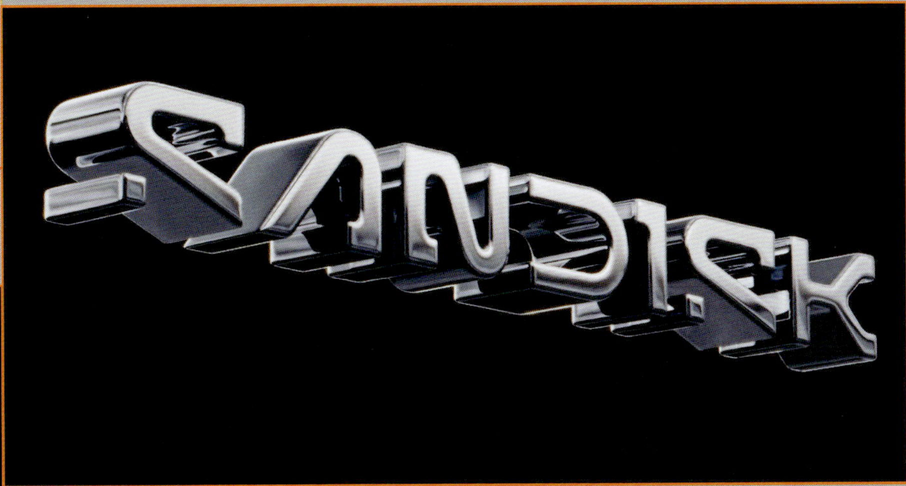

: Abra.network was approached by ELA agency to create a video that would tease and ultimately reveal SanDisk's new look to the world. Inspired by the voiceover script provided by ELA and the 2D motion toolkit from Daisy Chain Studio, Abra created a dynamic video that explores the idea of a world made of data.

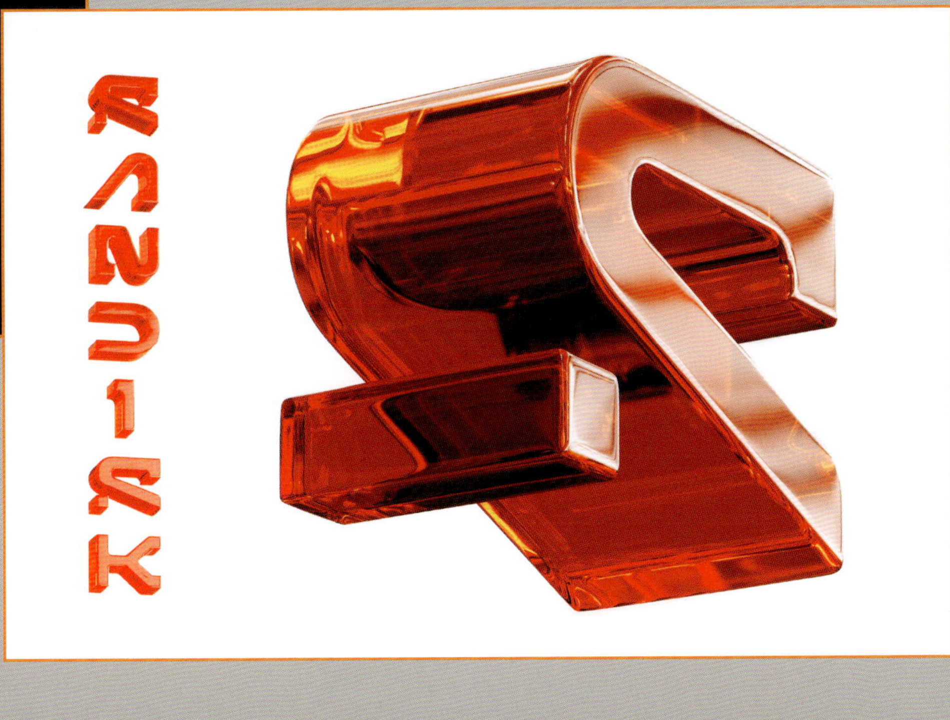

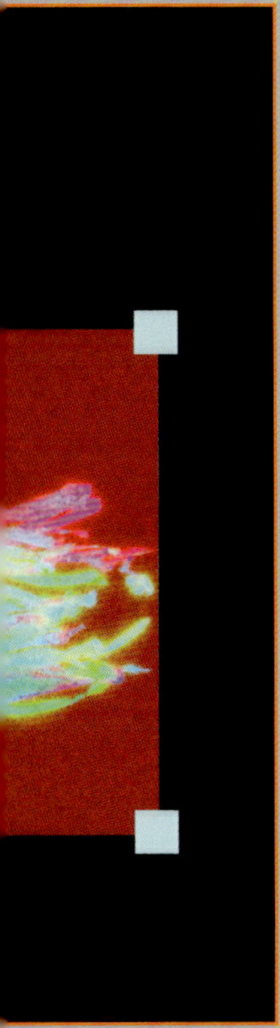

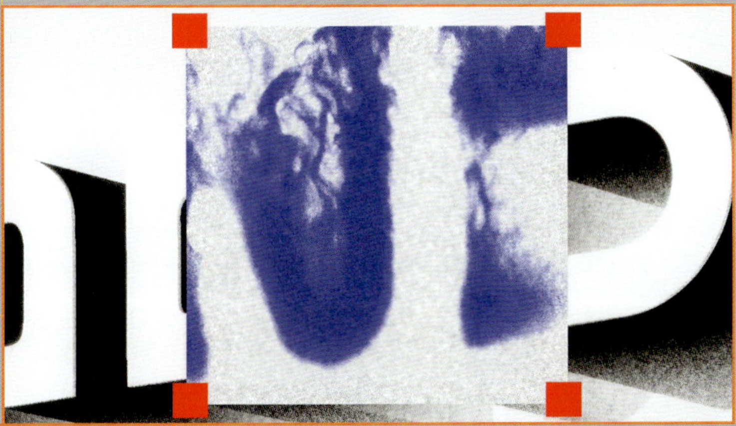

(67)

Studio/Designer Woodwork Amsterdam

Title Campaign Identity Formula 1 Etihad Airways Abu Dhabi Grand Prix Year 2024 Client Ethara

[3d]→ Formula 1

: Woodwork crafted a vibrant identity for the 2024 Abu Dhabi Grand Prix, blending bold typography and motion-driven graphics with a dynamic colour palette. The campaign channels the thrill of Formula 1 while celebrating Abu Dhabi's cultural diversity, ensuring visual consistency across digital and physical formats for a truly global and inclusive brand presence.

FORMULA 1
ABU DHABI
GRAND PRIX
2024

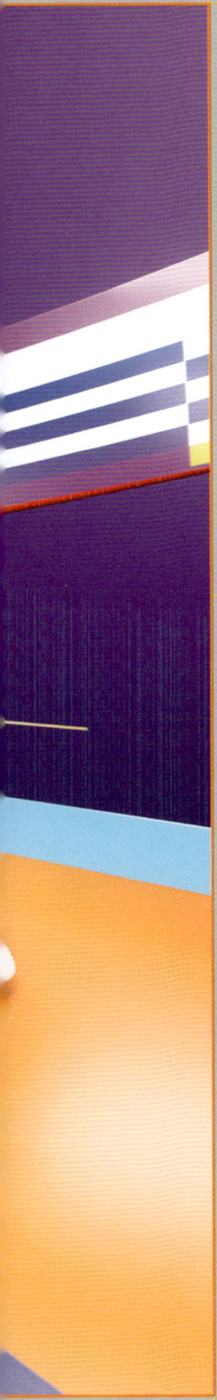

FORMULA 1
ABU DHABI
GRAND PRIX
2024

Studio/Designer Vincent Wagner Title Humanity
Year 2022 - Ongoing Client Self-initiated

(68) [3d]→ Human

: "Humanity" is an ongoing series that explores the human experience, specifically our connection to nature, our relationship with ourselves, and the increasingly central of media in shaping our lives.

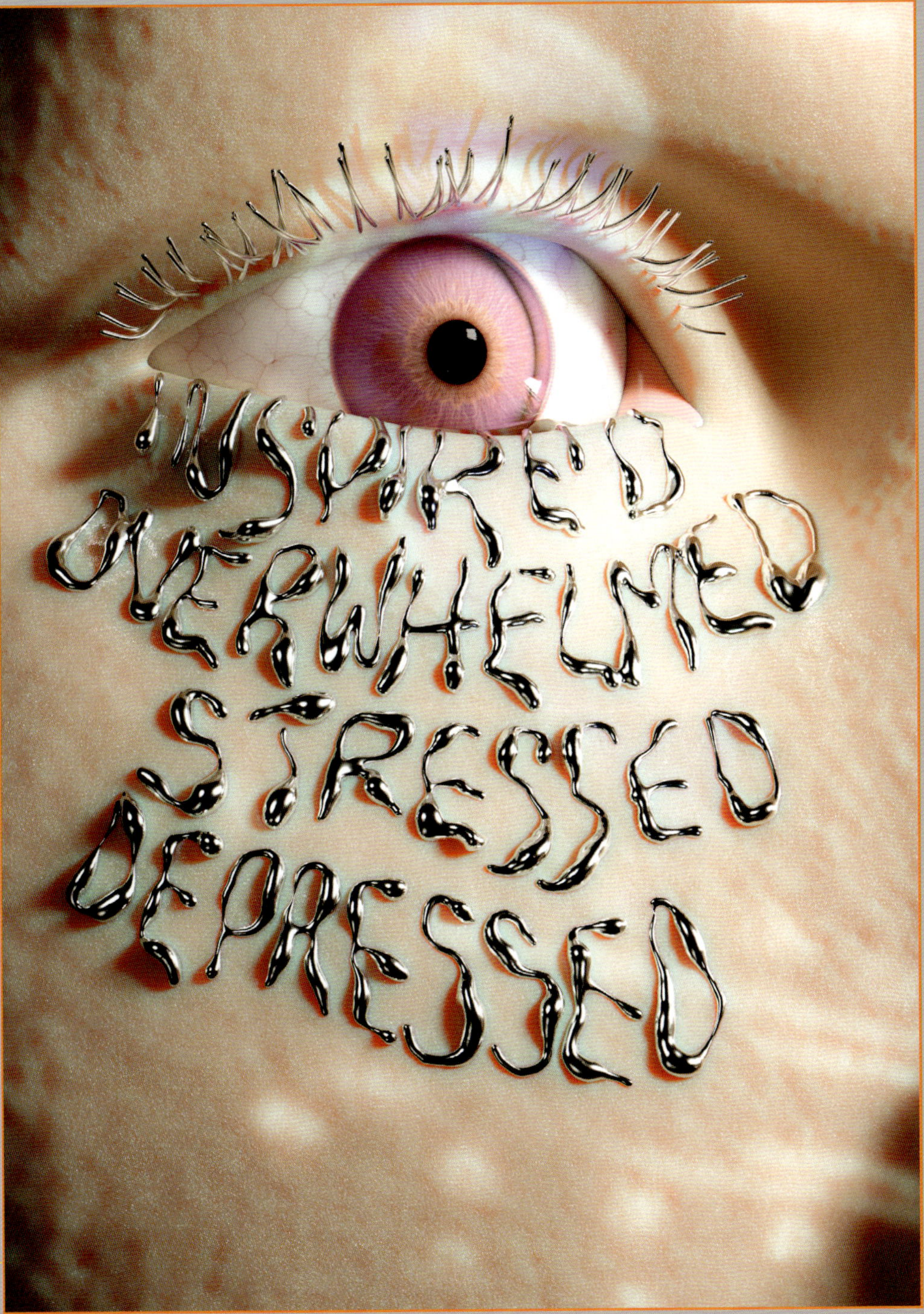
INSPIRED
OVERWHELMED
STRESSED
DEPRESSED

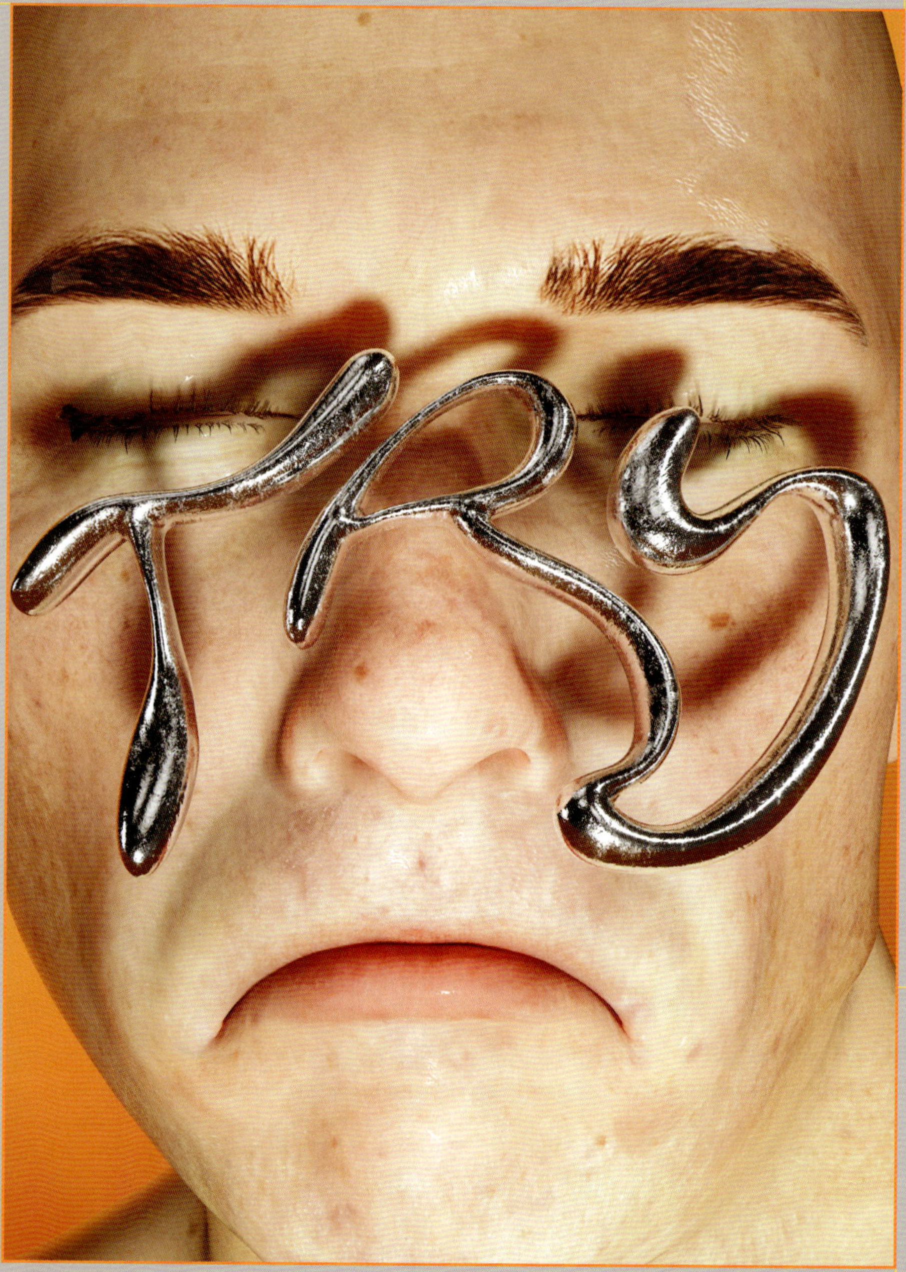
TRY

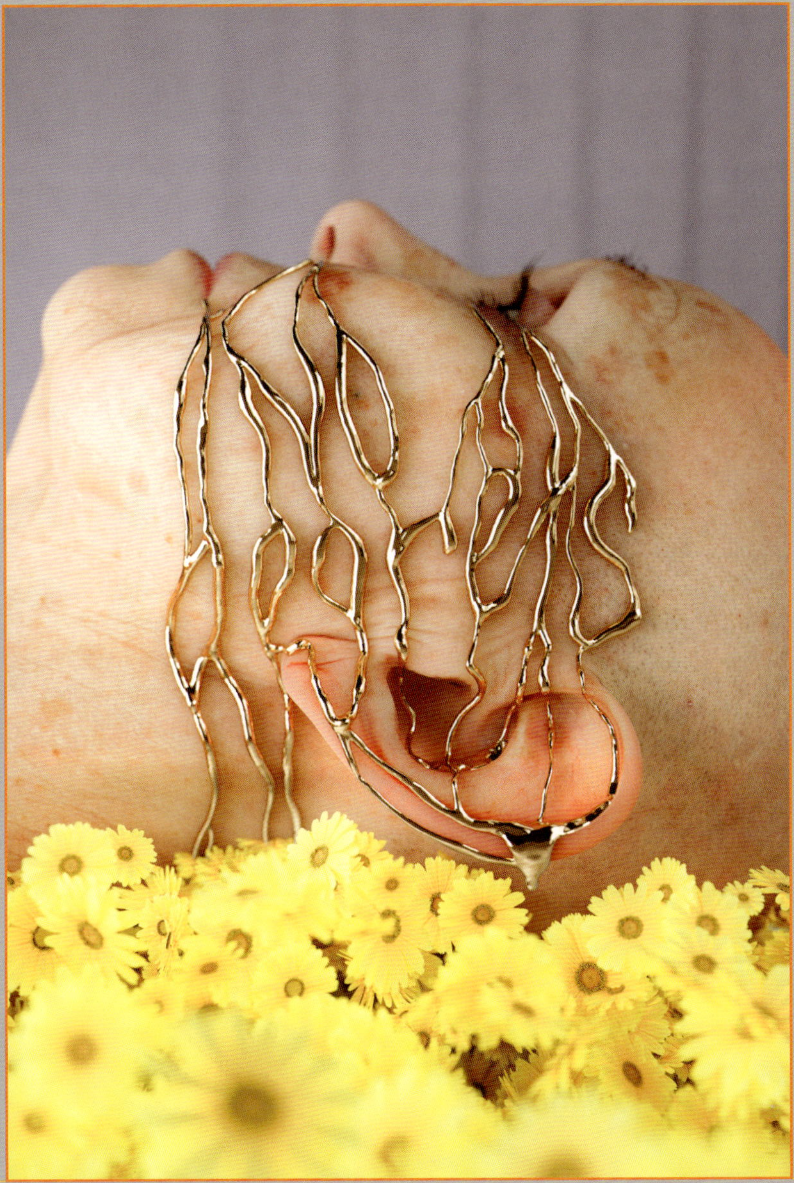

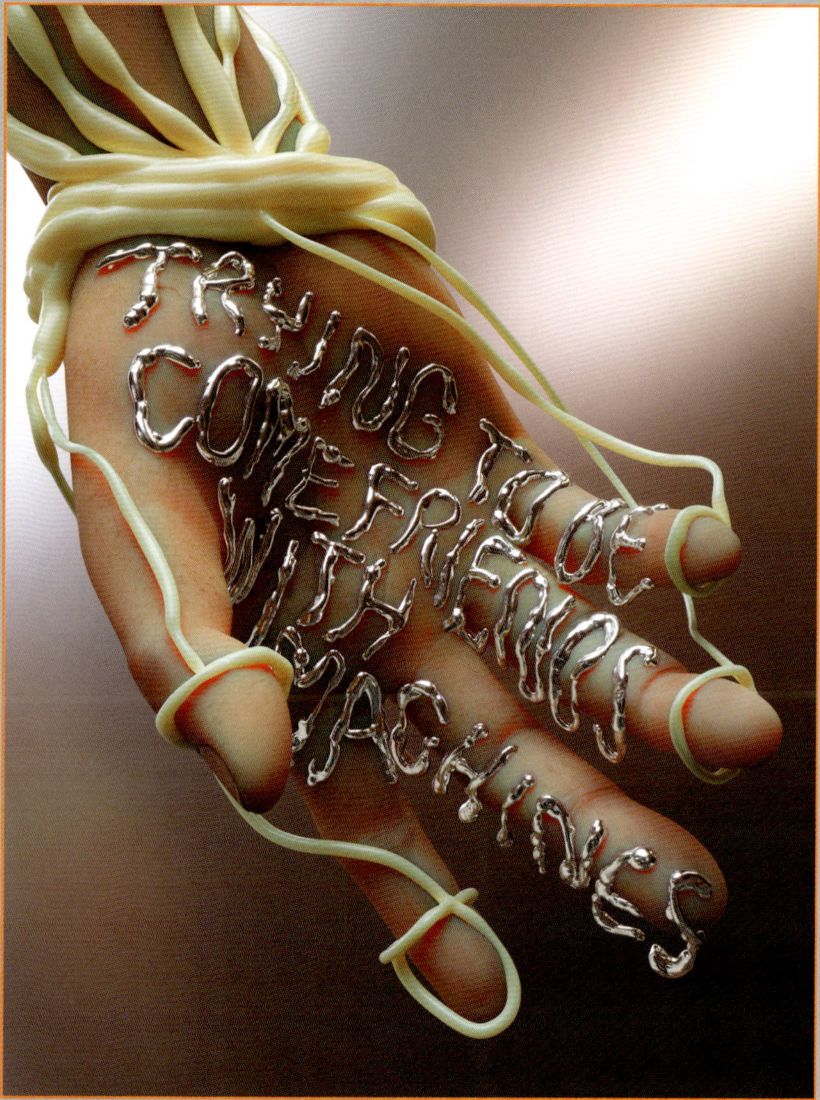
TRYING TO BE
COME FRIENDS
WITH
MACHINES

LISTEN
TO
YOUR
SELF

(69) [3d]→ Stone

Studio/Designer Michael Askew

Client Self-initiated

Title Stone Year 2025

Title Stoned Year 2025

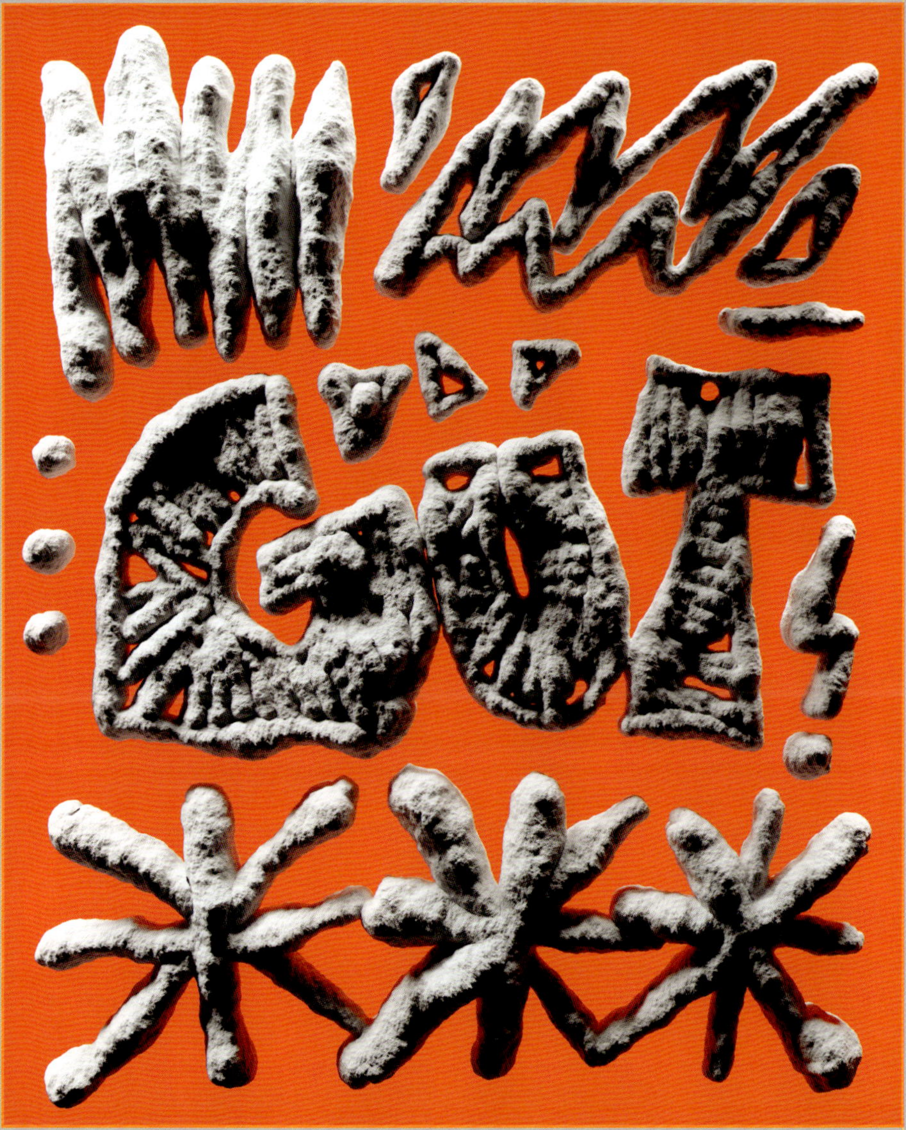

Title Gut Year 2025

Title Gateway Year 2025

Studio/Designer Goh Jing Min Title The Street Collection 2024 Year 2024 Client Self-initiated Typeface(s) Mochiy Pop One, HelloFont ID, LangRunTi, Dela Gothic One, Zen Kaku, Gothic New, Chirumiru Papercut Font

(70) [3d]→ Traffic

: Inspired by everyday street elements like lamp posts and traffic lights, Goh Jing Min's Street Collection 2024 reimagines urban fixtures with playful originality. By envisioning the world from an elevated viewpoint, she explores a whimsical shift in perspective. Subtle Japanese influences, including added text, reflect her fondness for Japanese culture and enhance the project's imaginative tone.

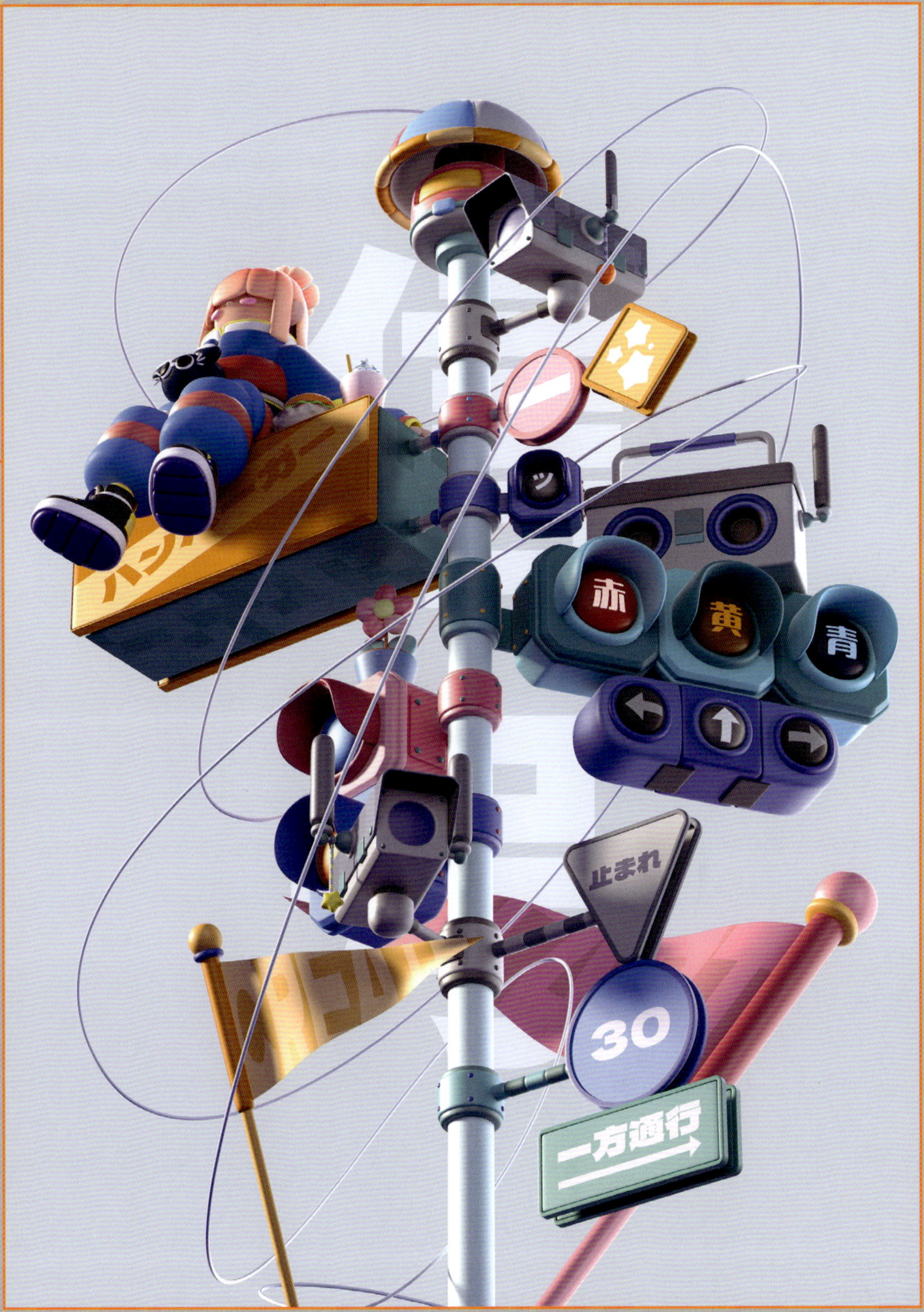
赤
黄
青
止まれ
30
一方通行

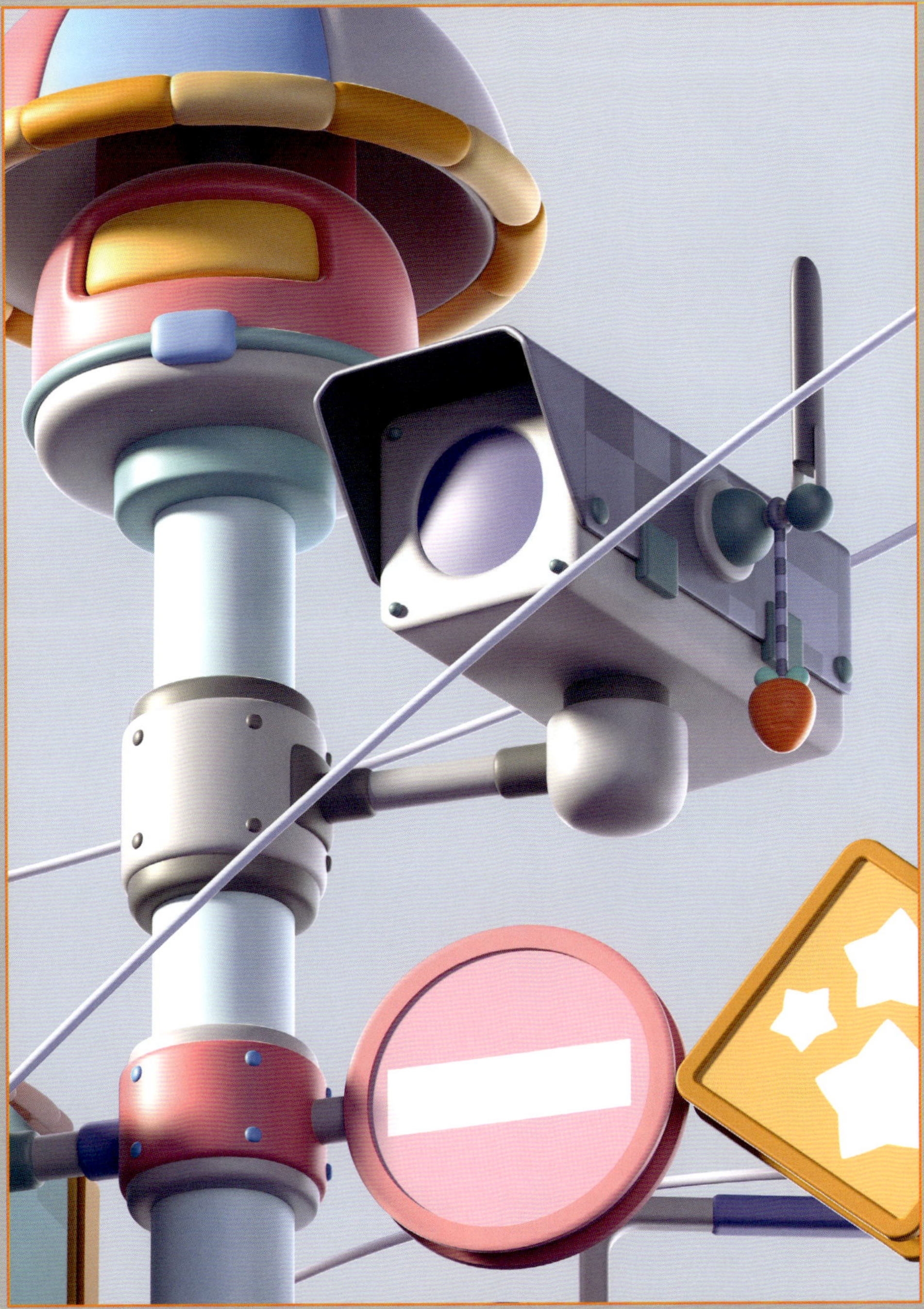

赤
黄
青
止まれ

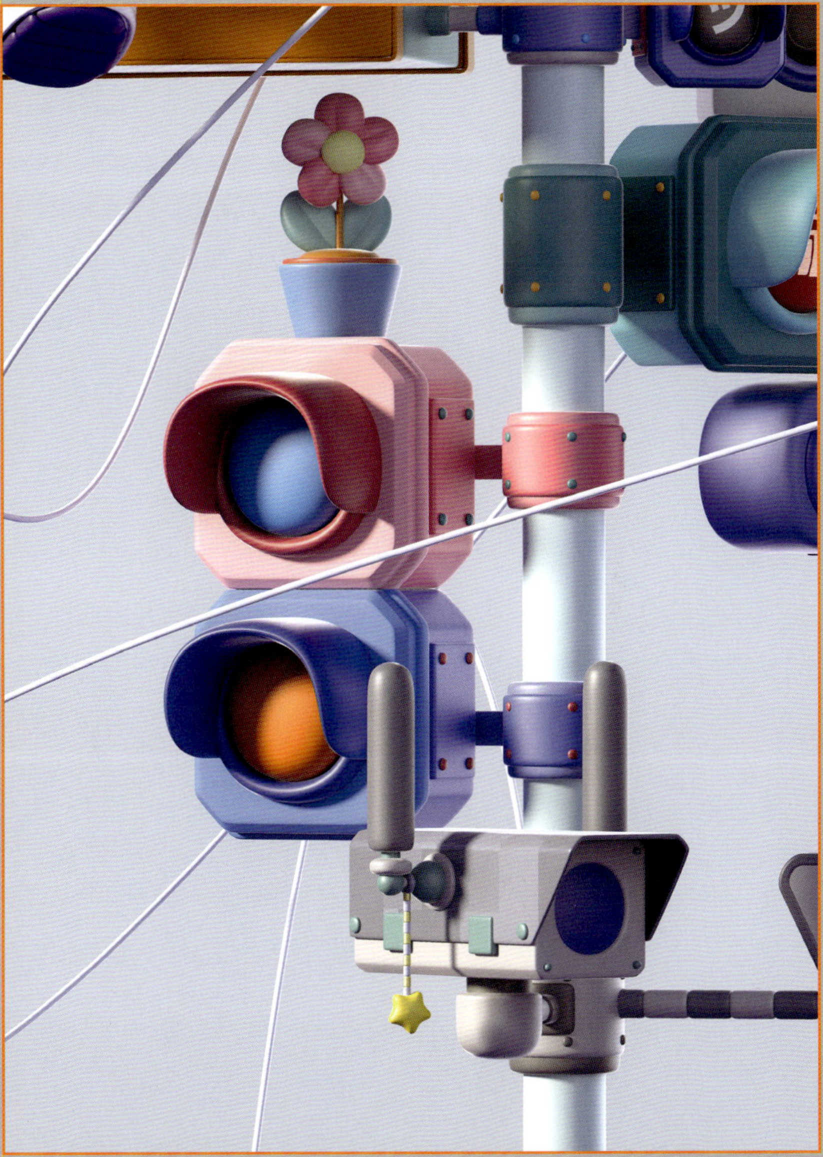

: TimTim collaborated with Filtrum, the home decor brand known for its unique products, to create a series of dynamic 3D animations and fun product shots. The project brings the brand's designs to life, highlighting their playful and distinctive style through bold, engaging visuals.

(71) [3d]→ Decor

Studio/Designer TimTim

Title Filtrum Home Collection Year 2023

Client Filtrum Home

: "Balloon Birds" transforms avian life into whimsical balloon sculptures, blending charm with environmental commentary. Each bird, rendered with lightness and intricacy, becomes a symbol of fragility – mirroring the delicate state of nature. The project celebrates creativity while gently reminding us of our ecosystem's vulnerability, encouraging viewers to see beauty and transience in equal measure.

(72) [3d]→ Avian

Studio/Designer Nastia Ibragimova
Title Balloon Birds Year 2021
Client Self-initiated

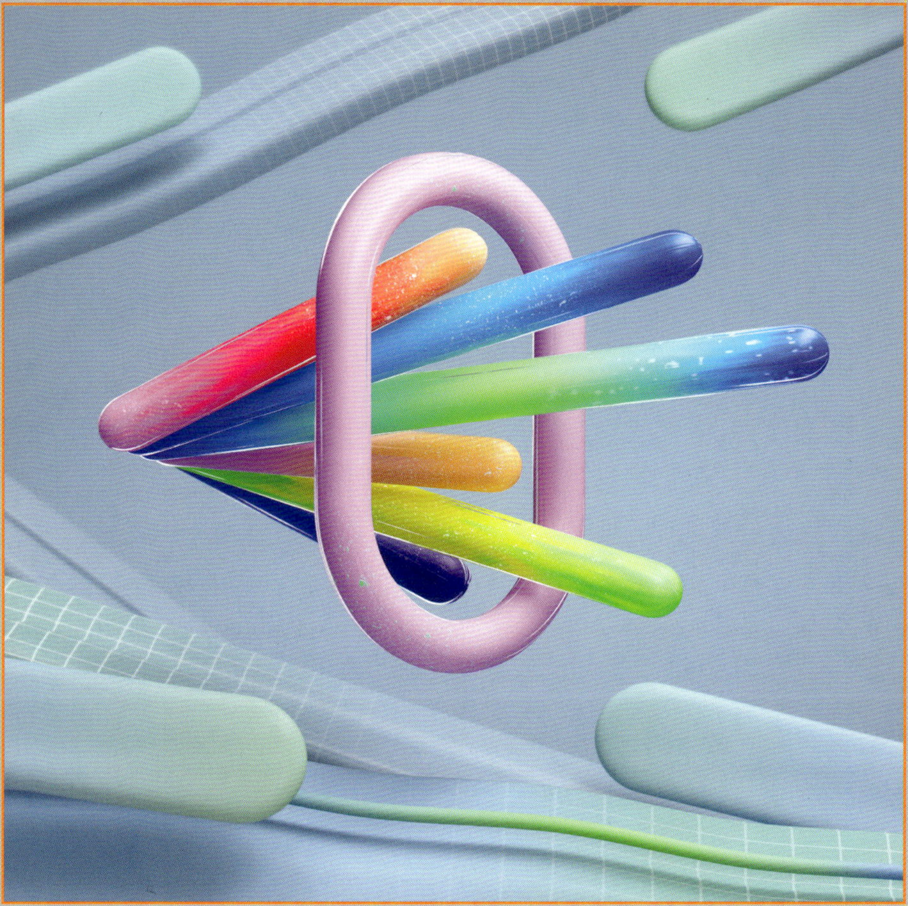

(73) [3d]→Symbol

Studio/Designer Danil Tabacari

Title Microsoft Praise Year 2021

Client Microsoft Viva, Stephen Bader

: Microsoft Design partnered with Datalands to reimagine traditional expressions of gratitude, creating a set of universal and emotional symbols. Aimed at conveying themes of inclusion and courage, they were designed to foster deeper connection. To enhance their dimensionality, Microsoft handed the 2D illustrations over to Danil Tabacari, who brought the designs to life through his visual exploration.

Studio/Designer Loop Studio

Title COP28 Opening Sequence Year 2024

Client Bloomberg Philanthropies

(74)

[3d]→

Manifesto

: Commissioned by Bloomberg Philanthropies, Loop Studio created an immersive opening sequence for the COP28 Local Climate Action Summit in Dubai. The large-scale film combined striking CG visuals with statements from global city mayors, delivering a powerful manifesto that highlights the vital role of local leaders in accelerating emission reductions, managing climate risks, and driving national climate progress.

Special Credit (Production Co) Aggressive

AIR
POLLUTION
PET

(75)

Studio/Designer Vincent Schwenk Title "K-Hit" Series
Year 2021–2023 Client Self-initiated

: Vincent Schwenk's "K-Hit" Series (2021–2023) explores digital fashion liberated from physical form. Dance-inspired, animated "garments" transcend the body to emphasise interactions between cloth, motion, and ideology. In collaboration with sound designers, each iteration abstracts fashion's essence – prioritising form, fluidity and expression in virtual space, free from corporeal constraints.

[3d]→ Dance

Studio/Designer Vincent Schwenk Title "Cycle of Life" Series
Year 2022 - Ongoing Client Self-initiated

(76)

[3d]→ Cycle

: Schwenk's ongoing "Cycle of Life" series features abstract, otherworldly forms in a continuous 360° rotation, symbolising perpetual growth, transformation. and renewal. Drawing from nature's rhythm, each composition balances vivid motion and colour to evoke organic evolution in a digital realm.

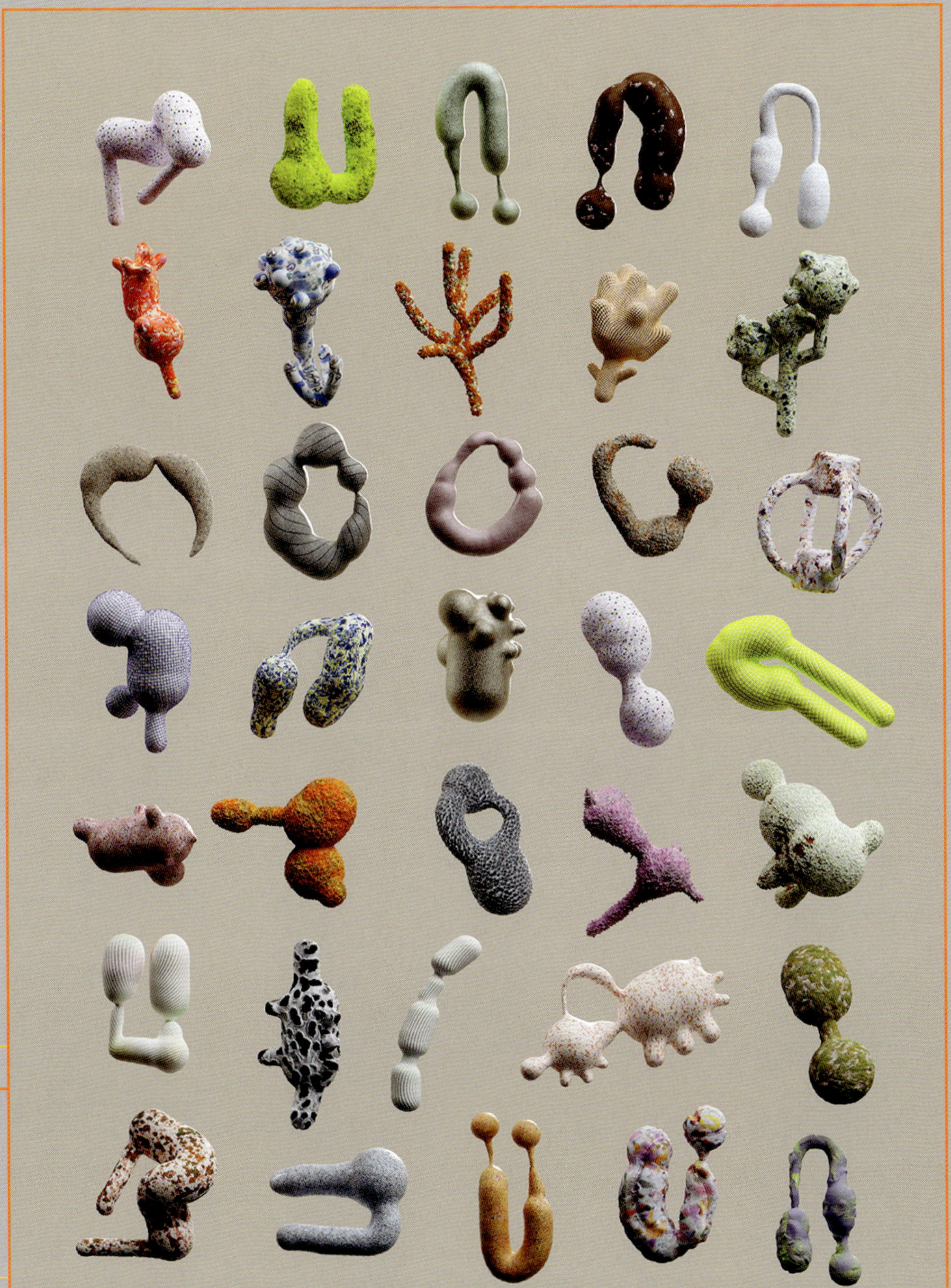

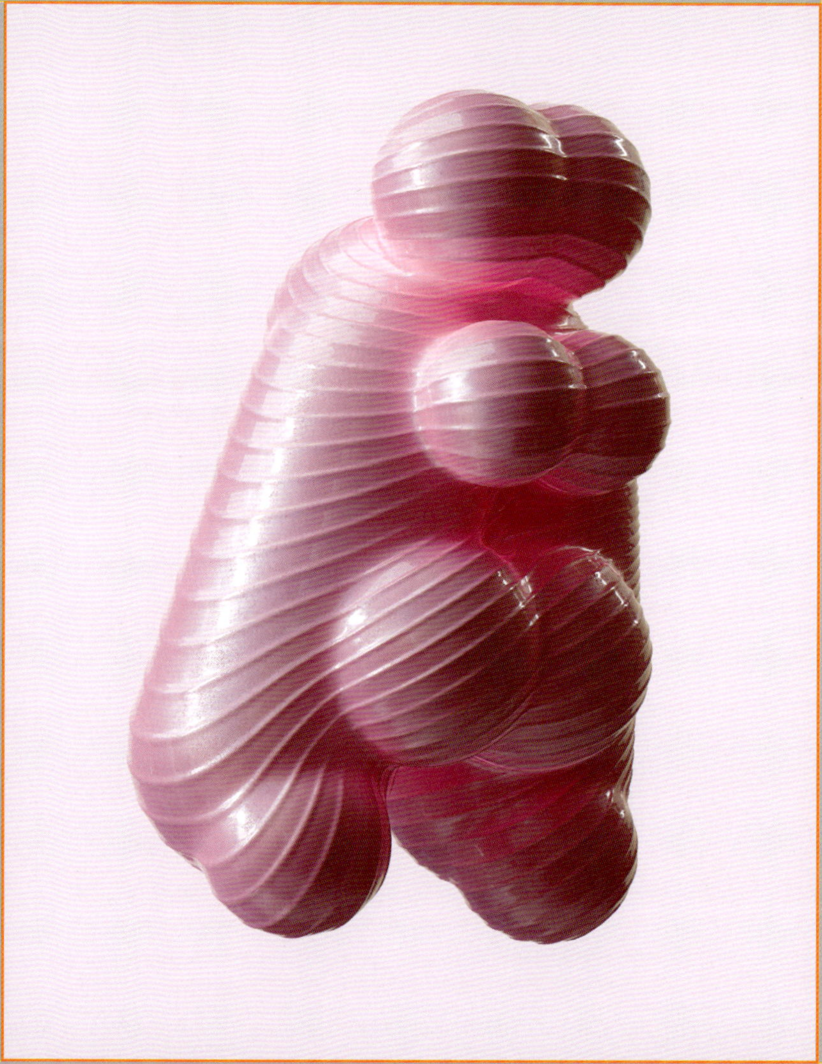

(77)

Shishimai

Studio/Designer Marina Nakagawa

Title Shishimai Boy Year 2024 Client Self-initiated

: “Shishimai Boy” is a vibrant 3D artwork that fuses traditional Japanese folklore with playful, modern aesthetics. Inspired by the lion dance (shishimai), the character bursts to life through bold colours, stylised forms, and rich textures. Marina’s whimsical and charming style shines throughout, blending myth with a sense of childlike wonder.

Studio/Designer Szu-Yu Hou Title Fairy Tales with Alphabet
Year 2024 - Ongoing Client Self-initiated

(78)

:   “Fairy Tales with Alphabet” is a 3D illustration series blending language, design, and cultural history. Each letter reimagines a classic fairy tale using playful typography and storytelling. Engaging for young learners and nostalgic for adults, it combines familiar stories with fresh visuals to create an imaginative, educational experience for all ages.

[3d]→Fairytale

Studio/Designer Juni Kweon

Title On the Way Home

Year 2025 Client Self-initiated

: Juni Kweon's "On the Way Home" depicts a solitary salaryman on a playground slide, lost in thought. The scene reflects the emotional contrast between childhood wonder and adult nostalgia, capturing how familiar places shrink with age. It evokes a quiet longing for simpler times, exploring the bittersweet nature of growing up.

(79) [3d]→ Salary-man

(80) [3d]→ Girl

Studio/Designer Untitled Army

Title Calendar Girl Year 2024

Client Self-initiated

: "Calendar Girl" is a surreal animation featuring a character who flips through various outfits like pages of a calendar. Her body and the calendar form merge into a 4D-like visual, symbolising the passage of time in contemporary life.

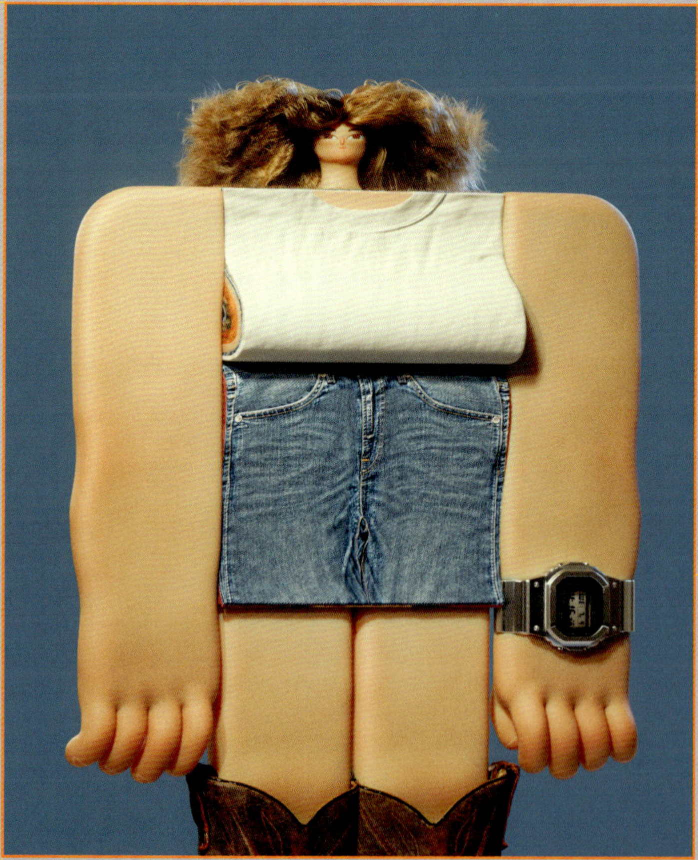

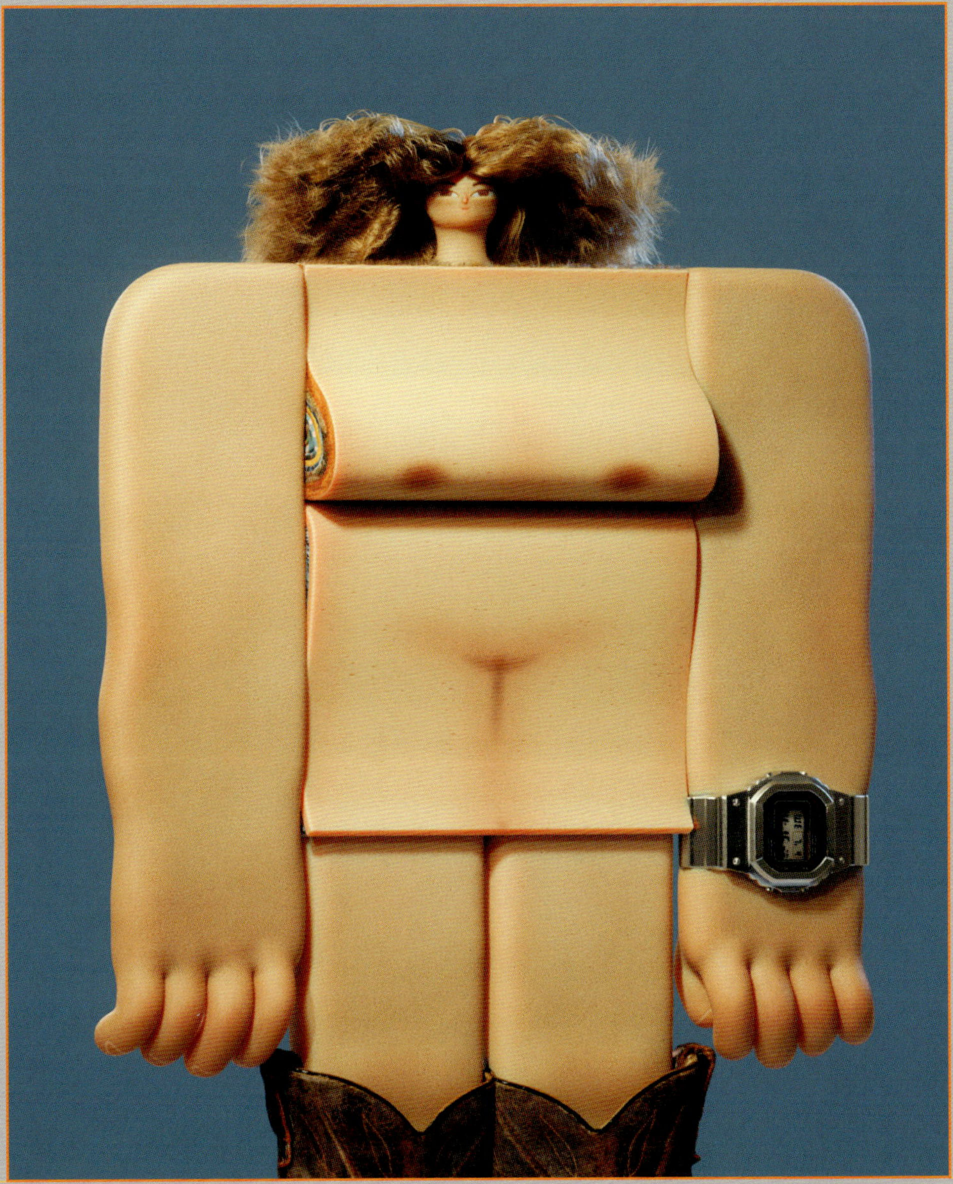

(81) [3d]→ Kindness

: "My Kind of Kind" celebrates kindness's boundless power to shape our world. Intertwined letters form a vibrant symphony of colours and textures, reflecting empathy's gentle curves and generosity's bold hues. The artwork invites reflection on the simple yet profound impact of kindness, inspiring us to embrace compassion and spread positivity across our shared humanity.

Studio/Designer Tina Touli

Title My Kind of Kind Year 2023

Client Type Campus Typeface(s) Custom

Studio/Designer Mohamed Basil

Title Blender Everydays

Year 2023 Client Self-initiated

(82)

[3d]→ Daily

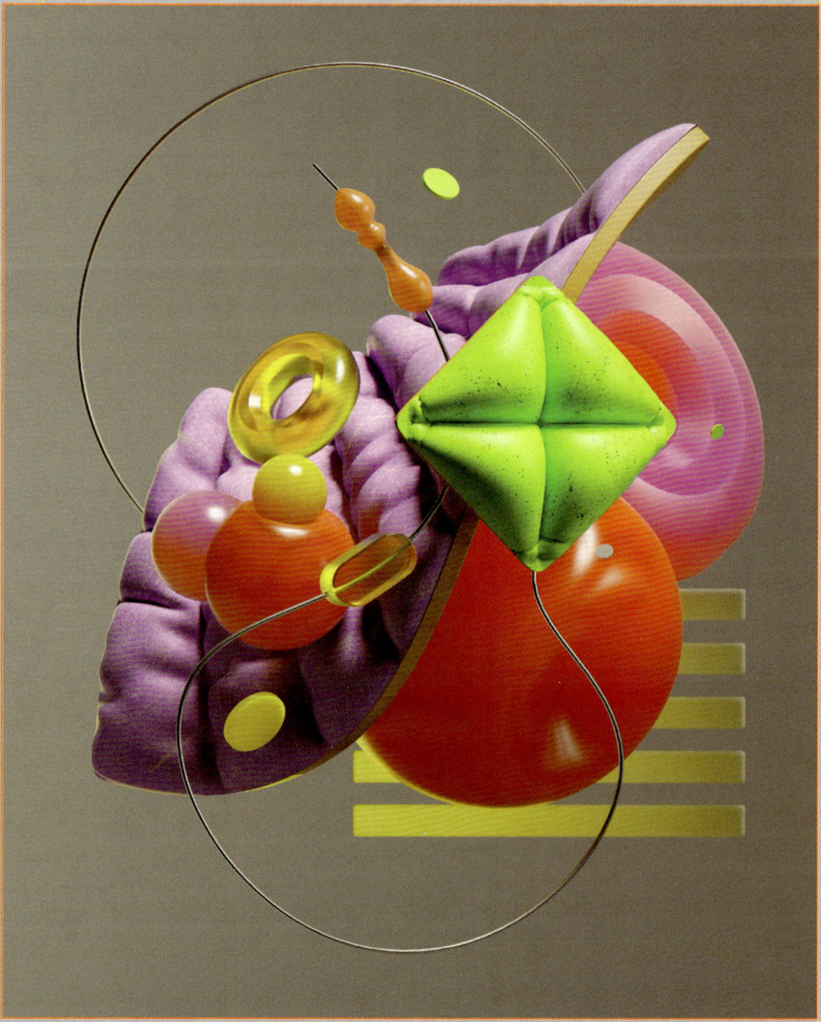

: Mohamed Basil's "Blender Everydays" is a long-term self-initiated project where he created daily artworks for three years. The goal was to master Blender and refine his design fundamentals through consistent practice. Drawing inspiration from diverse sources, he developed a distinct visual language by experimenting with forms, textures, and mood.

(83) [3d]→ Assemblage

: David Pocull created a whimsical 3D collage of interlocking forms and soft textures, blending organic curves with geometric shapes. Set against a dreamy gradient backdrop, the piece evoked toy-like objects in a pastel, retro-futuristic world – balancing materiality, colour, and composition with a lively, tactile rhythm.

Studio/Designer David Pocull
Title Playful Assemblage Year 2024
Client The Furrow

Special Credit (Creative Direction) Seth Eckert, The Furrow

Biography

Aaron Nieh Workshop

pp.102-113

Aaron Nieh Workshop specialises in brand identities across music, publishing, the arts, and the public sectors. Their practice is rooted in blending contemporary and pop culture references with varied visual languages to create layered, thought-provoking designs. This distinctive approach results in work that is both conceptually rich and accessible, inviting viewers to engage with graphic design on multiple levels.

Anna Fay

pp.232-237

Anna Fay is a graphic and motion designer specialising in brand identities, campaigns, and motion design, with a strong focus on typography and AI-driven design. Her AI work explores abstract, near-illegible typographic forms and investigates the automated creation of fonts.

Abra.network

pp.430-437

Abra.network is a Warsaw-based motion design collective led by Rafał Woźniak, Bartek Kalinowski, and Łukasz Partyka. Collaborating with skilled artists and studios, they craft original commercials, music videos, and interactive films, combining varied perspectives with advanced techniques and postproduction expertise to deliver bespoke campaigns.

Ayumi Tan

pp.224-231

Ayumi Tan is a motion designer and 3D artist based in Singapore, known for reimagining everyday objects through varied styles and textures. Her work explores the familiar with a fresh perspective, using tactile detail to create visually engaging and layered compositions.

ACRE

pp.020-029

ACRE is an independent London design studio specialising in brand identities, motion, and digital design. Known for its thoughtful culture and creative excellence, the studio crafts impactful campaigns and visual languages that resonate globally. ACRE aims to bridge the present and future with compelling design that drives meaningful, measurable results.

Bito

pp.080-087, 174-181

Bito is a pioneer of motion design and creative narratives in Asia, specialising in creating emotional, unforgettable experiences through motion, branding, and experiential design. Bito's mission is to push design boundaries by integrating innovative technology with emotionally impactful experiences, while empowering creative talent to influence the world.

Builders Club

pp.404-409

Builders Club is a global creative studio founded in 2015 by Jonas Hegi and Julien Simshauser, blending 3D motion, design, film production, and ideation. Partnering with brands and agencies worldwide, they craft bold, meaningful work. As a hybrid production company, creative agency, and design studio, their team thrives on curiosity, experimentation, and fun, redefining storytelling and creating impactful solutions.

BÜRO UFHO

pp.202-207

BÜRO UFHO is a Singapore-based creative studio founded by Yana and Jun. Known for their hyperreal, dreamlike aesthetic, they craft emotive visual experiences across branding, 3D, AR, and typography. Since 2008, they have worked with clients like Adobe, Apple, and Vogue, earning accolades from D&AD, ADC, and Tokyo TDC for their innovative and visually rich approach to design.

COLORS AND THE KIDS

pp.382-393

COLORS AND THE KIDS is an interdisciplinary studio based in Berlin, blending design, motion, and music to redefine brand identities and cultural expression. Collaborating with global brands and organisations, they create sensory, brand-led storytelling. Their name embodies their commitment to dreaming big and embracing curiosity, helping brands explore new genres and craft evolving identities through audio-visual landscapes.

Dada Projects

pp.352-369

Dada Projects is a female-led studio redefining 3D design through cutting-edge technology. They create distinctive visuals and animations that merge digital materiality with reality, pushing creative boundaries. With a diverse global portfolio spanning commercial, fashion, tech, and more, their clients include Google, Nike, and Calvin Klein.

Daniel Bornmann

pp.046-047, 066-067,
114-115, 126-127

Daniel Bornmann is a multidisciplinary 3D artist, graphic designer, and art director based in Berlin. With over seven years of experience in branding, CGI, and motion design, his work is deeply influenced by the electronic music and events scene. In 2024, he co-founded the Berlin-based design studio Stüdio with Lennard Makosch and Sophia Becker.

Danil Tabacari

pp.472-477

Danil Tabacari is a freelance 3D designer and art director. Inspired to create innovative visuals for multinational digital brands, focusing on conveying messages in a human-centric manner. Translating digital concepts into visuals that resonate with curated life moments.

David Pocull

pp.514-515

David Pocull is a seasoned freelance motion designer celebrated for his punchy, clean, and graphic style. He also steps into the director's chair, leading projects that fuse his love of animation and illustration, always with a dose of humour and heart.

Dennis Hoelscher

pp.058-059, 282-283, 302-303

Dennis Hoelscher is an independent motion and 3D artist based in Cologne, specialising in creative direction. His work explores the fusion of typography and abstract, procedural forms in the three-dimensional space, crafting dynamic visual experiences. By bringing these elements to life through motion, his creations engage and interact with audiences in unique and immersive ways.

Doris Lin

pp.370-373

Doris Lin is a motion designer and 3D illustrator inspired by animals and everyday life. She creates soft, friendly characters, often exploring 3D and clay as mediums. Passionate about movies, street photography, and life's details, Doris finds inspiration in the small things and knows her work is on the right track when it makes her laugh.

Erich Brechbühl

pp.018-019, 030-031, 100-101, 172-173

Erich Brechbühl is an independent graphic designer from Lucerne, known for his award-winning poster designs. After studying typography and apprenticing under Niklaus Troxler, he founded his studio, Mixer, in 2003. He co-founded the Weltformat Graphic Design Festival in 2009 and initiated Show & Tell in 2012. Erich has been a member of AGI since 2007.

Everyday Practice

pp.078-079

Everyday Practice was founded by Kwon Joonho, Kim Kyung-chul, Kim Eojin and a small community thinking about the role of design in the real world. Although its work is based in graphic design, the studio does not restrict itself to the two-dimensional space – experimenting with various design methods and applying its newfound knowledge to all of its work.

Facultative Works

pp.238-273

Facultative Works is a studio founded by Lesha Galkin and Olya Marchenko, blending architecture, art history, and cellular biology. Their interdisciplinary approach explores the relationship between the real and virtual, and the scientific and fictional, through product design, sculpture, 3D graphics, video, and sound installations. Their work seeks to offer new perspectives on the world, highlighting its uniqueness and value.

Fonts From Folch (FFF)

pp.284-285

Fonts From Folch (FFF) is a digital type foundry offering retail and custom typefaces.

FutureDeluxe

pp.374-381

FutureDeluxe is a global collective of artists, designers, and dreamers crafting cutting-edge visual experiences from studios in London, Los Angeles, and New York. Fuelled by curiosity and experimentation, they help brands imagine and design for tomorrow – boldly exploring what's next through innovation, artistry and a fresh perspective.

Get It Studio

pp.426-429

Get It Studio is a Tokyo-based creative studio founded by Swiss artists Sandra Golay and Alexandre Armand. Combining influences from fashion, product design, nature, and architecture, they create unique visual experiences using 3D tools. With clients like Google, Adobe, and Uniqlo, their work pushes creative boundaries with a playful, uplifting, and emotional approach since 2017.

Goh Jing Min

pp.452-457

Goh Jing Min is a motion graphics designer based in Singapore, passionate about creating innovative design solutions. Outside of work, she enjoys animated shows, photography, and art inspired by the world around us. She believes every piece of art tells a story, no matter how small, and that is what makes it feel real and alive.

High Tide

pp.116-125

High Tide is a full-service brand studio based in New York, partnering with emerging innovators such as Warby Parker and established icons including Spotify and New Balance. Working across strategy, design, and experience, they create brands that capture attention, grow with intention, and stand the test of time.

Indego Design

pp.128-145

Indego Design is a brand visual team specialising in corporate identities, event imagery, packaging, and multimedia design for commercial and cultural clients. Collaborating across creative fields, they explore new media visuals, earning recognition from clients and markets, along with numerous awards in Macau and internationally.

Independent Designers Collective (ID–C)

pp.088-099

Independent Designers Collective is a Swedish design duo, Niklas Rosén and Gustav Nordebrink, creating digital design and brand identities for global clients. As an officeless team, they collaborate with a trusted network to scale as needed, responding to modern demands for flexibility. Their work spans branding, industrial and print design, and apps, delivering functional, long-term solutions for people and businesses.

Joseph Töreki

pp.286-299

Driven by curiosity, Joseph Töreki blurs the lines between disciplines and draws inspiration from everything that sparks his imagination. Known for his hyper-realistic 3D renderings, his work evolves through unconventional experiments that embrace uncertainty. Influenced by craftsmanship, nature, and a passion for exploring new processes and materials, he pushes the boundaries of both the digital and physical worlds.

Juni Kweon

pp.502-503

Juni Kweon is a motion designer based in Los Angeles, inspired by her childhood dream of becoming a giraffe. As an illustrator and designer, she embraces a sense of limitless possibility in her work. She continues to dream with the heart of her seven-year-old self.

Kaan Iscan Ethem Cem Hazal Özkaya

pp.060-065

Kaan Iscan is a 3D designer and artist in Istanbul, creating branding, commercials, music, and product visuals, along with digital and physical sculptures that explore personal narratives.

Hazal Özkaya is a London-based designer focused on branding and visual identities.

Ethem Cem is a freelance designer and director in London, working in motion graphics and immersive media. His personal work blends science, art, and technology.

Kevin Jaeger

pp.394-397

Kevin Jaeger is a Hamburg-based digital artist and art director with over a decade of experience. Specialising in compelling concepts for international clients, he blends static and dynamic imagery, sculptural forms, and bold designs. His works, often revealing creative processes, have been featured globally, from billboards to exhibitions and magazines.

Kitasavi

pp.328-333

Nikita Savinov, known as Kitasavi, is a multimedia artist blending nostalgia and futurism. Through photography and 3D sculpting, he explores identities, urban energy, and the interaction of organic and synthetic forms. His layered, textural compositions invite viewers to reconsider perception, drawing inspiration from city landscapes and both popular and underground culture.

Kopfgestaltung

pp.306-313

Bernd Kopf, known as Kopfgestaltung, is a German artist and designer creating immersive works that evoke distinct atmospheres. With a master's in Media Design and a background in music and audio production, he blends CGI, sound design, and custom-created 3D models to craft unique, sensory experiences. His work spans still images, audio-visual scenes, and experimental short films.

Maximilien Vert

pp.314-321

Maximilien Vert is a French 3D artist specialising in procedural materials and complex texture design. With a passion for visual experimentation, his work blends technical precision and aesthetics, earning him recognition in the digital design industry.

Loop Studio

pp.478-483

Loop is an award-winning multidisciplinary studio specialising in creative and art direction, visual storytelling, and motion design. They approach each project personally, with a focus on honesty, professionalism, and reliability. Their passion lies in telling meaningful stories through design, ensuring every job is a journey toward crafting the best possible outcome for their clients.

Melvin Le Riboter

pp.322-327, 334-341

Melvin Le Riboter is a Paris-based artist and director specialising in visual arts and film. After studying at Gobelins, he began his freelance career in 2016, developing a style that blends hyper-detailed visuals with saturated colours and bold compositions. Melvin has collaborated with clients like Cartier, Decathlon, and Devialet, bringing his unique vision to high-end visual projects.

Marina Nakagawa

pp.496-497

Marina Nakagawa is a Japanese freelance 3D artist and motion designer based in London. Since 2016, she has worked at various studios before going freelance in 2019. She has collaborated with major clients like Netflix, Nike, Apple TV, Valve, and TikTok. Known for her stylised characters and playful animations, she draws inspiration from Japanese traditions and mythical creatures.

Michael Askew

pp.448-451

Michael Askew is a Sydney-based artist and creative director whose work bridges design, motion, and contemporary art. His commercial projects span music, fashion, and lifestyle, while his personal practice explores sensory perception through digital expression. Using 3D tools, light, and sound, he crafts immersive ambient works that blur the line between the virtual and physical.

Mohamed Basi

pp.512-513

Mohamed Basil is a self-taught designer who began with graphic design and typography out of a love for designing. He later transitioned to 3D design, with the fundamentals of design, colours, and composition from graphic design helping to make the shift easier.

Monga Design

pp.008-017

Monga Design is a Brazillian, two-person design studio. Since August 2020, they have been searching for their dreams and creating awesome, beautiful things.

Nastia Ibragimova

pp.466-471

Nastia Ibragimova specialises in character design and illustration. Known for her unique storytelling through visuals, she infuses her works with vibrant, dynamic characters, each carrying their own personalities and narratives.

Ordinary People

pp.048-057

Ordinary People is a multidisciplinary design studio founded in 2006, focusing on brand strategy and art direction. Blending cultural insight with modern technology, they create distinctive visual communications through ongoing experimentation across media.

Sass Scimirö

pp.416-419

Sass Scimirö is the creative alias of Fabio Salvadori, an Italian designer. His multidisciplinary practice spans motion design, 3D modelling, and type design, often blending these disciplines to explore the spaces in between. His work is marked by a distinctive sense of form, movement, and visual experimentation across both commercial and personal projects.

Sawdust

pp.274-281, 304-305

Sawdust is the creative duo of Rob Gonzalez and Jonathan Quainton, known for their award-winning work with global brands like Apple, Nike, and NASA. Their practice explores atmospheric themes through light, form, and sound, blending futurism and typography. With work featured in major publications and galleries, they remain driven by curiosity and a commitment to aesthetic and creative exploration.

Sebastian Koseda

pp.032-045

Studio Koseda, led by Sebastian Koseda, collaborates with leading cultural institutions and brands to craft forward-thinking, socially conscious identities, visuals, and experiences.

Studio Nari

pp.410-415

Studio Nari is a London-based design and branding agency that champions a human-centred, collaborative approach. Guided by the ethos "Not Always Right Ideas", they celebrate individuality and cultural nuance in their work. Operating across sectors, the agency focuses on projects with cultural or social relevance – crafting strategies, identities, and experiences that aim to connect authentically with people.

SMLXL

pp.402-403

SMLXL is a full-service design company based in New York and Barcelona, known for creating influential projects across various scales – from visual identity systems for sports events to packaging for Seth Rogen's Houseplant line. Their approach blends strategic thinking with an intuitive, playful sensibility, collaborating with experts to achieve technical precision. They aim to evoke wonder through exceptional design.

Szu-Yu Hou

pp.498-501

Szu-Yu Hou is an animation director, motion graphics designer, and visual artist, working internationally across London, Taipei, and beyond. Her work combines playful storytelling with cultural heritage, drawing inspiration from myths, historical objects, and everyday scenes. Known for her distinctive style, she blends geometric forms and tactile textures in both 2D and 3D media.

Studio Dumbar/DEPT®

pp.342-351

Studio Dumbar/DEPT® is an international agency with Dutch roots, specialising in visual branding and motion. Known for attracting global talent, its diverse portfolio spans industries, from business and government to culture and non-profits. Notable projects include the Dutch Railways' identity, Adidas Futurenatural, the Van Gogh Museum refresh, and DEMO – the world's largest design-in-motion festival.

The Royal Studio

pp.068-077

The Royal Studio is a communication studio that uses design as a tool for disruption rather than decoration. Blurring the lines between authorship, identity, and corporate communication, it treats storytelling as strategy and campaigns as performative outcomes. With a conceptual, word-driven approach, the studio crafts experiences that challenge conventions and provoke cultural reflection, designing not just visuals but societal impact.

TimTim

pp.458-465

TimTim (Timea Balo) is a 3D artist and motion designer, known for her bold colours, playful shapes, and tactile style. After eight years in graphic design, she transitioned to 3D, driven by curiosity and experimentation. Her work has reached major brands like Apple, Samsung, and Pepsi, but she remains passionate about creating fun, vibrant art that brings joy.

Untitled Army

pp.504-509

Lucas Camargo, the visionary behind Untitled Army, is a Brazilian artist renowned for his distinctive style and imaginative characters. Initially starting in stationery design and advertising, he shifted focus to his art in 2017. His daily sketches evolved into 3D characters and animations, earning global recognition. He continues to blend illustration, animation, and character design, creating an immersive surrealist universe.

Tina Touli

pp.398-401, 510-511

Tina Touli is a London-based creative director, multidisciplinary graphic designer, artist, and speaker. She collaborates with diverse clients such as Adobe, CNN, and Converse. Recognised by Print Magazine as one of the world's top 15 young designers under 30 in 2017, she has presented at renowned events including OFFF and Adobe MAX.

Untitled Macao

pp.148-163

Untitled Macao, founded by Au Chon Hin in 2017, specialises in branding, visual identities, web design, wayfinding, and signage systems. Known for its forward-thinking, bold vision, the studio has earned recognition from prestigious international awards, including the ADC Annual Award, The One Show, D&AD Awards, and the Taipei Design Award.

Toby Ng Design

pp.164-171, 208-217

Toby Ng Design is a Hong Kong-based branding consultancy known for crafting impactful design solutions rooted in strong ideas. The studio has earned recognition from D&AD, ADC, One Show, Red Dot, and Tokyo TDC, among others. Twice listed in Campaign Brief's Creative Rankings, it has also been highlighted by Monocle as a key voice in defining Hong Kong's design identity.

Vincent Schwenk

pp.484-495

Vincent Schwenk is a multidisciplinary 3D artist with a background in graphic design. He creates vibrant, fluid digital sculptures that explore artificiality through candy-coloured, futuristic forms. His work spans album covers, branding, and digital installations, often focusing on the physical irregularities of abstract objects.

Vincent Wagner

pp.300-301, 442-447

Vincent Wagner is a Vienna-based motion designer whose work spans both cultural and commercial realms. He often focuses on type-led visuals, blending experimental 2D and 3D motion design. Known for his fascination with 3D lettering, he explores spatial dynamics and expressive movement to push the boundaries of typographic storytelling.

Woodwork Amsterdam

pp.438-441

Woodwork Amsterdam is a design and direction company focused on bold visual storytelling. Through visual identities, motion branding, and film, their work delivers visual firepower that informs and entertains, sparks vision, and inspires brands to connect with audiences in meaningful ways.

Vladyslav Kuchaiev

pp.420-425

Vladyslav Kuchaiev is a multidisciplinary designer exploring the intersection of artificial and organic through generative and dimensional visuals. His work blends structure, texture, and motion to create expressive forms that challenge traditional design boundaries. Drawing inspiration from natural systems and computational aesthetics, he crafts visuals that evoke emotion and curiosity, balancing futuristic and tactile elements.

Zuzanna Rogatty

pp.146-147

Zuzanna Rogatty is a Polish designer based in New York. With over a decade of experience, she pushes the boundaries of typography as a lettering artist and creates intricate brand identity systems as a creative director, seamlessly transitioning between the two roles.

Whitelight Motion

pp.182-201

Established in 2016, Whitelight Motion is an internationally awarded creative team known for its innovation. The studio offers solutions across visual design, motion graphics, and brand consulting, including brand strategy, image films, and new media strategy. With numerous awards from global design competitions, Whitelight Motion demonstrates its unwavering commitment to excellence and creativity.

First published and distributed by
viction workshop ltd.

viction:ary™

viction workshop ltd.
Unit C, 7/F, Seabright Plaza,
9-23 Shell Street, North Point, Hong Kong SAR
Website: www.victionary.com
Email: we@victionary.com

@victionworkshop
@victionworkshop
Bē @victionary
@victionary
小红书 @Victionary Books

Edited & produced by viction:ary
Creative direction: Victor Cheung
Design: Hazan Yeung
Editorial: Ynes Filleul, YL Lim
Coordination: Katherine Wong, Kristine Ng
Production: Bryan Leung
Typefaces: PP Mondwest by Pangram Pangram® Foundry,
Aeonik Fono by CoType Foundry

ISBN 978-988-76845-1-0
Printed and bound in China

ACKNOWLEDGEMENTS

We would like to specially thank all the artists and illustrators who are featured in this book for their significant contribution towards its compilation. We would also like to express our deepest gratitude to our producers for their invaluable advice and assistance throughout this project, as well as the many professionals in the creative industry who were generous with their insights, feedback, and time. To those whose input was not specifically credited or mentioned here, we also truly appreciate your support.

FUTURE EDITIONS

If you wish to participate in viction:ary's future projects and publications, please send your portfolio to: we@victionary.com